Britain and Defence 1945–2000

Pearson
Education

We work with leading authors to develop the
strongest educational materials in politics,
bringing cutting-edge thinking and best
learning practice to a global market.

Under a range of well-known imprints, including
Longman, we craft high quality print and
electronic publications which help readers to understand
and apply their content, whether studying or at work.

To find out more about the complete range of our
publishing, please visit us on the World Wide Web at:
www.pearsoneduc.com

Britain and Defence 1945–2000

A Policy Re-evaluation

Stuart Croft, Andrew Dorman, Wyn Rees and Matthew Uttley

An imprint of **Pearson Education**

Harlow, England · London · New York · Reading, Massachusetts · San Francisco · Toronto · Don Mills, Ontario · Sydney
Tokyo · Singapore · Hong Kong · Seoul · Taipei · Cape Town · Madrid · Mexico City · Amsterdam · Munich · Paris · Milan

Pearson Education Limited
Edinburgh Gate
Harlow
Essex CM20 2JE

and Associated Companies throughout the world.

Visit us on the World Wide Web at:
www.pearsoneduc.com

First published 2001

ISBN 0 582 30377 X

British Library Cataloguing-in-Publication Data
A catalogue record for this book is available from the British Library

10 9 8 7 6 5 4 3 2 1
05 04 03 02 01

Typeset in 10/12pt Garamond by 35

Printed in Malaysia (VVP)

Contents

Contents

List of Abbreviations

ANZAM	Australia, New Zealand and Malaya Pact
ARRC	Allied Command Europe Rapid Reaction Corps
ASW	Anti-Submarine Warfare
BAOR	British Army on the Rhine
C3	Command, Control, Communication
CDS	Chief of the Defence Staff
CENTO	Central Treaty Organisation
CJTF	Combined Joint Task Force
CND	Campaign for Nuclear Disarmament
DERA	Defence Evaluation and Research Agency
DESO	Defence Export Services Organisation
DFID	Department for International Development
DPA	Defence Procurement Agency
EDC	European Defence Community
EC	European Community
EEC	European Economic Community
EPC	European Political Cooperation
EU	European Union
FCO	Foreign and Commonwealth Office
FRG	Federal Republic of Germany
FY	Financial Year
GDP	Gross Domestic Product
GNP	Gross National Product
IFOR	Implementation Force
ISTAR	Intelligence, Surveillance, Target Acquisition and Reconnaissance
JRDF	Joint Rapid Deployment Force
JSCSC	Joint Services Command and Staff College
KFOR	Kosovo Force
LTC	Long-Term Costing
MoD	Ministry of Defence
MINIS	Management Information System for Ministers
NATO	North Atlantic Treaty Organisation
NMS	New Management Strategy
NWFZ	Nuclear Weapons Free Zone
OCCAR	Organisme Conjointe de Cooperation en matière d'Armament
PFI	Private Finance Initiative
PJHQ	Permanent Joint Headquarters

PPP	Public/Private Partnerships
PUS	Permanent Under Secretary
R&D	Research and Development
RAF	Royal Air Force
RMA	Revolution in Military Affairs
RSI	Rationalisation, Standardisation and Interoperability
SACEUR	Supreme Allied Commander Europe
SDI	Strategic Defence Initiative
SDP	Social Democratic Party
SDR	Strategic Defence Review
SEATO	South East Asian Treaty Organisation
SFOR	Stabilisation Force
TOW	Tube-launched Optically-tracked Wire-guided [missile]
UK	United Kingdom
UKMF	United Kingdom Mobile Force
UN	United Nations
UNPROFOR	United Nations Protection Force
US	United States
USSR	Union of Soviet Socialist Republics
WEU	Western European Union
WUDO	Western Union Defence Organisation

Introduction

Stuart Croft

This volume considers change in British defence policy across more than a fifty year time period. There are four dangers with a project with such a scope. The first danger is that the book becomes overly descriptive, focusing upon narrative to the exclusion of analysis, becoming a far too narrow examination of one aspect of British and/or international politics. The second danger is that change is taken for granted, without there being any clear identification of the sources of change; again, this would encourage description over analysis, and a false presumption of 'inevitability' with hindsight, without understanding the complexity of the issue to the decision-makers of the time. In short, the danger of reinterpreting the past in terms of the present. The third danger is that unless the analysis is conceptually grounded it risks being quickly overtaken by events; that is, themes outlined here should have relevance beyond the time period selected for analysis. The fourth danger is that of too much generalisation, and insufficient attention to details, in the attempt to be comprehensive.

To address these potential pitfalls, this volume will be based upon a clear conceptual framework, one that will be developed in this opening chapter. Five central themes will be identified. First, the epistemological position taken, which will stress the role of the ideational without excluding the material. That is, it is not sufficient to simply focus on Britain's declining material power in the period after 1945; rather, what is important is to focus on conceptual prism(s) through which those material factors were interpreted. And those interpretations were often rooted in different political perspectives, making it impossible to allow agreement and consensus.

The second theme to be outlined focuses on the nature of 'change'. Too often in the literature on British politics generally change is taken for granted, or is explained rather too simply. This volume will attempt to examine complex reasons for thinking about change, in part in order to frame discussions about Britain's 'decline'. Decline is usually assumed in reviewing Britain's relations with the world. In this book, that assumption will be investigated.

Third, and linked to the previous theme, there will be an examination of the nature of structure and agency, crucial again in considering the nature of British 'decline' and the scope of national policy in an anarchic international structure. Given the first theme, this book will not accept the view that the United Kingdom had no choices given its declining material power in the international structure; but neither will it be suggested that decline was purely a constructed concept.

The fourth theme will be the inadequacy of the international–domestic dichotomy for understanding policy. Traditionally, British politics on the one hand, and British foreign and defence policies on the other have been analysed separately. As the analysis in this volume unfolds, it will be clear that the domestic and the international cannot be treated in this fashion.

The fifth and final theme will be the significance of the definition of 'defence' in different periods of time. Clearly the 1998 Strategic Defence Review would be unintelligible to defence planners in the 1950s as *defence* policy, for it incorporates much broader security themes and issues. Contemporary defence debates now incorporate a range of 'soft' security issues (drugs, crime and so on) and make links to 'foreign' policy in novel and evolving ways.

From this Introduction, a notion of 'the British way of defence policy' will emerge. The Introduction will therefore comprise three parts. In the first section, the five themes will be further developed. The second part will examine this notion of a 'British way in defence'. The third will explain the structure of the book.

The five themes of the book

The role of epistemology

Much, if not all, of the literature on British defence policy operates from an unstated positivist conception of knowledge. Largely, this is due to the historical dominance of positivism in both the study of British politics and in the discipline of international relations. This volume does not seek to refute positivism. Rather, the book operates from a non-positivist conception of knowledge, and this has important implications for the analysis.

Simply expressed, three epistemological positions may be identified: positivist, relativist, and the 'middle ground'. Allowing for simplification, the three positions may be described as follows. Positivists assume that the world exists independently of human knowledge, that there is objective truth that can be discovered through reason and tested through empiricism. Perhaps this is best summed up by Jan Aart Scholte, who rejects the four essential premises of positivism: that it 'purports that there is one truth; . . . that a clear distinction can be drawn between "logical" and "mythological" accounts; . . . that empirical observation provides the whole essential link between human consciousness and social reality; and that facts and values are discrete elements of thought, with social science incorporating the former without the latter.'[1] In stark contrast to the positivists, relativists make a series of contrary assumptions. Rather than seeing the world as existing independently of human knowledge, relativists argue that it cannot; rather, there is no 'real' world beyond discourse. If nothing 'real' exists outside of discourse, it follows that 'objective' knowledge is impossible, and that there are no independent or foundational grounds for judging between different discourses. Relativists therefore criticise '[t]he modern project [which] is seen as a cultural construction that attempts to extend one particular mode of thinking – rationality – to all corners of the world, destroying diversity in the name of progress.'[2] The middle ground between positivism and relativism is sometimes referred to as constructivism.[3] Like positivism it assumes that there is an objective world; like relativism, it suggests that discourse, or social construction, is central to our understanding. Structures do not determine outcomes, but instead they constrain and facilitate.[4]

Perhaps the easiest way to conceive of differences between these three epistemological positions is to consider the relationship between the material and ideational levels of explanation. For positivism, it is the material that is central; in international relations terms, this includes all shades of realism, neo-liberalism and structuralism – i.e. that whole of the discipline as explained by Michael Banks' notion of the inter-paradigm debate.[5] For relativism, it is the ideational that is central, incorporating postmodernists in international relations such as Ashley, Der Derian, and Walker. For constructivism, however, the relationship is more complex; there is a material base, mediated through the ideational level.[6] Taking a constructivist position is of vital importance to this book, and is one of the issues that makes this analysis different from other examinations of British defence policy. Positivist accounts of British defence policy essentially focus on the objective decline in Britain's position. As the UK lost weight in geo-political and geo-economic terms, policy-makers had to readjust. Thus, the major changes in British defence policy – the Sandys review, withdrawal from East of Suez – were inevitable readjustments to global decline. The constructivist position does not reject the notion of material decline (as relativists would), but instead argues that what is of importance to understanding policy is the ideational as much as the material; that is, what is important is not the evaluation of whether policy-makers were objectively correct in their assessments of Britain's material position at any period of time but, rather, how the discourse of decline created its own policy requirements. Thus, it is not appropriate to ask whether proponents of particular positions in these debates were objectively correct, but rather to examine how the ideational created different interpretations of material 'reality'.

One can see this clearly with the example of the first Thatcher administration, which sought to reverse the 'decline' in British defence policy that had been a key plank in the election manifesto. Positivist accounts would focus on the 'reality' of British defence decline in the 1970s, and the 'objective' problems faced in overturning this decline. Constructivism, in contrast, would focus on the construction of the idea of defence policy decline and its role in political discourse in the late 1970s and throughout the 1980s.

The nature of change

Change is one of the most difficult concepts in the social sciences. In the discipline of international relations, one that largely focused on the Cold War conflict, the end of that conflict came as a surprise, and the discipline as a whole has struggled to come to terms with explanations for such revolutionary events as those witnessed in Central and Eastern Europe in the period from 1989 to 1991. In terms of British defence policy, change is usually interpreted in one of three ways.

The first of these is that which emphasises the 'dominance of decline'. In the tradition of grand history, Britain's decline has been the key theme in British defence policy throughout the 1945–98 period (indeed, one could argue from earlier than 1945). Thus, an examination of British defence policy is essentially one concerned with tactical adjustments of policy and doctrine to the overarching theme of declining power and resources in the international arena.

The second way of looking at these issues is through the notion of the 'turning point'. There is widespread consensus on four of the turning points – the end of the Second World War and the election of the Attlee government, the withdrawal from East of Suez, the rejection of decline with the election of the first Thatcher government and the emergence of a renewed Cold War, and the fall of Margaret Thatcher from the premiership and the collapse of the Cold War structures. Thus it would be possible to focus a book on British defence policy into four sections, focusing on each period.

A third interpretation might be termed 'concepts and policy'. Here the focus is on the level of change: should the focus be on policy changes, or on conceptual changes? Clearly in one sense, the two are linked: conceptual changes can lead to policy changes. But the purpose of opening up the conceptual level is to examine when dominant ideas came under criticism, even when they did not lead to specific policy changes. That is, it opens up space for a consideration of the ideational level among policy-makers (a feature of agency that will be examined later) to address notions of consensus and argument.

This book does not reject the interpretation of the 'dominance of decline' but rather seeks to put it into ideational, rather than a purely material, context. Similarly, it accepts the 'turning point' thesis, while recognising the importance of continuities. A key interpretation here is a third element: opening space for conceptual change. Thus, this volume seeks to develop a more sophisticated notion of change by examining the interplay between each of these three types of change.

Structure and agency

The relationship between structure and agency is another particularly problematic area in the social sciences, but an issue of great importance for an examination of British defence policy in the second half of the twentieth century. The nature of this relationship revolves around issues already introduced, notably; what scope has the British government (agent) had for action (policy) given its decline in the international system (structure)?

The answer to this question points in two directions. The 'dominance of decline' approach would suggest a structural answer, that Britain has had very little space for action, instead essentially responding to the pressures of the international system. The 'turning point' approach would, in contrast, emphasise agency in, for example, initiating the British bomb project, going to war in the Falklands, or seeking to create a new world order with the Americans in the Gulf.

However, there is a problem for this book in seeking to answer the question set out above, for it is in essence a positivist question.[7] There are two aspects to reordering this question into one that a constructivist project could seek to investigate.

First, it is unhelpful to see the relationship as either structure *or* agency. Constructivism suggests that it is the material plus ideational environment that provides agents with their understandings of both interests and identities. This means, importantly, that structure and agency must be *mutually* constituted, not separately privileged. In this conception, agents have structural positions, but structures are interpreted by agents and indeed changed by agents' actions.[8] In short, they are mutually constituted like the concepts of 'Self' and 'Other', in that one cannot be understood without its partner.

Second, the literature actually deals with two levels of structure and agency: one, that of the role of Britain in the international system; and the other, that within the British state. At the first level, agency is that of the British state; its policies and statements of position. At the second level, the structure is not that of bureaucratic position, but rather of discourse, which includes critics who may have sat outside official positions. This will be further examined in the next section, but the point here is that there is mutual constitution at both of these levels.

The international–domestic dichotomy

The issue of structure and agency seemingly operating at two levels seems to reinforce the notion that there is an international–domestic dichotomy of central importance to an examination of British defence policy. Indeed, that is what one tends to find in the literature. It has generally been the case that the literature on British politics has tended to ignore foreign and defence policy issues, while that on international relations has treated 'domestic' issues as at best secondary. Thus, British defence policy has been seen by both sets of analysts as being qualitatively different from, say, agricultural policy.

However, this book does not argue for such a dichotomy between the international and the domestic; indeed, it positively argues against it. The 'turning point' argument set out below has both domestic and international roots to focus on: the election of Attlee plus the postwar era; the election of Thatcher plus renewed Cold War hostility; the end of the Thatcher period plus the end of the Cold War. The conception at work here is again that of mutual constitution; it does not make sense to talk of the British domestic debate within an international context; and one cannot talk of Britain's foreign and defence policies without concern for the domestic context. Thus, although organisationally it has been the case that we are dealing with two sets of structure–agency mutual constructions, these constructions themselves are mutually interrelated. As an example, the Westland helicopter crisis of the late 1980s was an important issue domestically, but also had significant international ramifications in terms of procurement policy and, indeed, in terms of European integration.

Definitions of defence

The final theme concerns the broadening definition of defence issues. It has become commonplace in the 1990s to talk of *security* rather than *defence*, to indicate clearly the broadening of the debate away from questions of the military balance towards a wider and more holistic conception of protection from threat. However, the focus in this book is on defence, not security. This is because defence provides a tighter set of issues for the consideration of the broader themes set out in this introduction than does security across the time period under examination. Security may be considered in its political, environmental, social and economic variants, while defence is essentially limited to military security matters. It is also the case because notions of security problematise the referent for security, whereas in this study these issues are short-circuited by the focus on the British state. And it is also the case because security had no real meaning in the debate about Britain's relations with the non-British before, at best the 1970s. That is, to examine British security policy before, say, 1975 would be to impose later conceptions onto the policy-makers of the time.

However, although the concentration on defence allows a clearer focus on the thematic issues, the nature of defence itself has changed. For example, the 1998 Strategic Defence Review introduces the notion of 'defence diplomacy'. This is clearly a vital area of work for Britain in the post-Cold War environment, but it is not an area that would make any sense to defence planners in the 1950s or 1960s. This takes us back to an earlier point. Defence is clearly at one level concerned with material issues: a tank has substance, it is not simply discursively constructed. But defence has also an ideational aspect – how it is understood – and this ideational aspect has changed over time. The longitudinal approach underlying this book will allow those changes to be more fully mapped and understood.

A British way in defence

The five themes of this book outlined above are designed to overcome the four principal dangers that face an undertaking of this kind. They will prevent an overemphasis on narrative; question notions of change, and limit the tendency to interpret the past in terms of the present; provide an epistemological grounding to create foundations for analysis against the shifting sands of events; and allow for the detailed empirical work that follows in subsequent chapters, thus avoiding the danger of rootless generalisation. And by examining the period from 1945 to 1998, a sufficient scope is created for a longitudinal analysis of the themes above.

But all of this needs to lead to at least one analytical question. The positivist question outlined earlier would be: what scope has British government (agent) had for action (policy) given its decline in the international system (structure)? This, it will be recalled, was rejected because of its overemphasis on objectivity, and on the distinction between structure and agency. Instead, for the constructivist, the question needs to be rephrased as: can a British way in defence be identified? This in turn needs further definition.

What is not sought here is an answer in relative terms; we are not seeking to compare a British way with a French, or American, or Russian. Instead, we are looking for key continuities in several areas, such as: key agents of change and decision-making within the UK; central assumptions in the British discourse, including policy-makers, elites and critics outside those groupings; arguments and debates over particular issues such as threats or the defence industrial base; attitudes to allies and to Europe; and to the use of force and Britain's role in the world. It may be that there are continuities across the time period of 1945–98; it may be that there are continuities, but only within shorter time periods; or it may be that there are no significant continuities at all.

The focus, then, is on the ideational constructs of the material reality of British defence from 1945 to 1998. Emphasis on the 'British' aspect should not be seen as favouring agency over structure, for the two are mutually constructed. And 'defence' will be defined in the terms of the time, while recognising changes in that definition over time. The final section of this Introduction will explain the structure of the book.

The structure of the book

Having set out the key themes to be examined in this volume in this Introduction, it remains to explain how these issues have structured the empirical analysis of the book. Seven chapters follow, concentrating on different aspects of the British defence story. The attempt here is to be comprehensive and multi-dimensional; to examine issues that have been traditionally seen as high politics (for example, nuclear weapons) as well as low (such as the defence industrial base), and to examine the bureaucracy of defence decisions along with policy outcomes.

Chapter 1 views British defence policy since 1945 as a product of a symbiotic or dialectical relationship between 'crises' and 'defence reviews'. Crises (such as the Korean War), have led to reviews of Britain's defence posture (e.g. the Sandys Review); but similarly, reviews have been deeply affected by subsequent crises (e.g. the Nott Review and the Falklands War). Examining British defence policy through this relationship indicates several of the themes outlined in the introduction, notably mutual constitution and the role of the ideational.

One of the most visible changes in the nature of British defence policy from postwar to post-Cold War comes in the move from the global to the regional, and this is the focus of Chapter 2. However, decolonisation led to a series of conflicts in colonial and post-colonial conflicts (e.g. the Indonesian confrontation), and indeed even after Britain seemed to signal its withdrawal from a global role with the withdrawal from East of Suez, the UK has been involved in colonial power balances (Hong Kong and Belize) and conflicts (the Falklands and the Gulf). How has the material – the use of force – interacted with the ideational?

Historically Britain believed that it was concerned with preventing a single power from dominating the continent, and it is certainly possible to see the formation of NATO in this light. But NATO has been more than this, as the UK has sought to develop a relationship with a major power (the US) that is without historical parallel for that state. And how has the process of European integration affected UK defence policy? The European dimension is the focus of Chapter 3, which questions the nature of change in policy terms through different ideas of the British–European relationship.

The British nuclear bomb has been seen to be more of a constant in British defence policy than perhaps any other single element of policy. Yet what is perhaps most striking about that consistency is not in the policy, but in the nature of debates between proponents and opponents of the British bomb which can be traced from the 1940s to the 1990s. Consensus on the bomb in the UK has not been the norm, but is rather a constructed idea. Chapter 4 examines a further aspect of the relationship between the material, in this case nuclear weaponry, and ideational constructs and interpretations.

A further aspect of the agent–structure issue will be the focus of Chapter 5. When did the defence consensus emerge between the parties, how was it maintained, how far did the consensus stretch, and how and when was it challenged? What factors produced greater periods of consensus, and what factors encouraged discord?

Chapter 6 moves the analysis towards the agent–structure aspect of the enquiry. Defence policy, as with all policy, is at least in part a product of the policy-making environment. This chapter will examine the evolution of the machinery of defence policy-making in order to ascertain where the key decision-making centres have been, and how they have been affected by change and reform.

Chapter 7 examines the lines of argument regarding the defence industrial base and, as a logical extension, the arms trade. The defence industrial base has survived periods of nationalisation and privatisation, periods of industrialisation and post-industrialisation, rapid technological change, globalisation, debates over ethics and the relative economic decline of the UK economy. Why and how?

The Conclusion will interpret the findings of the empirical chapters through the lens of the research questions set up in this Introduction. How should British decline be interpreted? Can a British way in defence be defined?

Notes

1. J. A. Scholte, *International Relations of Social Change*, Buckingham: Open University Press, 1993, p. 134.
2. T. Porter, 'Postmodern Political Realism and International Relations Theory's Third Debate' in C. T. Sjolander and W. S. Cox (eds), *Beyond Positivism: Critical Reflections on International Relations*, Boulder, CO: Lynne Rienner, 1994, p. 108.
3. On this attempt to create a middle ground, see E. Adler, 'Seizing the Middle Ground', *European Journal of International Relations*, 3 (3) September 1997, p. 322; and also A. Wendt, *Social Theory of International Politics*, Cambridge: Cambridge University Press, 1999.
4. Of course there is a great deal of simplification here; the central point though, is to emphasise the way in which interpretation of material reality must be considered through its discursive construction.
5. M. Banks, 'The Inter-Paradigm Debate', in M. Light and A. J. R. Groom (eds), *International Relations: A Handbook of Current Theory*, London: Pinter, 1985, pp. 7–26.
6. Critical theory is here used in its European sense, i.e. to refer to a specific area of enquiry based on the work of Jürgen Habermas and the Frankfurt School, rather than in the American sense which is generally taken to mean 'critical of the mainstream'. For a classic statement of the constructivist position, see A. Wendt 'Constructing International Politics', *International Security*, 20 (1) 1995, pp. 71–81.
7. On the problems for positivism in IR (specifically realism) on this question, see A. Wendt, 'The Agent–Structure Problem in International Relations Theory', *International Organisation*, 41(3) 1987, pp. 340–4.
8. A. Wendt, 'Anarchy is What States Make of It: The Social Construction of Power Politics', *International Organisation*, 46 (2) 1992, pp. 391–425.

Chapter 1

Crises and Reviews in British Defence Policy

Andrew Dorman

Introduction

The period from 1945 to 2000 has witnessed a series of crises in British defence policy. Indeed, much of the defence literature has been focused either on specific reviews and crises or on their cumulative effects. Frequently they have been identified as key 'turning points' in the evolution of policy, both during and after the end of the Cold War. This is particularly true for those involved in the declinist debate who have often used the various reviews and crises as evidence to support their arguments. For example, Jackson points out that one of the most visible changes in the nature of British defence policy during the Cold War was the move from a global to a regional power and implies that this change in defence policy was part of a general decline in Britain's economic position *vis-à-vis* the rest of the world.[1] In this argument he points to the series of reviews conducted under the auspices of Denis Healey. Such a view is supported by the majority of defence economists who see the effect of decline impacting upon defence policy. In contrast Malcolm Chalmers argues that defence spending has been one of the causes of Britain's economic decline.[2] He has argued that the costs of this investment have restricted the capacity for future production in other areas, that defence investment has utilised a disproportionate share of scarce high-technology inputs and that it has had an adverse effect on the balance of payments.

There are a number of problems with such approaches. Firstly, they are very structurally orientated and generally fail to take account of a number of other factors influencing British defence policy, such as the role of individuals and the interaction of domestic and international factors upon defence policy. Secondly, they assume that reviews and crises lead to significant policy changes that are incurred virtually immediately. Such an approach generally focuses on declared policy, rather than considering the other aspects of policy – military strategy and procurement policy. All too often, as this chapter will show, changes in policy were often internally disconnected and not fully implemented. This chapter will therefore take a slightly different approach. It will look at the nature of crises and reviews in British defence policy between 1945 and 2000 as a means of understanding how policy evolved. Each crisis and review will be considered in turn, looking at the events that led up to them, briefly outlining their impact upon defence policy and making some conclusions about them individually.

The chapter will then draw together some overall lessons about change and the role of crises and reviews in British defence policy. In this chapter crises and reviews have been defined as those occasions where one of the three dynamics of defence policy (declaratory, military and procurement) have undergone significant change. They are not, therefore, defined purely by those occasions where significant defence cutbacks are formally announced and justified within an overarching strategic context or merely where the government formally made reference to a review. Such an approach is markedly different from the traditional view which invariably starts with the 1957 review.

The Korean War and the 1950 and 1952 Defence Policy and Global Strategy Papers

The first articulated defence policy to emerge after the end of the Second World War was the 'Three Pillars Strategy' in 1948. This was based on the premise that 'the security of the British Commonwealth depended on: protecting the United Kingdom; maintaining vital sea communications; and securing the Middle East as a defensive and striking base against the Soviet Union.'[3] This avoided a formal commitment of troops to the defence of Europe; instead reliance was to be placed on air power deployed from bases in the United Kingdom and the Middle East to counter the Soviet Union supported by the Royal Navy. To support this a subcommittee of the British Cabinet, GEN 75, approved the construction of fissile production facilities to produce a British atomic weapon in 1946.[4] At the same time, the first British strategic jet bomber specification was conceived and issued as an operational requirement.[5] In reality the whole strategy was flawed because of capability deficiencies. It would take some time to develop the British bomb; meanwhile the existing bomber force was incapable of striking targets in the Soviet Union even with conventional munitions. However, the condition of Britain's armed forces encouraged such a policy.

The 1950 'Defence Policy and Global Strategy Paper' was agreed immediately prior to the outbreak of the Korean War.[6] It reflected the defence realities in which Britain found itself and sought to implement a consistent 'Hot War' and 'Cold War' policy based on a three-phase strategy.[7] The first phase depended upon the deterrent value of US atomic supremacy over the Soviet Union and the ability of the United States and Britain to sustain a long war. This required Britain to provide secure bases from which the United States could launch its aircraft against Russia together with sufficient naval support to allow for the long-term invasion and re-conquest of Europe (i.e. a second Normandy landing).[8] Meanwhile, the second phase would witness the build-up of NATO's conventional forces to a size capable of overcoming a Soviet invasion of western Europe. The final phase then required that the West maintain its ability to strike the Soviet Union with conventional and atomic weapons from the air in the face of technological developments in Soviet air defences. The paper therefore represented a logical implementation of the 'Three Pillars Strategy' using the American nuclear capability to offset British deficiencies in this area.

In response to the outbreak of the Korean War the British accelerated the programme and defence spending was planned to rise rapidly from 1951.[9] A major rearmament programme was initiated despite rationing still being in existence in some areas of the economy.[10] Particular attention was given to conventional forces in both their Hot and Cold War roles. The Korean War also led to the formal commitment of British land and air forces to the defence of Germany in support of a similar American move.

Although generally grouped together, the subsequent 1952 'Defence Policy and Global Strategy Paper' marked a decisive shift in policy at two levels. Firstly, the balance between Hot and Cold War activities was decisively shifted in favour of the former.[11] By the time the 1952 variant of the paper was constructed, the Americans had pressed ahead with their hydrogen bomb programme in response to the Soviet testing of an atom bomb and serious doubts had started to be raised about the realities of a long war. The revised paper concluded that:

> [t]he opening phase . . . will be of unparalleled intensity. It may last only a few weeks; but at the end of that period it seems certain that both sides, particularly Russia and the United Kingdom, will have suffered terrible damage. No one can foretell what kind of war – assuming it continues – will follow this intense period. It may be a long-drawn-out period of chaos with an intermittent struggle spreading worldwide, but the results of the previous phase are bound to limit considerably the capabilities of the contestants and the scale of their operations. If this general picture is accepted, the logical conclusion is that in their preparations for war the Allies should concentrate on measures that will contribute to their defence in the opening phase and to the violence of the initial assault upon the enemy.[12]

Secondly, the paper changed the balance of conventional forces, with land and air forces being given priority. With the Cold War role for armed forces diminishing *vis-à-vis* Hot War, the role of the Royal Navy became much less clear. However, to placate the Navy the 1952 paper adopted the idea of 'broken-backed hostilities'. This assumed that after the initial short intensive period there might be an indefinite period of broken-backed warfare in which each side would attempt to recover from its wounds and strike again. In such a situation everything would depend upon the relative speed of recovery of the two opposing sides.[13] As a result, the Navy retained the task of keeping the sea-lanes open for the reinforcement of Britain and the Middle East.[14] The degree to which this was believed remains debatable, but it served as a sop to the Navy which altered its naval programme to reflect the requirements of a third battle of the Atlantic.[15] This led to a move away from large aircraft carriers and amphibious warfare in favour of convoy escorts and mine countermeasures.

The two Defence Policy and Global Strategy Papers, together with the impact of the Korean War, marked the first fundamental review of British defence policy since the end of the Second World War and the adoption of the 'Three Pillars Strategy'. The evolution of the review between the two Defence Policy and Global Strategy Papers reflected the internal disconnects within the 'Three Pillars Strategy', the successful Soviet development of the atomic bomb and the US hydrogen bomb programme. While the 'Three Pillars Strategy' had planned to launch conventional and atomic strikes against the Soviet Union, as a means of countering Soviet superiority on land, the Royal Air Force's decision to skip a generation of bombers and the lack of a British atomic bomb during this period undermined the linkage between the different elements of defence policy. The new policy was internally more consistent, although there were still inherent contradictions. By the time of the 1952 paper it was already conceded that Britain could not be successfully defended from atomic attack, yet the momentum of the 1951 rearmament package meant that significant funds continued to be invested in Britain's air defences. Moreover, this review witnessed the first sign of an ongoing theme within British defence policy – finding a role for the Navy if the planning assumptions were for a war in Europe to go nuclear early. In this review the 'broken-backed hostilities' strategy attempted to paper over this question.

Both the papers were noticeably military led, with the three Service Chiefs working out the overall policy and submitting their proposals to the Prime Minister for approval. This was partly a reflection of the weak position of the Ministry of Defence *vis-à-vis* the three Services, which all had their own minister at this time. However, this would increasingly become an infrequent occurrence as the power balance between the Services and the Ministry of Defence altered throughout the period in favour of the latter. The 1952 paper, therefore, left Britain with a defence policy emphasising its Hot War requirements. However, it was a Cold War problem, the Suez Crisis, which was the principal cause of the major rethink in defence policy.

Suez and the Sandys Review

The Suez Crisis of 1956 proved to be the next watershed in postwar defence policy and the lessons the government drew from it were manifold.[16] The rearmament package announced by Attlee in 1951 had proven to be financially unsustainable and had failed to produce the forces required to deal with the Suez Crisis. The Anglo-French response to Nasser's nationalisation of the Suez Canal took three months to organise, mainly because of a shortage of available forces. Recourse had to be taken to the recalling of reservists and the redeployment of air, sea and land units from other theatres.[17] In the first six days of November 1956 British gold and dollar reserves fell by 15 per cent[18] and the government turned to the International Monetary Fund for emergency loans. However, after prompting from the United States, these loans were refused. The ensuing financial crisis proved to be one of the main reasons why the British government halted the invasion and accepted a ceasefire, much to the consternation of their French allies.[19]

The failure of the Anglo-French expedition served as the trigger for a major reconsideration of British defence policy. In the background lay the issue of the cost of defence. This was acknowledged in the 1957 paper which noted that:

> Over the last five years, defence has on average absorbed 10 per cent of Britain's gross national product. Some 7 per cent of the working population are either in the Services or supporting them. One-eighth of the output of the metal-using industries, upon which the export trade so largely depends, is devoted to defence. An undue proportion of qualified scientists and engineers are engaged on military work. In addition, the retention of such large forces abroad gives rise to heavy charges which place a severe strain upon the balance of payments.[20]

However, this rethink did not consider abandoning commitments. Despite the experience of defeat at Suez, the government still wanted to maintain the world role and the review focused on the implementation of existing policy. As a result, there were some quite substantial changes in the composition and outlook of Britain's armed forces. Whereas the 1950, and to a lesser extent the 1952, Defence Policy and Global Strategy Papers had seen the West's nuclear supremacy as a means of buying time while the West matched the perceived conventional superiority of the Soviet-led forces, the 1957 Defence Review effectively removed this second phase and relied almost exclusively on phases one and three. Consequently, the 1957 Defence White Paper placed much more emphasis on Britain's nuclear forces as a means of reducing the financial cost of defence on Britain. By 1957 the deployment of the V-bomber force was already underway and the construction of Britain's first thermonuclear bombs continued.[21] To preserve the deterrent beyond the mid-1960s the Blue Streak intermediate-range ballistic missile and an extended range version of the Blue Steel stand-off missile for the V-bombers were under development as priority programmes.[22]

The government, therefore, looked to its conventional forces to provide the greater proportion of the reduction. It looked to its European allies to shoulder more of the conventional responsibility in NATO and announced a significant reduction in the land and air forces deployed in West Germany. At the same time the remaining air component was given a nuclear role to compensate for the overall reduction in numbers.[23] There were other cutbacks in conventional forces as the assumptions of the 1952 paper were fully implemented. For example, the White Paper announced significant reductions to the Royal Air Force's (RAF) Fighter Command and redefined its mission in terms of solely defending the V-bomber bases.[24] This brought the policy into line with the military assumptions outlined in the 1952 Defence Policy and Global Strategy Paper. The Navy also came in for significant review. Sandys, the minister responsible for running the review, was an opponent of the Navy's aircraft carrier force:[25] 'The Defence White Paper of 1957 ran into thirteen so-called "final" drafts and ultimately appeared with wording which had been inserted only minutes before it went to press.'[26] The aircraft carriers were only saved by the unanimity of the Service Chiefs against Sandys, yet the White Paper contained no defined role for the Navy. Only slowly over the subsequent six months was Mountbatten, as First Sea Lord, able to sell the East of Suez role to a sceptical Sandys. Without it there was no need for the Navy to maintain a balanced fleet. The Navy, therefore, changed its emphasis again, away from the protection of the transatlantic convoys towards the provision of a small number of strike carrier groups and amphibious warfare. The Navy's role in NATO became somewhat clouded with the 'broken-back' strategy effectively retained, but the reserve fleet earmarked to underpin it was scrapped as part of the defence cost savings coming out of the review.[27] The Territorial Army's commitment to Germany was also withdrawn and, more significantly, National Service was ended as part of the substantial reduction in its forces committed to NATO.[28]

While a reaction to the Suez débâcle and the government's needs to reduce the financial and manpower costs of defence, the 1957 Defence White Paper also reflected the implementation of the 1952 Defence Policy and Global Strategy Paper in full. The reality of a short war was accepted with the significant reduction in the RAF's Fighter Command and the Navy's scrapping of much of the reserve fleet. However, the key difference lay in the use of the new tactical nuclear weapons to offset the original plans for large NATO conventional forces (phase 2).[29] Britain's and NATO's nuclear forces now offered a means of defending Europe on the cheap, thereby allowing Britain to continue to play the world role it sought. As a result, Britain's declaratory, military and procurement policies were brought into line with one another for the first time since the end of the Second World War.

Unlike the previous review, Duncan Sandys ran the 1957 defence review through the Ministry of Defence (MoD) and sought to override the Service departments. This was a significant step forward for the MoD and represented quite a considerable coup for the department against the previously all-powerful Service departments. Nevertheless, the Service Chiefs were able to have a considerable input into the process and this was reflected most clearly in Sandys' change of view about the future of the Navy's aircraft carriers.

The Nuclear Review, 1958–69

A number of issues and mini-crises arose between the 1957 review and the series of reviews put through by Denis Healey from 1965 onwards. Most prominent were the series of decisions linked to the strategic nuclear deterrent. While never articulated as a review, or acknowledged in mainstream literature, the fundamental changes that were made to Britain's nuclear forces substantiate the argument that the crisis that resulted was as significant as some of the more official reviews.

Sandys had agreed a twin-track replacement for the high flying V-bomber force and the Thor ballistic missiles, then being deployed to the United Kingdom under dual-key arrangements with the United States. In the short term he sought to retain the V-Force in operation at a reduced scale, initially equipped with an early version of the Blue Steel missile. In the longer term he wished to deploy the Blue Streak intermediate-range ballistic missile and an extended range version of the Blue Steel missile on the existing bomber force. The reasoning was straightforward – the V-bomber force offered flexibility in its mode of operation and deployment while the Blue Streak was invulnerable to interception.[30]

However, these plans were subject to reconsideration quite soon after the 1957 review. The development of both the Mark 1 and Mark 2 variants of the Blue Steel bomb, together with the Blue Streak ballistic missile and TSR-2 strategic bomber placed too high a burden on Britain's scarce scientific and engineering facilities and all were suffering from delays as a result. The options available to the government were limited. The Blue Steel Mark 1 variant was about to enter service and was needed in the short term to sustain the credibility of the nuclear deterrent. Much of the capital investment had already been made and it made little sense to cancel the programme. The TSR-2 was already earmarked as the next generation of strike aircraft for the Royal Air Force. Cancelling this programme would fundamentally undermine the future composition of the Air Force. This left a choice between Blue Streak and the Mark 2 variant of Blue Steel. In the case of the latter there was a direct overlap in the physical and manpower resources required to develop this programme with the earlier Mark 1. It made sense, therefore, to abandon this programme, particularly as the Americans had their own air launched system under development – Skybolt – which they offered to Britain.[31]

Meanwhile the Blue Streak ballistic programme also ran into problems. It was originally conceived as an above ground liquid-fuelled weapon designed to complement, rather than replace, the existing V-bomber force. It was to have been deployed to bases in the UK and Middle East to ensure that it could cover the appropriate target sets in the western part of the Soviet Union.[32] However, its main asset, its invulnerability, was called into question with the development of Soviet ballistic missiles. As a result, consideration was given to underground basing of Blue Streak, but this option was eventually abandoned as the projected costs of Blue Streak continued to rise,[33] and the decision was taken to cancel the programme in 1960. No comparable American system was under development so it was decided to rely instead on the US Skybolt missile carried aboard the existing V-bomber force. Thus, the replacement of both elements of the British strategic deterrent converged upon the American Skybolt missile.

Unfortunately, a crisis emerged when the US subsequently decided to cancel the Skybolt system.[34] This caused a major dispute to occur between the American and British governments. Eventually it was agreed at the following Nassau meeting that the British would purchase the Polaris missile system less warheads from the Americans.[35] The US made the purchase conditional upon the assignment of the British Polaris boats to NATO, with the exception that supreme national interests could take pre-cedence. In the meantime the V-bomber force, with its Blue Steel Mark 1s, was left to fill the void while the Polaris programme was begun. The government accepted that a period of heightened vulnerability would have to be accepted and once Polaris entered service in 1969 the remaining V-bombers were officially switched to the tactical role, although they retained the ability to undertake strategic operations using free-fall bombs.

Thus, between the Sandys Review in 1957 and the Navy's Polaris boats becoming operational in 1969, Britain's strategic nuclear forces underwent a quite substantial change. In 1957 the force had relied entirely on a single weapons platform, the manned aircraft, which had been entirely developed independently from the United States. By 1969 the United Kingdom had become entirely dependent upon the United States for the provision of its strategic nuclear platform, although the government emphasised that it retained operational independence. This marked a partial climb down on the original reasoning behind the acquisition of nuclear weapons as a symbol of being a world power and the growing emphasis upon defence policy being threat based.

The Healey Reviews

The incoming Labour government of 1964 had a different ideological perspective to the preceding Conservative administration. In the late 1950s the Labour Party had flirted with unilateralism as a significant minority within the party voiced concern over the new NATO doctrine of Massive Retaliation.[36] The new administration therefore favoured a conventional rather than nuclear emphasis in NATO together with the maintenance of the East of Suez role.[37] However, these goals came into conflict with their other stated priority of restoring Britain's economic strength. This situation was summed up in Labour's first Defence White Paper:

> The present Government has inherited defence forces which are seriously over-stretched and in some respects dangerously under-equipped. . . . There has been no real attempt to match political commitments to military resources, still less to relate the resources made available for defence to the economic circumstances of the nation. . . . To continue along these lines would mean imposing an increasing burden on the British people which none of their competitors in world trade are carrying.[38]

The government therefore sought to reduce the level of defence spending planned by the Conservatives and set themselves the target of reducing defence's share of government expenditure. Denis Healey, the Secretary of State for Defence, believed that these conflicting objectives were achievable if the MoD was subjected to the appropriate management efficiencies and the defence reviews of 1965–66 sought to meet the requirements of conventional force improvements at a lower cost.[39]

Initially a 'buy American' policy was adopted to try and reduce the cost of various aircraft programmes.[40] This resulted in the cancellation of three domestic aircraft programmes in favour of American alternatives (TSR-2 replaced by F-111s, HS681 replaced by C-130s and the P1154 replaced by F-4s).[41] However, these changes looked as though they would provide only half the necessary cutbacks required to bring defence expenditure to a level of 6 per cent of Gross National Product (GNP) by 1969–70.[42] As a result, a review of defence policy was carried out between 1965 and 1966 and published as the 1966 Defence Estimates. This did not seek to change policy *per se*, but simply look to more efficient means of implementing it in order to provide the requisite savings. A number of cutbacks were announced, most noticeably to the Army's reserve forces. These followed on from the 1957 review assumption that war in Europe would be relatively short and that there was little need for an ill-equipped reserve capable of mobilising over several months.[43] However, these cuts were insufficient to achieve the target reductions and focus quickly settled on two programmes which promised to consume considerable funds. The Navy was looking to replace its existing force of aircraft carriers, while the Air Force was looking to purchase American F-111 strike aircraft in place of the cancelled TSR-2 as a means of bridging the gap in its capabilities before the introduction of the Anglo-French variable-geometry aircraft.[44] Sustaining both programmes within the planned defence budget looked unlikely. The Air Force therefore argued it could undertake tasks of the Navy's aircraft carriers East of Suez at less cost using the proposed F-111 aircraft and the F-4 Phantom aircraft previously ordered in 1965. The Navy disagreed and argued that both new carriers and F-111 aircraft were required if the armed forces were to be able to perform all their required military missions outside Europe.[45] After considerable debate the government concluded that:

> Experience and study have shown that only one type of operation exists for which carriers and carrier-borne aircraft would be indispensable: that is the landing, or withdrawal, of troops against sophisticated opposition outside the range of land-based air cover. It is only realistic to recognise that we, unaided by our allies, could not expect to undertake operations of this character in the 1970s – even if we could afford a large carrier force.[46]

The first of the new carriers, CVA-01, was therefore cancelled and the Navy began to reconfigure itself towards its NATO rather than out-of-area tasks.

By 1967 the continuing failure of the government's economic policy resulted in further calls for reductions in defence spending. This situation was reinforced by the devaluation of the pound which put considerable pressure on the government to reduce its foreign currency expenditure. The main drain on foreign currency stemmed from the stationing of significant air and land forces in Germany and the sizeable forces deployed East of Suez. Given the existing economic climate one of these commitments had to be drastically reduced. While the government's preference was for maintaining the world role, it was also in the midst of Britain's second application to join the European Economic Community (EEC). It therefore wanted to emphasise its European credentials in order to try and prevent another French veto. As a result, any action that could be construed as anti-European, such as the significant withdrawal of troops from Germany, was politically unacceptable. This position was reinforced by NATO's adoption of Flexible Response in 1967 which gave a greater emphasis to conventional forces.[47] Any withdrawal of British forces from Germany would have undermined this new strategy and encouraged other NATO members to do likewise. Fortunately, the confrontation with Indonesia had come to an end and offered the prospect of releasing the forces committed to this,[48] while the 1967 Arab–Israeli War highlighted the lack of British influence in that region. Moreover, the new transport aircraft then entering RAF service offered the opportunity to rapidly deploy UK-based formations East of Suez when needed rather than permanently station units in the area.[49] If stationed at home these forces could also be earmarked to NATO and thus cover both commitments. Given these tensions the decision to withdraw forces from East of Suez was the only real option

The Supplementary Statement on Defence Policy in 1967 therefore announced the decision to withdraw half of the forces deployed in Singapore and Malaya by 1970–71 with further cutbacks to occur later on.[50] However, these cuts proved to be insufficient and the complete withdrawal of units from East of Suez was announced in 1968 together with the cancellation of the F-111 order.[51] However, Britain's commitment to both CENTO and SEATO remained and it was envisaged that units would be flown out from the United Kingdom as necessary to support these obligations.[52]

The series of defence reviews conducted by Healey initially focused on the procurement dimension to policy in an attempt at preserving declaratory policy. When this proved insufficient attempts were made to alter the military dimension of policy through substitution. Thus the initial step was to abandon the replacement aircraft carrier programme and substitute their role with RAF F-4s and F-111s. However, the economic problems confronting Britain, culminating in the devaluation of the pound, led to the large-scale withdrawal of Britain's forces deployed outside Europe and their replacement by forces based in the United Kingdom. Thus, declaratory policy was allowed to remain largely unchanged although in reality the majority of commentators recognised that this marked the beginning of the withdrawal from East of Suez and the down-playing of the world role. During this phase the primacy of the Ministry of Defence and the position of the Secretary of State for Defence was confirmed. The trend towards the centralisation of defence gained momentum with the individual Services now falling under the ambit of the Ministry of Defence.

Détente and the Mason Review

The late 1960s and early 1970s witnessed a change in East–West relations which became known as détente. By 1974 the changing environment within Europe was matched by a change of government in Britain. In opposition, the Labour leadership accused the Conservative government of being too negative about détente and the negotiations that accompanied it. Under the Conservatives defence spending, as a percentage of GNP, had risen once again but this increase failed to keep pace with the rising cost of defence. The Conservatives had also slowed the rundown in forces East of Suez.[53] The new Labour Government therefore again inherited a position where 'the economic situation of the country and the burden of defence expenditure at the level of the plans costed in February 1974 were incompatible'.[54] The 1975 Defence Review aimed to reduce the burden of Britain's defence still further from 5–6 per cent of GNP to 4.5 per cent over ten years.[55]

To achieve this the British government planned to concentrate the British defence effort on NATO and the independent nuclear deterrent.[56] This allowed the government to remove the last vestiges of Britain's worldwide role by withdrawing its forces completely from the Five Power Agreement and CENTO, and dispensing with those forces earmarked for these worldwide roles.[57]

However, this policy of abandoning Britain's non-NATO forces did not provide the requisite reductions in expenditure. The government therefore decided to focus its efforts within NATO on four areas: the deployment of land and air forces in Germany; the protection of supply routes in the Eastern Atlantic and Channel Areas; the defence of the UK; and the strategic nuclear deterrent.[58] This meant completely withdrawing all permanent air and sea forces from the Mediterranean and abandoning Malta as a main base and the virtual elimination of the amphibious assault capability.[59] However, these reductions were still insufficient to provide the required savings and, as a foretaste of the 'Front Line First: Defence Costs Study', infrastructure and support services were slashed to minimise the effect on frontline forces earmarked to NATO. Indicative of this was the Army's abandonment of the brigade level command within its forces.[60]

The Mason Review marked the end of Britain's world role with the virtual elimination of Britain's out-of-area capability[61] and the withdrawal of many of the residual forces deployed beyond Europe. It therefore marked the logical implementation of the Healey Reviews after the holding period of the intervening Conservative government. With the realisation that Britain was not and could not afford to be a world military power within the Cold War structure the Mason Review marked a move towards minimalism – namely, the minimum contribution that Britain needed to make in order to remain part of the NATO alliance. Four core areas were openly identified. The problem that John Nott would subsequently be confronted with was the priority within them. By emphasising the Navy's role in the Eastern Atlantic and Channel Areas the review also marked a shift towards accepting a longer war scenario which conflicted with the reduced sustainability of the conventional forces deployed in Germany.

The review was conducted with the Chiefs of Staff working to achieve the financial targets set by the ministerial team. They established early on the minimum levels required in the four main areas in order to maintain Britain's treaty obligations to NATO. Other areas were then discussed and significant cutbacks made. In this the Chief of the Defence Staff had a prominent role in arbitrating between the Services and selling the case to ministers. Throughout the review the government was very concerned about the reaction of Britain's NATO partners and their views were taken on board before the final document was presented, and the document included a section on the government's reactions to NATO suggestions.[62]

The 1981 Nott Review

The Nott Review, like the subsequent 'Options for Change' and 'Front Line First: The Defence Costs Study',[63] was never formally a review but instead a realignment of forces to meet the financial situation of the time. Nevertheless, the outcome and changes put through by all three warrant their consideration as formal reviews for all were preceded by financial crises within the defence estimates. In many respects the position Nott found himself confronted by was similar to that facing Denis Healey in 1964. He inherited an overspend from the previous financial year (FY) of £200 million and a projected overspend of £400 million for FY 1980/81.[64] Moreover, he felt that the long-term costings (LTC) were overly optimistic and failed to include the decision to purchase the Trident C-4 system in 1980. He decided to undertake a review of the defence programme, rather than a full-blown defence review, in order to bring the procurement programme and available resources into line.

In searching for savings Nott quickly established that the prime areas for savings were in either the continental or maritime commitments to NATO. Home defence and the independent nuclear deterrent were deemed to be sacrosanct while little remained beyond Europe to be cutback. Moreover, the Prime Minister, Margaret Thatcher, was keen to resurrect this role and Nott required her support to successfully implement the review.[65] Within a short space of time he presented the Chiefs of Staff with a single sheet of paper which 'came as a bombshell, they had not expected a Secretary of State to act so decisively, and so quickly to their detriment. On one side of the paper were guidelines for Britain's defence policy in the future and on the other side figures for the three services over the next ten years.'[66]

In part the paper reflected Nott's desire to move away from the conflictual nature of the MoD, but it also reflected his desire to bring the various dimensions of defence policy back into line. It made two basic assumptions. Firstly, that the British armed forces should be geared towards combating the threat posed by the Soviet Union and that this threat was predominantly in Europe. This followed along the lines that had developed over the past twenty years and was not in itself particularly revolutionary. Secondly, that such a war would involve little or no warning, and that it would be a short, intense war. It was, therefore, a return to the policy outlined in the 1952 Defence Policy and Global Strategy Paper but without the broken-backed element. Policy was to be based upon the requirement to buy time on NATO's Central Front in Germany while the NATO Alliance either managed to agree a peace or decide to use nuclear forces. Given this latter assumption the reinforcement convoys traversing the Atlantic became less important.

As a result, the paper indicated that the sea–air function would be substantially affected and that the defence of the home base should become a priority. It advocated a reduction in the Navy's share of defence budget by the end of the 1980s from 29 per cent to 25 per cent, despite the fact that it was now to contain the Trident programme, and removed £7,600 million from the Navy's building programme within the LTCs.[67] For the Navy, the consequences of these conclusions were immediate and substantial cutbacks throughout its fleet. With such a substantial reduction in size of the fleet and the abandonment of the ongoing programme of mid-life updates for surface ships a major reduction in the number of Royal Dockyards was possible. As

Rosyth was busy with Polaris work Nott decided to close Gibraltar and Chatham, and to substantially run down Portsmouth.[68] The reorganisation of Britain's Rhine Army (BAOR) suggested by its new commander went ahead with the reduction of BAOR to 55,000 men. By way of compensation, Nott announced a significant expansion in the size of the Territorial Army from 70,000 to 86,000.[69] Their use and the use of the headquarters units returning to the UK from Germany remained unclear. The latter was subsequently used as part of the Army's transformation to manoeuvre warfare initiated by Field Marshal Sir Nigel Bagnall.[70] The Royal Air Force proved to be the chief beneficiary of the review. Nott sought to increase the number of air defence squadrons as part of the revitalisation of Britain's air defences[71] and announced the initial purchase of 60 Harrier GR5s to support Britain's military capabilities deployed in Germany and a reduction in its forces committed to the eastern Atlantic.[72]

In many ways the changes brought about under Nott marked the fruition of trends begun by Healey and continued by Mason. Where it differed was in Nott's attempts to fully integrate the different elements of defence policy. Mason's minimalist approach did not require that these different aspects be fully integrated because his review was essentially about reducing the defence budget with minimum political damage to Britain. Nott's prioritisation of the continental commitment over the maritime dimension required him to justify the reductions he planned. Moreover, his whole approach to the Ministry of Defence was to achieve a fully integrated defence policy. While the premises he adopted have been questioned, especially after the Falklands War, the inner logic remained intact. His review was, therefore, more akin to that of Sandys than of the other reviews to date.

His approach to review was far more confrontational than had gone in the past, the nearest equivalent being Duncan Sandys. Like Sandys, Nott used a small central team to put his review together but went much further in initiating policy than had been the case with his infamous 'Bermudagram'. Unlike the Sandys review the Services did not unite over the carrier issue and Nott was able to make use of the divisions between the Services to push his policies through.

Options for Change and the end of the Cold War

The Options for Change exercise was announced to the House of Commons in July 1990 with more detailed plans revealed in the 1991 White Paper.[73] The language used was that of an exercise rather than a review and it was presented by the government as the first adjustments to the changing strategic agenda following the breach of the Berlin Wall.

> In the Options for Change studies, we have sought to devise a structure for our regular forces appropriate to the new security situation and meeting our essential peacetime operational needs. . . . Our proposals will bring savings and a reduction in the share of GDP taken by defence. We need force levels which we can afford and which can realistically be manned, given demographic pressures in the 1990s. The aim is smaller forces, better equipped, properly trained and housed, and well motivated. They will need to be flexible and mobile and able to contribute both in NATO and, if necessary, elsewhere.[74]

This was somewhat misleading. The financial pressure upon the defence budget in the late 1980s had been steadily increasing to the extent that a review was already underway. Surprisingly this had been initiated by the Service Chiefs in conjunction with the Chief of the Defence Staff (CDS). They had felt that the procurement programme had become so far removed from the rest of policy that a review was needed to bring it back into line and force the government to make some politically difficult decisions. As a result of the financial pressure on the LTCs the Service Chiefs, under the auspices of the CDS, had already agreed to a sweeping across-the-board cut. What was left to consider was how they would manage these changes and the level of cutback required. In the end the cut represented the minimum that the Service Chiefs thought they could legitimately get away with and it was accompanied with the condition that there would be no further cutbacks for the subsequent five years in order to provide some sort of stability for the defence planners.[75]

What was different about this review was its conduct in a strategic vacuum. The threat posed by the Soviet Union was at an end and NATO was in the throes of substantial change. Before defence policy had been principally based around the Soviet threat. With the dissolution of the Warsaw Pact, and later the Soviet Union, defence policy could no longer be formed around a single threat. Options for Change therefore began the shift towards a capability-based rather than threat-based defence policy. Not surprisingly, there was a considerable amount of liaison between the government officials involved in formulating NATO's New Strategic Concept and those involved in working out the details for Options for Change.[76] In particular, the former had a considerable bearing on the restructuring of the army as the government sought to obtain the coveted command of Allied Command Europe's new Rapid Reaction Corps (ARRC) which required a significant commitment amounting to two divisions and a headquarters staff.[77]

The Options for Change process therefore left all three Services with essentially the same basic force composition as they had during the Cold War but on a smaller scale. The agreement of the Air Force and the Army to this was perhaps not surprising. The Navy had borne the brunt of the reductions in the 1980s and they were therefore content to maintain the existing balance of forces. The Navy's acquiescence was also understandable. Throughout the late 1980s the increasing divergence between the procurement plans envisaged within the LTCs and fiscal reality had particularly affected them as the strategic nuclear deterrent, home defence including the air defence of the UK, and the commitment of land and air forces to West Germany remained the government's priority. As a result, the Navy had suffered continuing delays to its procurement programme. Options for Change allowed the Navy to retire many of its older manpower intensive ships and retain the newer vessels in service while ensuring that the other two Services also equally bore the cutbacks.

Unlike the Nott review Options for Change was a largely CDS–Service led review. The government of the time did not actually want to be confronted with the issue of a review, hence the title Options for Change. Having been saved by the end of the Cold War the government's objective was to achieve a sizeable peace dividend without significant political fallout. As a result, the Services were able to choose which areas they cut back while preserving many of their existing Cold War programmes, such as the Challenger 2 main battle tank and the European Fighter Aircraft. In a sense this was the first review undertaken without recourse to the government's declaratory policy because there wasn't really one. The end of the Cold War had transformed the state of world affairs but nobody was quite sure how.

Front Line First: The Defence Costs Study

The first half of the 1990s witnessed a government ideologically committed and a MoD reacting to the need to quantify defence. The end of the Cold War had heralded considerable talk about a 'peace dividend' at a time of economic slump. The MoD therefore found itself the prime target of the Treasury, which sought to reduce government expenditure where it could. The response to this pressure was 'Front Line First: The Defence Costs Study' which sought to find the necessary savings without reductions to the frontline. It was therefore clearly a response to the government's needs to reduce defence spending in the midst of a recession. In the introduction to the document the Secretary of State for Defence, Malcolm Rifkind, acknowledged this and set himself two goals:

- To ensure that every pound contributes directly or indirectly to fighting capability.
- To spend every pound as efficiently as possible to minimise the overall burden on the public.[78]

Three trends in defence policy emerged under the auspices of this review: firstly, that the defence effort could, in some way, be quantified; secondly, that the ongoing privatisation of many of the defence functions should be enhanced through the Private Finance Initiative (PFI); and thirdly, that joint solutions were a means to enhance Britain's defence capabilities at a significantly reduced cost.

These areas were intentionally targeted because the government wanted to leave declaratory policy unchanged so the frontline could not be seen to suffer further reductions. Cuts to the support services were easier to sustain politically and they fitted more easily into the ideological framework of the Conservative Party at that time. The result was a significant number of cutbacks in the supporting services principally through contracturalisation and the centralisation of defence functions. For example, it was decided to merge the three separate Service Colleges with the existing joint college into a single college to be financed using the Private Finance Initiative.[79]

While these cuts did not look as though they would have an effect on the frontline the reality was somewhat different. They raised a number of questions about the ability of Britain's armed forces to sustain the number of different types of operations that British forces became involved in. Moreover, the ongoing shift away from a threat-based defence policy centred upon the Central Front towards a capabilities-based policy requiring the dispatch of forces outside the European region required a significant logistical tail, the area most affected by this defence review. As a result, this review led to a complete disconnection in the different strands of defence policy as declaratory policy largely divorced itself from military capability. Interestingly the review itself was conducted and run largely by the Top-Level Budget Holders in conjunction with the Secretary of State for Defence. It was therefore far less coordinated than in previous reviews and the internal disconnections were therefore perhaps not surprising.

Strategic Defence Review

The new Labour government entered office in 1997 with a defence review forming part of its election manifesto. In opposition the Labour front bench had been very critical of the government's handling of defence policy and highlighted the hollowing out of capabilities brought about by the reductions to the support services. Initially it was thought that such a review would take about six months and the government sought to canvass a wider range of views than had previously been the case in defence reviews. The result was a review that took fourteen months to publish and which remains to be fully worked out. Robertson virtually admitted this when he stated that Strategic Defence Review (SDR) was only the first step in the process.[80]

SDR sought to address the defence requirements to 2015[81] but retained the existing military tasks and defence roles that were promulgated under the previous administration.[82] The one obvious change has been the creation of an eighth defence mission – defence diplomacy.[83] In part this drew together a number of existing tasks under a new heading but it also reflected the government's internationalist agenda and the desire that Britain should be a force for good in the world.

At the same time attention was now drawn to Britain's position as a leading member of the European Union (EU) and this was linked into Britain's membership of NATO and the importance of the United States.[84] This was a reversal over previous policy and marked a return to a European rather than transatlantic focus. The document was noteworthy in its overt linkage of the use of military force to support Britain's economic interests. Thus not only was defence policy now tasked to promote Britain as a force for good but it was also more explicitly tasked to support the national interest.

To manage the expeditionary nature of Britain's use of force a new Joint Task Force Headquarters has been created which is capable of rapid deployment overseas with the nucleus of a second formed to allow the management of simultaneous operations. This marks a significant advance over the previous situation and, if fully implemented, will mean that more than one operation can be undertaken outside the United Kingdom without recourse to the callout of a significant number of reserve personnel. This will, therefore, give the government a greater degree of flexibility than it has had to date. This is important as defence policy incorporates more of the new internationalist agenda and reflects the changing power balance within Whitehall following the emergence of the Department for International Development (DFID) in place of the previous Overseas Development Administration. SDR also contained a number of structural changes, such as the reordering of the Army's brigades, which underpinned the declared policy. In addition, it contained a number of procurement commitments, such as to two large aircraft carriers and strategic sea and air lift, which will ensure the different elements of policy will have a more harmonious relationship.[85]

The document highlights a number of changes with emphasis given to the importance of technology, particularly the ability to gather information about an opponent and use it to maximum advantage. ISTAR (intelligence, surveillance, target acquisition and reconnaissance) and improved C3 (command, control and communication) are stressed within the SDR document and one of the first announcements after the SDR document was released was the decision to go ahead with the next generation of military communications satellites.[86] However, the concept of information warfare has only five lines devoted to it.[87] This reflects the innate conservatism that still persists within the MoD to anything that is radically different from that which has gone on before together with a desire to see what emerges from the United States before making a decision.

SDR was also novel in its approach. This review was the most open to date and included three seminars attended by selected academics. It set out to be openly foreign policy led, although the failure to publish the foreign policy assumptions led some to question the reality of this. The savings wrought were also relatively minor in comparison with the previous two reviews, although the financial calculations have assumed in-built efficiency savings which may not prove to be quite so easy to achieve. Thus, many of the novel features of SDR surround its conduct rather than its findings and the force composition and future procurement plans are rather conventional. The one new defence mission – defence diplomacy – is merely a relabelling of existing defence tasks rather than a more fundamental change to policy. What SDR has achieved has been the realigning of the three dimensions of policy with one another; whether this can be sustained in the long term is a separate question.

Conclusion

The period from 1945 to 2000 was one of immense change in British defence policy. Within this transformation four interlinked assumptions remained consistent throughout the period: concern about the Soviet Union and its successor states, the 'special relationship' with the United States, the creation and maintenance of a nuclear deterrent, and the ability to influence decisions on the world stage. Their underpinning of British defence policy was inevitable given the position with which Britain was confronted in 1945 but their continuation into the post-Cold War era is perhaps surprising and in some respects they have become stronger under the present Labour government.

Clearly fiscal pressure placed upon the defence budget was a major factor leading to a number of the crises and reviews. However, this was not the sole explanation for many of the changes in policy brought about by the various reviews. The reviews were as much about government spending priorities as Britain's relative decline. Government spending priorities not only reflected the international environment in which Britain found itself, but were also indicative of the domestic environment. For example, the expectations of a peace dividend in the early 1990s proved to be one of the main drivers behind the Front Line First review when the international situation provided a basis for arguing that further defence reductions were premature. Equally defence spending was not and is not governed solely by the domestic agenda. Britain's involvement in a number of defence alliances had a significant impact upon the decisions taken within the Ministry of Defence. Thus the declinist argument that defence policy slowly contracted as the escalating costs of defence forced Britain to abandon its immediate postwar ambitions is somewhat overstated. While few would disagree that overall policy has contracted, what these reviews have shown is that some of the contraction was effectively voluntary as successive governments altered their spending priorities.

Comparisons between the various reviews also highlight a number of common threads. Firstly, that virtually all the reviews had internal inconsistencies which were frequently legacies of previous reviews. For example, the 1952 Defence Policy and Global Strategy Paper concluded that the defence of the United Kingdom from strategic air attack was no longer feasible, yet it continued the build-up in the Royal Air Force's fighter strength. As a result, no review was ever fully carried out and decisions made in one review would often take another review or two to be implemented.

Secondly, the role for the Royal Navy was a perennial issue. This was most evident in the 1957 paper which ignored the Navy's role because agreement could not be reached. This was a reflection of the quandary that defence planners continually faced: whether policy should be threat-based or capability-based. The problem with the former was most evident with the 1952 Defence and Global Strategy Paper which focused on Hot War tasks and left Britain ill-prepared for the Suez Crisis and the 1981 Nott Review which almost left Britain ill-equipped to deal with the Falklands issue in 1982. The problem of the latter is a lack of focus; particularly when there is an obvious threat. Nott's main criticism of the armed forces in 1981 was their weakness in supporting their primary missions, deterring the Soviet Union. This dilemma remains with SDR emphasising capabilities.

Thirdly, what is also apparent from the various reviews is the changing power balance among those involved in the formulation and implementation of defence policy. The reviews have indicated the key roles played by some individuals within the review process and this would indicate that the traditional structure-orientated approaches to policy analysis have weaknesses. For example, John Nott's lead within his own review or that of the Service Chiefs in producing the Defence Policy and Global Strategy Papers reflects the influences individuals can have, while the sheer time-scale involved in altering procurement programmes is an indication of the potential for structural dominance.

Notes

1. See General Sir W. Jackson, *Britain's Defence Dilemma: An Inside View*, London: B. T. Batsford, 1990.
2. M. Chalmers, 'Military Spending and the British Economy', in David Coates and John Hillard (eds), *UK Economic Decline*, London: Harvester Wheatsheaf, 1995, p. 287.
3. Ritchie Ovendale, *British Defence Policy since 1945*, Manchester: Manchester University Press, 1994.
4. H. Wynn, *RAF Nuclear Deterrent Forces*, London: HMSO, 1994, p. 13.
5. Idem.
6. 'Report by the Chiefs of Staff on Defence Policy and Global Strategy', D.O. (50) 45, CAB 131/9, 7 June 1950, London: PRO.
7. Ibid., paras 5 and 13.
8. See J. J. Sokolsky, *Seapower in the Nuclear Age: The United States Navy and NATO, 1949–80*, London: Routledge, 1991, especially pp. 7–75.
9. *Defence Programme*, Cmnd. 8,146, London: HMSO, 1951, reprinted in Rear Admiral H.G. Thursfield (ed.), *Brassey's Annual: The Armed Forces Yearbook, 1951*, London: William Clowes & Sons Ltd, 1951, p. 408.

10. Ibid., pp. 407–8.
11. 'Report by the Chiefs of Staff on Defence Policy and Global Strategy', PREM 11/49, COS (52) 362. fos 85, 80, 15 July 1952, London: PRO.
12. Ibid., paras 32–3.
13. Ibid.
14. Ibid., paras 103–4.
15. Eric Grove, *Vanguard to Trident*, London: Bodley Head, 1987, pp. 84–5.
16. See S. Kelly and A. Gorst, 'Whitehall and the Suez Crisis', Special edition of *Contemporary British History*, 13 (2) 1999, pp. 1–11.
17. P. Ziegler, *Mountbatten: the Official Biography*, London: William Collins Sons, 1985, pp. 537–8.
18. C. J. Bartlett, *A History of Post-war Britain, 1945–74*, London: Longman Group, 1977, p. 135.
19. H. Thomas, *The Suez Affair*, London: Weidenfeld & Nicolson, 1967, p. 147.
20. *Defence Outline of Future Policy*, Cmnd. 124, London: HMSO, 1957, para. 7.
21. Ibid., paras 10 and 12.
22. H. Wynn, op. cit., p. 373.
23. *Defence Outline of Future Policy*, op. cit., para. 22.
24. Ibid., p. 3.
25. E. Grove, op. cit., p. 199.
26. P. Ziegler, op. cit., p. 552.
27. *Defence Outline of Future Policy*, op. cit., para. 38.
28. Ibid., p. 4.
29. Ibid., para. 23.
30. H. Wynn, op. cit., pp. 373–4.
31. Ibid., pp. 401–3.
32. Ibid., p. 374.
33. Ibid., p. 383.
34. Ibid., p. 399.
35. Ibid., p. 421.
36. D. Keohane, *Labour Party Defence Policy since 1945*, Leicester: Leicester University Press, 1993, p. 22.
37. P. Ziegler, *Wilson: The Authorised Life*, London: Weidenfeld & Nicolson, 1993, pp. 210–11.
38. *Statement on the Defence Estimates, 1965*, Cmnd. 2,592, London: HMSO, 1965, p. 1.
39. D. Healey, *The Time of My Life*, London: W. W. Norton, 1989, pp. 270–7.
40. *Statement on the Defence Estimates, 1965*, op. cit., p. 10.
41. Ibid., para. 150; B. Reed and G. Williams, *Denis Healey and the Politics of Power*, London: Sidgwick and Jackson, 1970, p. 172; S. Straw and J. W. Young, 'The Wilson Government and the Demise of TSR-2, October 1964–April 1965', *Journal of Strategic Studies*, 20 (4) December 1997, pp. 18–44.
42. *Statement on the Defence Estimates 1966, Part 1: The Defence Review*, Cmnd. 2,901, London, HMSO, 1966, p. 1.
43. *Reorganisation of the Army Reserves*, Cmnd. 2,855, London: HMSO, 1965.

44. *Statement on the Defence Estimates 1966, Part 1: The Defence Review*, op. cit., paras 8–9.
45. E. Grove, op. cit., pp. 270–7.
46. *Statement on the Defence Estimates 1966, Part 1: The Defence Review*, op. cit., p. 10.
47. See J. E. Stromseth, *The Origins of Flexible Response*, Basingstoke: Macmillan, 1988, pp. 151–74.
48. *Supplementary Statement on Defence Policy, 1967*, Cmnd. 3,357, London: HMSO, 1967, p. 5.
49. Ibid., p. 4.
50. Ibid., p. 5.
51. *Statement on the Defence Estimates, 1968*, Cmnd. 3,540, London: HMSO, 1968, p. 2.
52. Ibid., p. 5.
53. *Supplementary Statement on Defence Policy, 1970*, Cmnd. 4,521, London: HMSO, 1970, pp. 4–5; *Statement on the Defence Estimates, 1975*, Cmnd. 5,976, London: HMSO, 1975, p. 1.
54. R. Mason, *House of Commons Parliamentary Debates*, vol. 883, fifth series, session 1974–75, 9–20 December 1974, Statement to the House, 12 December 1974, col. 1,148.
55. R. Mason, *House of Commons Parliamentary Debates*, vol. 882, fifth series, session 1974–75, 25 November–6 December 1974, Statement to the House, 3 December 1974, col. 1,352.
56. *Statement on the Defence Estimates, 1975*, op. cit., p. 7.
57. The air portable division and parachute brigade were disbanded and replaced by an airportable formation of brigade strength which contained a limited parachute capability earmarked for deployment in the Central and Northern regions of NATO. The Air Force suffered comparable cutbacks in its air transport fleet and strike aircraft were withdrawn from Cyprus. *Statement on the Defence Estimates, 1975*, Cmnd. 5,976, London: HMSO, pp. 14–15, and p. 18.
58. Ibid., pp. 9–10.
59. Ibid., p. 15.
60. Ibid., p. 16.
61. See table Ibid., p. 12.
62. See M. Carver, *Out of Step: The Memoirs of Field Marshal Lord Carver*, London: Century Hutchinson, 1989, pp. 448–57; *Statement on the Defence Estimates, 1975*, op. cit., p. 13.
63. Tom King, *House of Commons Parliamentary Debates*, vol. 177, sixth series, session 1989–90, 23 July–19 October 1990, Statement to the House, 25 July 1990, cols. 468–86; *Statement on the Defence Estimates, 1991: Britain's Defence for the 1990s*, Cmnd. 1,559, London: HMSO, 1991; *Front Line First: The Defence Costs Study*, London: HMSO, 1994.
64. D. Fairhall, 'The Battle of the Cuts', *The Guardian*, 7 January 1981.
65. M. Thatcher, *The Downing Street Years*, London: HarperCollins, 1993, p. 162.
66. M. Macintosh, *Managing Britain's Defence*, London: Macmillan, 1990, p. 116.

67. D. Wettern, *The Decline of British Seapower*, London: Jane's, 1982, p. 384.
68. *The United Kingdom Defence Programme: The Way Forward*, Cmnd. 8,288, London: HMSO, 1981, p. 12.
69. Ibid., p. 6.
70. See C. McInnes, 'BAOR in the 1980s: Changes in Doctrine and Organisation', *Defense Analysis*, 4 (4) 1988, pp. 377–94.
71. *The United Kingdom Defence Programme: The Way Forward*, op. cit., p. 6.
72. Ibid., p. 8.
73. *Statement on the Defence Estimates, 1991*, op. cit.
74. T. King, *House of Commons Parliamentary Debates*, op. cit., col. 468.
75. Private discussion.
76. Agreed at the NATO Heads of State and Government meeting, Rome, 7–8 November 1991, *NATO Press Communiqué S-1 (91) 85*, 7 November 1991.
77. *Statement on the Defence Estimates, 1991*, op. cit., p. 47.
78. *Front Line First: The Defence Costs Study*, op. cit., p. 3.
79. Ibid.
80. *Strategic Defence Review*, Cmnd. 3,999, London: The Stationery Office, 1998, p. 7.
81. Ibid., p. 6.
82. See *Statement on the Defence Estimates, 1996*, Cmnd. 3,223, London: The Stationery Office, 1996.
83. *Strategic Defence Review*, op. cit., pp. 14–15.
84. Ibid., p. 6.
85. Ibid., pp. 24, 26–7, 29.
86. Ministry of Defence Press Release no. 213/98, 12 August 1998.
87. *Strategic Defence Review*, op. cit., p. 21.

Chapter 2

Britain's Contribution to Global Order

Wyn Rees

Introduction

A superficial inspection of Britain's global military role in the latter half of the twentieth century appears to accord with the standard 'declinist' thesis. At the end of the Second World War Britain was a triumphant power, one of the 'Big Three' powers that sat at the top table of world diplomacy. Admittedly, the country's material resources had been denuded by the war and it had become dependent on US financial assistance, but its industrial base had not been devastated and it had escaped occupation by a hostile power. The British government swiftly reasserted its imperial position and began the process of policing its extensive overseas territories. But by the end of the century, Britain's reduced circumstances were apparent for all to see. It had withdrawn its military forces from around the world and relinquished the overwhelming proportion of its empire territories. No longer could it claim to be a superpower but a middle-ranking European power.

The story of postwar British global policy as an inevitable process of recognising reduced material power is, however, insufficient. Such an approach tells us little about the evolving perceptions of British policy-makers and why critical changes of direction occurred at particular moments. In particular, it fails to take account of Britain's sense of its special contribution in the world, derived from its history and sense of responsibility. At the end of the century, despite its reduced global military presence, the UK is still an actor involved in most substantial world issues and it still retains a seat on the United Nations Security Council.

A more discriminating and nuanced approach to postwar British global policy than that of the 'declinist' school, has to be made in order to understand the position Britain finds itself in today. Postwar British defence planners were faced with a complex task. On the one hand, they had to develop security policy in the face of an external environment that was dominated by US-Soviet rivalry, the breakup of colonial empires and the multiplication of sovereign states. On the other hand, planners inherited a mindset that affirmed that Britain was a major world power with a unique set of obligations in the world. Although policy-makers were aware of the reduced financial strength of the UK after the war there was every expectation that this was a temporary phenomenon. It was assumed that the UK would continue to hold a place in the top tier of countries leading the west.

The complexity of Britain's position was exacerbated by the lack of clarity surrounding the relationship between defence and foreign policy. A government's defence policy is usually designed to protect those interests that it determines to be vital: in this sense, defence policy is expected to be the servant of foreign policy. Yet successive British governments, determined to preserve the country's great power status, were unwilling to reduce Britain's foreign policy commitments to match the declining resources available to defend all these interests. What resulted was an absence of a clear foreign policy vision. As Denis Healey, a long-serving Minister of Defence in the 1960s noted,[1] defence obligations, rather than being subordinate to foreign policy interests, actually came to determine foreign policy due to the fact that all commitments were considered to be vital.

The characteristic pragmatism of British policy-makers rendered it unlikely that any of the three policy objectives of protecting the country's relationship with its empire, the US and Europe would be fundamentally challenged or dramatically revised. Sketching out new and innovative visions of Britain's role was something that would have made civil servants at the time feel distinctly uncomfortable. Those responsible for executing Britain's defence policy were preoccupied with immediate demands and numerous crises. Consequently, short-term tactical assessments of policy tended to take precedence over long-term strategic thinking. The resulting defence planning became focused on the maintenance of Britain's place in the world.

This chapter will proceed to look at Britain's conception of postwar order. It will analyse its attitudes towards its treaty partners and the United States and will compare the differing priorities that were attached to these relationships. It will focus on the decision to withdraw from its Far East and Middle East military roles in the latter part of the 1960s and it will seek to illuminate the extent to which, at the present time, the UK regards itself as a global actor.

A British concept of order

The perception of policy-makers about Britain's global status provided a prism through which they viewed the world. Foremost among the responsibilities that they believed their country possessed was the preservation of 'order' around the globe: an order that was understood to represent the *status quo* and the existing distribution of power. As the 1948 Defence Estimates made clear: '[t]he United Kingdom, as a member of the British Commonwealth and a Great Power, must be prepared at all times to fulfil her responsibility not only to the United Nations but also to herself'.[2] Even though it had been unable to protect all of its empire from invasion and annexation during the Second World War, there was never any question about the reassertion and protection of Britain's overseas colonies after the conflict was over. Failure to have re-established its position would have undermined Britain's conception of its status and represented an abdication of its responsibilities. It was determined to protect its interests and regarded the use of force as a legitimate instrument for this purpose.

In addition, the fact that sterling served as one of the two major international reserve currencies, alongside the American dollar, and as a medium for conducting international trade, also gave the UK a sense of its special status. A Cabinet paper from 1960 declared that, 'the United Kingdom's first economic responsibility, and the necessary condition for maintaining our place in the world, is to keep sterling strong'.[3] This meant that it was considered vital for Britain's international standing to be maintained: a loss of confidence in the UK could have resulted in significant ramifications for the value of the pound and vice versa. British policy-makers believed it was necessary to deploy military power to protect overseas trade and investments. For example, the 1973 Statement on the Defence Estimates drew an overt link between Britain upholding stability without which, 'Britain's world wide political and trading interests cannot flourish'.[4] This was a questionable assumption as other trading countries, such as Japan and West Germany, did not protect their export partners and trade routes with military forces.

There was a consensus around these views for long periods in British domestic politics: differences of emphasis existed between the main two parties but both adhered to the fundamental conviction that the UK must uphold the existing international order against all challenges. For example, even when the Labour government of 1964 came to power after a period of criticising the external policies of its predecessor, the new Prime Minister Harold Wilson was still willing to state that Britain's line of defence began on the Himalayas. Few people in positions of authority were prepared to question the assumption of the UK's role. One notable exception was the Chief Scientific Adviser at the Ministry of Defence, Sir Henry Tizard, who feared that if Britain continued to overreach itself it would hasten its own demise. He warned that 'if we continue to behave like a Great Power we shall soon cease to be a great nation'.[5]

In seeking to uphold its conception of international order, the UK was at the same time protecting and furthering its own interests. It became impossible to differentiate between these two objectives: on the one side, the maintenance of stability within the international system and on the other, the protection of British interests. In the Middle East, for instance, Britain's security efforts were often portrayed as a contribution to upholding a western inspired order. But they also served the purpose of safeguarding vital lines of communication between the UK and the Far East as well as ensuring oil supplies for the UK economy and protecting the investments of national oil companies.[6]

In order to police its worldwide commitments, the postwar Labour government reintroduced conscription in 1947. By the end of that decade it was estimated that approximately 300,000 British military personnel were involved in extra-European responsibilities.[7] But it was doubtful whether even resources on this scale were commensurate with the demands that a global defence presence imposed. The sense of military overstretch, of forces being spread too thinly around the world, was evident from the early 1950s onwards. For the armed services, standing at the sharp end of these policies, the implications were apparent in the long tours of duty for personnel, often unaccompanied by their families, and the inability to replace expensive weapons platforms such as ships and aircraft.

Policy-makers had to balance the needs of the armed forces against the pressure of defence spending that they considered the British economy could support. Competition for labour was fierce after the war and defence spending absorbed valuable resources away from scientific research and development. After the Second World War, Britain was dependent on the provision of US loans. In 1947 Britain signalled to America the parlous state of its economy when it announced its inability to sustain economic assistance to the governments of Greece and Turkey. There was a very real fear that Britain's long-term strength to resist Soviet pressure during the Cold War could be put at risk by short-term military priorities.

Even though resources for defence were under constant pressure, the UK's sense of its obligations and responsibilities as a great power precluded radical cuts in commitments. For Britain to disengage from any of its overseas military commitments risked increasing the instability of a region and presenting a power vacuum for an adversary to exploit. This rendered it difficult for Britain to reassess its international obligations if in so doing it might lead to damaging global repercussions. This helps to explain why leaders of every political hue were so reluctant to reduce the military commitments that the armed forces considered themselves to be incapable of sustaining without substantial additional resources. Even the opportunity to review Britain's obligations presented by the granting of independence to India did not cause a substantial questioning of the UK's role. India, after all, had been the linchpin around which Britain's imperial interests were constructed[8] yet after its independence the UK remained committed to essentially the same obligations east of the Suez Canal.

When change was found to be inevitable, the UK took upon itself the task of ensuring that the process of withdrawal occurred in an ordered and structured fashion. As Darby notes: 'It was a British interest to [see that change] took place in a controlled manner'.[9] It became an article of faith that the UK could not afford to lose face as it was feared that this might encourage enemies to pressure Britain to leave other parts of the world. Territories had to be vacated with honour, leaving behind a semblance of good government and administration even if this required the fighting of wars before the retreat took place. Even after withdrawal had occurred from former colonies, Britain tended to enter into defence obligations that left it with long-term responsibilities. For example, in 1957, Britain committed itself to the defence of Malaysia after it granted that country independence and in return, the UK obtained the right to station a limited number of forces on Malaysian soil. After the withdrawal from East of Suez, Britain retained its obligation to assist in the Five Power defence agreement with Singapore, Malaysia, Australia and New Zealand, that promised to consult with these governments in the event of an emergency. Similar obligations were entered into in the early 1970s with states in the Persian Gulf, such as Bahrain and Qatar.

Threat perceptions and alliance commitments

Throughout the postwar period, threats to British interests were perceived to emanate from a variety of sources. Most potent was the threat from the expansionist ideologies and great power interests of adversaries such as the Soviet Union and China and those countries that were part of their spheres of interest. There was also the danger posed by states that had territorial designs on countries within the British Commonwealth as well as the threat from indigenous anti-western nationalist movements. In the light of this complex array of threats, Britain chose to construct a global network of alliances to protect its interests. In the West it was a member of NATO; in the Middle East it assisted in the creation of the Baghdad Pact[10] and in Asia it became party to the South East Asian Treaty Organisation (SEATO).[11]

That the UK was engaged in a series of conflicts, of varying types and levels of intensity throughout the postwar period attests to the seriousness with which the UK treated these threats. Successive British governments demonstrated their preparedness to expend considerable military resources and suffer casualties in overseas conflicts. It is a tribute to the adaptability of the three armed services that they were able to fight in widely differing regions, at relatively short notice, yet still produce enviable results. Tasks ranged from colonial policing in Hong Kong to counter-insurgency warfare in the jungles of Borneo; from peacekeeping missions in Cyprus to high intensity warfare in the Falklands. Bartlett wrote that 'since 1950 Suez had been the only disaster'.[12] Even in the case of Suez, the reasons for the curtailment of the operation were due to political pressures rather than the failure of forces on the ground to achieve their objectives. The success of British military engagements since the Second World War appears to justify the rationale that in training for the most demanding types of warfare, forces were rendered capable of performing a wide range of operations.

In order to respond to the various types of threats, British military planners placed them in three distinct categories. The foremost threat was that of global conflict against the Soviet Union and its allies. This was likely to involve the use of strategic nuclear weapons on national homelands and Britain intended to launch its strategic attacks from the UK and from bases in the Middle East and possibly Asia. It was envisaged that Europe would be the decisive theatre in such a conflict and the UK would be fighting for its very survival. Based upon these premises, the British were reluctant to plan to send reinforcements to other areas of the world in the event of a global war taking place. It was difficult to see how fighting by regional allies in Asia or in the Middle East would have an appreciable impact on what was likely to be a short and immensely destructive war.

Nevertheless, UK planning priorities for global war brought it into tension with alliance partners in the Baghdad Pact and SEATO who wanted guarantees of western assistance against what they perceived to be the likely threats to their regions. In the 1950s and 1960s, the Far East tended to be lower down the UK list of priorities than the Middle East. It was considered unrealistic to expect to send reinforcements to the SEATO area in the event of all-out war: the British had limited capabilities for such a task, the distances involved were too great and too much time would elapse. As for the forces already located in the theatre, these were primarily concentrated in just two bases, Singapore and Malaya. As a result, the UK was content to accord primary responsibility for the area to the United States, who had been most active in this region during the Second World War and retained the closest links with many Asian states.

Even in the Middle East, where the UK enjoyed more influence than the US, little serious planning was devoted to defending the region against a determined Soviet incursion. The Middle East did have great strategic significance for Britain in the Cold War: it was the Soviet Union's gateway to Africa and it was an important transport route and source of raw materials for Britain. Yet with the advent of thermonuclear weapons the Middle East could no longer be seen as the key to the security of the UK. The UK also lacked the resources to be able to assist the region in global war. Nuclear-armed aircraft, for example, were not available in sufficient numbers to be able to offer to CENTO before 1959.[13] The UK was against reinforcing the theatre with conventional forces because it did not believe this would make any significant difference. Its attitude led to perpetual frictions with alliance partners who regarded themselves as dependent on western help in such a conflict.

The second level of threat was limited war: a conflict in which some form of restraint was exercised, either in relation to the weapons used or its geographical extent. There was an increasing likelihood of limited conflict occurring during the Cold War because the nuclear armouries of the Superpowers deterred the initiation of global war. One possible form of limited war was the threat of Soviet aggression against a country with whom Britain maintained alliance obligations; for example, Pakistan or Iran. This was thought to be unlikely, however, because the Soviets would fear the possibility of escalation to all-out war. Instead, the USSR might encourage one of its surrogates to initiate a limited conflict on its behalf, enabling it to provide assistance to its protégé without being directly involved.

Once again, alliances were deemed by Britain to be of little use in the face of limited war as they would be heavily dependent on military assistance from either the UK or the US. British planners had a low opinion of the military capabilities and fighting efficiency of states in the Baghdad Pact and SEATO. The alliances were seen as weak because of the diversity of states within them and the differences of view among their members. The British were suspicious that many of their allies were trying to involve them in regional quarrels with their neighbours that had nothing to do with the over-arching East–West competition. For example, the British suspected that pressure from Pakistan, throughout the 1950s, to mount a stronger conventional defence of its territory was principally aimed at obtaining security from the threat posed by India.[14]

In addition, the UK found that many of the limited conflicts in which it became involved were national obligations that took place outside of the parameters of the alliances. Some of Britain's key territorial interests were not covered within the formal treaty arrangements, such as Muscat and Aden in the Persian Gulf, Cyprus in the Mediterranean and Hong Kong and Borneo in the Far East. This rendered the alliances of questionable value to UK policy. In the case of Malaya, to which Britain felt itself to have a powerful obligation, it was necessary for a dedicated regional agreement to be established – the Australia, New Zealand and Malaya Pact (ANZAM) – because the territory was outside the ambit of SEATO. After Malaysia was granted independence in 1957, Britain entered into a period of sustained 'confrontation' with President Sukarno's Indonesia in the early 1960s because of threats to the security of Malaysia. As part of this commitment Britain deployed a large contingent of troops to Borneo who became engaged in both low-level border incursions and in plans to resist a large-scale invasion.

Other examples also highlight the fact that Britain was unable to rely on its alliances to defend its global interests. The conflict in Oman in 1957 and the Kuwaiti crisis in 1961 saw Britain take unilateral action to defend countries that were not part of CENTO. In the latter case, Iraq seemed to be poised to attack Kuwait and, although British troops were not engaged in actual hostilities, it was judged that their rapid insertion into Kuwait prevented an inter-state war. A final example was the Falklands War of 1982 which was a case of a British dependent territory being the victim of external aggression. A task force was dispatched to the South Atlantic that decisively defeated a numerically superior Argentinean force.

The third level of threat occurred with the greatest frequency and was often the hardest to counteract. This was the threat of conflicts that took place within states, that were inspired by nationalist insurgency movements. These conflicts might originate either from domestic factors, such as Arab nationalism in the Middle East, or might be fomented by countries outside of the region, such as the USSR or China. A paper written by the British Chiefs of Staff in 1958 stated that such conflicts could encapsulate 'subversion, civil wars and insurrections inspired by the basic ideological [communist] conflict'.[15] Dealing with such situations was inherently problematic because it was both difficult to target the source and because the insurgents could melt into the host population. It was judged necessary to develop a political campaign that would maintain popular support in order to complement the action.

Despite the complexity of these sorts of conflicts, Britain proved extremely adept at countering insurgencies. The British Army, in particular, was able to develop new techniques and combat skills to successfully prosecute campaigns and developed a reputation for pioneering many of the techniques of this form of warfare. Names such as Sir Gerald Templar and Sir Frank Kitson became synonomous with these ideas.[16] Britain fought long and gruelling conflicts against communist subversion in the minority Chinese population in Malaya; against the Mau Mau in Kenya and against anti-government forces in Aden and Oman. The Malayan campaign began in 1948 and continued, at varying levels of intensity, for twelve years. The British acquitted themselves more successfully in these conflicts, with markedly poorer resources, than the United States did in its subsequent conflict with North Vietnam.

In relation to this form of conflict, the British appreciated the value of CENTO and SEATO. These alliances gave the member states a sense of solidarity, both with their neighbours and with western countries. This contributed to their ability to resist external intimidation and internal subversion. Although the British, like the Americans, were reluctant to commit their forces to supporting their allies, they were supportive of the political value of the alliances.

The major alliances, other than NATO, were largely political agreements that were designed to demonstrate political support, rather than for war-fighting purposes. The fulfilment of alliance obligations provided a justification for Britain's military presence abroad, alongside the protection of UK colonies, but they were never blueprints for the type of military action that the UK would undertake in times of global conflict. A British Joint Planning Staff document from 1958 illustrates this point well: 'The UK . . . has viewed the military affairs . . . of the [Baghdad] Pact rather as a framework for its political aims than as a serious military undertaking.'[17]

Ally of the US

While the UK saw its Middle Eastern and South East Asian alliances as having only limited value, it placed the highest priority on its bilateral relationship with the United States. Consistent with policy-makers' beliefs of Britain's rightful place in the postwar order, the UK–US relationship provided the cornerstone of western security. Britain regarded the US as the only other state in the western alliance that held a world, rather than a regional perspective. It was therefore imperative from the British perspective that these two countries worked together in a partnership, based upon the cooperation that had been established in the Second World War. This approach received a mixed response in Washington: some US administrations seemed to appreciate the value of another 'global perspective' among their allies,[18] while for others the UK was just another fading power.

There were two other considerations that motivated British policy towards the US. The first was the need to be able to influence US policy on matters that affected the interests of all western powers. The British felt that their diplomatic experience was necessary to temper US policies, due to the fact that America was relatively new to its position of leadership in international affairs. In essence, the aim was to prevent extremist US policies, what could be termed the 'crusading spirit' of US policy. For example, the UK sought to provide a counterbalance to hard-line US views on China, particularly in the 1950s during the Korean War and later with the standoff over Taiwan and the islands of Quemoy and Matsu.[19]

The second consideration was that US assistance to Britain was vital in sustaining the UK's international position. US recognition enabled the UK to sit at the top table of international diplomacy, particularly in relation to western dialogue with the USSR. The British were also mindful that US strength could potentially be harnessed to compensate for deficits in Britain's resources. A Cabinet paper during Harold Macmillan's premiership acknowledged: 'the US will be the only Power capable of supporting our interests in the world. . . . We shall become increasingly dependent on their support . . . and our status . . . will largely depend upon their readiness to treat us as their closest ally'.[20] The US possessed the capability to relieve the perennial overstretch of British forces stationed abroad and to underwrite the UK's defence obligations through the provision of American power.

These policy objectives of cooperation with the United States were not without their problems however. Britain was seeking a partnership with a much more powerful state and that raised the issue of what the UK could offer in return to the relationship. Apart from sharing a common appreciation of many global problems, it was not readily apparent what the US stood to gain from cooperation with the UK. The British judged that they had to be capable of making a contribution to global security that would justify being treated as a partner; in effect, they had 'to make consultation necessary'.[21] Britain had to be seen to be serving alongside its transatlantic ally in order to be taken seriously. Yet in doing so this exacerbated some of the very resource questions that cooperation with the US was intended to resolve.

Another problem was that the two countries often differed in their policy prescriptions. The objective of influencing American policy was rendered especially difficult when the British disagreed with their ally's political stance. For example, in the 1950s the UK saw the threat of insurgency and subversion presenting the greatest threat in the Far East, but this was not a view that was held by policy-makers in Washington. A British Chiefs of Staff paper declared that the US was 'more concerned with overt aggression than with subversion or covert aggression which are now recognised as the main danger'.[22] Britain found itself in disagreement with US policy towards such issues as China and the hard-line American policy towards Cuba. In the 1980s, the difference in approach between the two powers was demonstrated in British reservation over the US invasion of Grenada.[23]

By attempting to act alongside the US in various regions of the world and in seeking to influence US policies, Britain found itself involved in issues that were peripheral to its own interests. The dispatch of British troops to the Korean War, for example, was an early attempt to demonstrate solidarity with the US, but this came at a time when the UK was still trying to overcome wartime rationing. In the Far East in the 1960s, where the US was more heavily involved than the UK, there was a long-term US policy of trying to engage Britain more closely in the region and the Johnson Administration pressured its British counterpart to send troops to Vietnam. The US Defense Secretary at that time, Robert McNamara, indicated that he saw Britain's contribution in Asia as relatively more important in the Cold War than its presence in Europe. Sufficient pressure was exerted upon Downing Street for the British Foreign Secretary, Michael Stewart, to fear that if the UK pulled out of the Far East then the US might withdraw its forces from Europe.[24] It was ironical that American attitudes towards Britain and South East Asia had come full circle: in the past the US had castigated Britain for its imperial overseas role and had called for its withdrawal, while now it was calling for a British military presence to be reasserted.

A final factor complicating Britain's calculations was that decision-makers in Washington were often antagonistic towards British policies. In particular, the postwar continuation of Britain's empire was a cause for criticism in the US and there was reluctance to be associated with any UK policies that could be labelled 'imperialist'. This was exemplified by US unwillingness to accede to the Baghdad Pact in the 1950s because America calculated that such a move might be interpreted as supporting British imperial interests in the Middle East.[25] A similar American attitude was present during the Suez Crisis in 1956, where the United States took active steps both politically and economically to frustrate the Anglo-French expedition.[26] After the experience of Suez, there was a decline in Britain's interest in countries surrounding the Mediterranean and a shift in focus towards Aden and the Persian Gulf area. Furthermore, a central tenet of British policy became the avoidance of another such catastrophic split with the US.

In the light of these tensions, fundamental questions were raised over the extent to which the UK could afford to become dependent on the US for its security policy. Alternatively, was it necessary for the UK to preserve its independence and capacity to act alone? The answer was in the affirmative but it had to be qualified. In policy areas such as intelligence gathering and nuclear collaboration, the relationship was markedly favourable to the UK and British policy-makers were content to become heavily dependent on the United States. Yet across the broader spectrum of defence interests, because of the reluctance of the US authorities to engage in detailed planning with Britain outside of Europe, the British chose to preserve their ability to act independently. As Lord Carver, a former Chief of the Defence Staff, has argued, the UK preserved the concept of 'balanced forces'.[27] This was the capability to execute all types of military operations independently of allies. Even with a partner as close as the US, the British believed that the capacity to make independent choices was fundamental to the maintenance of their Great Power status.

Withdrawal from East of Suez

By the early 1960s the situation of nuclear stalemate with the USSR diminished the likelihood of global war and threw into sharper relief the succession of minor conflicts and tensions in which the UK was engaged outside of Europe. Speaking in 1962 the former Field Marshal, Viscount Montgomery, declared that: 'The Atlantic is safe; the Mediterranean is safe: the potential trouble spots lie elsewhere, in the Near East, the Middle East and Africa.'[28] Similarly, in a meeting in 1964 between the Prime Minister and the Chiefs of Staff, Wilson stated that, 'the greater danger [than in Europe] lay in overseas theatres. The role of helping to keep the peace there was one which the UK was particularly fitted to maintain.'[29] The contribution of the UK to preserving global order had never appeared to be more important than at this time. The British government emphasised to its western partners at every opportunity the value of the forces that were deployed around the globe as a contribution to the broader strategic interests of the West.

The services provided a powerful constituency supporting Britain's global role. Like their political masters they shared an emotional and psychological affinity with the Commonwealth as it was the foundation upon which British greatness had been constructed. From a more selfish perspective, all three services were only too aware that the overseas roles were often far more interesting and exotic than the British Army of the Rhine (BAOR). Such global roles accorded military personnel the opportunity to use the skills that they had developed in training. By contrast, exercising in Germany against an enemy that never came was relatively mundane. As Minister of Defence Denis Healey noted in his memoirs, 'they [the services] much preferred fighting in the glamorous Orient to patrolling the North German plain or the East Atlantic'.[30]

More fundamentally, both the Army and the Navy predicated their force structures around the rationale of conducting a worldwide role. In an era when nuclear weapons appeared to have revolutionised warfare, both services had to justify retaining large conventional forces. The Army pointed to the need for large contingents of soldiers to be ready to fight in manpower-intensive insurgency conflicts, as well as to be based in overseas garrisons for policing purposes. For its part, the Royal Navy had embraced the limited war role after the Suez operation.[31] It justified the retention of its capital ships, especially expensive aircraft carriers, as vital to force projection capabilities to provide aerial support to amphibious landings undertaken at long distances from friendly bases. Such missions only made sense in the context of military operations conducted outside of Europe and therefore the Navy was eager to see a global military role perpetuated.

However, a variety of factors arose to remove the foundations of Britain's global role. The first of these was the process of decolonisation that had increased in intensity from the latter years of the 1950s. This was openly acknowledged by Prime Minister Harold Macmillan, in February 1960, in his famous 'Winds of Change' speech in Cape Town which recognised 'the growth of national consciousness'[32] around the world that was undermining the concept of empire. Conflicts, such as in the British protectorate of Aden, demonstrated both the impossibility of holding the empire by force and the inability to retain sufficient overseas bases to police the UK's dependencies. The failure of the British government to be able to respond militarily to Ian Smith's Unilateral Declaration of Independence in Rhodesia in 1965 was a further example of the weakness of the UK in the face of such a broad range of potential tasks.[33] These lessons gradually convinced UK political and military decision-makers that the empire was fading away and that a global military presence was no longer a justifiable source of defence spending.

A second and related change was a re-evaluation of the economic benefit to Britain of this empire. Ernest Bevin's vision of rebuilding Britain's Great Power status upon the resources of its empire had never been realised. A Cabinet paper from 1960 noted that, 'The Commonwealth is likely to become less of an economic unit' and that 'Britain cannot expect to increase her proportion of the trade of other Commonwealth countries'.[34] While the relative proportion of Britain's overseas trade with its Commonwealth had declined, UK trade with other European countries had grown significantly. This led Britain to reconsider its earlier rejection of the European Economic Community and to proceed to apply for membership. In the light of this change in orientation, it was no longer easy to justify spending a large proportion of the defence budget on protecting Britain's dependencies.

A third factor was that the strategic concept for the defence of Britain's overseas dependencies was being called into doubt. The termination of conscription by the Sandys defence review in 1957 severely reduced the manpower levels for the armed services: from 690,000 to a target figure of 375,000.[35] Senior Army commanders expressed the view that a force of 165,000 was inadequate to carry out the UK's military tasks. They argued that a complement of 200,000 troops was the minimum required.[36] Nevertheless, the political decision had been taken and the lower figure was retained. There was no accompanying reduction in the breadth of Britain's military commitments and so the forces used to police the UK's commitments had to be stretched more thinly.

The resulting strategy reflected the predilection of British policy-makers to seek to avoid making painful choices by pursuing the same objectives but in different ways. Instead of spreading forces evenly around the world, the British chose to concentrate their dwindling resources in a smaller number of fixed locations. These bases would provide the links between the UK's chain of overseas interests and forces would be able to deploy from these centres to local trouble spots in times of emergency. A key factor in the execution of the plan was the building up of a 'Strategic Reserve', located in the UK, that would reinforce a theatre in the event of a large-scale conflict. Bases such as in Aden, Kenya and later even in Australia[37] were regarded as potential focal points for the maintenance of Britain's reduced military presence.

This strategy of developing overseas bases never fulfilled the expectations of its authors. First, it was realised that the concept was vulnerable to the emergence of 'air barriers': territories in the Middle East and Indian Ocean which would deny Britain the right to fly through their airspace with reinforcements during a crisis.[38] This would render it impossible for the UK to reinforce areas such as the Far East with troops flown from national soil or from overseas. Second, the spread of independence movements raised doubts over the dependability of establishing bases. It made little sense to invest in costly infrastructure and building programmes at a location only to witness those assets becoming forfeited when self-government was demanded. This logic undermined the UK's choice of Kenya as a base to fly reinforcements to the Far East. Finally, there proved to be insufficient forces to maintain a Strategic Reserve in the UK. Evidence of the overstretch of the armed services was painfully clear.

Yet by far the single most important factor that accounted for the reduction in the UK's global military presence was resource constraint.[39] Despite a desire to maintain its role, the growth in the postwar British economy proved inadequate to sustain ever increasing defence expenditures alongside the simultaneous demands of domestic spending priorities. In the period between 1950 and 1973, for example, growth rates for the UK economy averaged only about 2.6 per cent per year.[40] The pressure to allocate more resources to defence risked weakening the fabric of the country's economic base, rendering it incapable of maintaining its competitive position in the future. As Harold Wilson stated in December 1964, 'we cannot do all that so far has been thought ideally desirable without fatally weakening our economy'.[41] The Labour government then proceeded to experience a series of balance of payments difficulties which culminated in a devaluation crisis in 1967. Pickering notes that the series of financial emergencies that occurred in this period 'struck the decisive blows' against perpetuating Britain's defence commitments.[42]

The decision was taken to withdraw British forces from East of the Suez Canal, a role that had come to consume approximately 25 per cent of the defence budget. The opposition of allies, such as Australia and Singapore, to this development was overridden. An agreement of June 1966 ended the 'confrontation' between Britain and Indonesia and enabled the UK to begin to dismantle its role in the Far East, bringing its troops home rather than redeploying them within the theatre. Although the European defence role experienced some reductions at this time, the brunt of the cuts were inflicted on Far East deployments. There followed a debate over how quickly the withdrawal should occur: initially Britain intended withdrawing from the bases but retaining its military capability to intervene. Eventually it was decided that this would be cut as well. In January 1968, the Prime Minister announced that British forces would be removed from Singapore, Malaysia and the Persian Gulf by the end of 1971.[43]

This crucial turning point in British global policy can only be explained by the interplay of a variety of complex factors. The pressure of resource constraint and the overstretch of the armed services had been apparent since the early 1950s, yet Britain's worldwide military deployments had continued. It was the political priorities of a particular government that determined the precise timing of the change: in 1964, Minister of Defence Denis Healey had ruled that defence spending would not exceed £2 billion and the East of Suez role was the casualty of this ceiling.[44] But the policy change has to be set against a wider backcloth that made this paradigmatic shift possible. For these factors one needs to take account of the evolving foreign policy environment in which decolonisation had altered the perceptions of where British interests lay and a shifting strategic calculation about the military power that Britain was able to wield around the world.

A post-imperial role?

The proportion of British forces that were dedicated to a global role after the 1960s was strictly limited. Although the Conservative government of Prime Minister Edward Heath questioned the extent of the cutbacks in the Far East undertaken by the 1964–70 Labour government, these were not reversed but only slowed down.[45] The obligations that the UK had assumed in CENTO and SEATO, albeit small, were withdrawn and forces on standby for out-of-the-NATO-area deployments were kept to a minimum. By the 1980s only the lightly equipped 5 Airborne brigade plus 3 Commando brigade were held in readiness for action outside of Europe. As for the Royal Navy, its capability to project power was severely limited by the modest size of its Invincible class of 'Through-Deck Cruisers'. This position would have been compounded, had it not been reversed, by the decision in 1981 to sell one of the cruisers to Australia and scrap the two amphibious assault carriers.[46]

Yet it would be inaccurate to suggest that the withdrawal from East of Suez marked the end of the UK's sense of global responsibilities. The UK continued to perceive itself as more than just a European power. For one thing, there were still millions of UK citizens who either lived or worked abroad and to whom the government felt a duty to protect. For another, Britain did not divest itself of all its dependent territories after the withdrawal from East of Suez. It needed, therefore, to preserve its capacity to protect those areas to which it retained an obligation. Throughout the 1980s, Britain contributed to the security of such areas as Hong Kong, Gibraltar and Brunei. In Belize, the British stationed a small garrison of troops and aircraft to deter aggression by neighbouring Guatemala, while in Brunei the Sultan paid for a limited British force to ensure the kingdom's territorial integrity. Naval task forces also conducted flag-showing visits around the world to promote good relations with other countries and perpetuate a sense of the UK's worldwide interests.

Although the UK never gave up its psychological preparedness to act outside the NATO area, it always expected to be able to undertake major operations in conjunction with its Alliance partners and the US. This assumption proved incorrect in the case of the Falklands conflict. The invasion by Argentina in 1982 demanded that the UK assemble a national task force – contrary to the sorts of missions for which the UK had been preparing in NATO. The majority of British naval forces dedicated to the eastern Atlantic had to be diverted to the Falklands operation.[47] The actual recapture of the islands required a very substantial military effort with relatively high casualties. Nevertheless, the impact of the Falklands experience on both British self-perceptions and perceptions of the country overseas should not be underestimated. By demonstrating the political will to fight to preserve sovereignty over one of its territories, the UK re-emphasised its international status and helped to arrest the perception of a declining international power in which it was held by ally and foe alike. In the words of the then Prime Minister, 'we have ceased to be a nation in retreat'.[48]

The UK judged it necessary to be capable of participating in overseas interventions with the United States in regions outside of Europe. For the Thatcher government in the 1980s this was a particularly important requirement, chiefly from a political point of view. It was motivated both by a sense of domestic ideological affinity and in order to demonstrate burden sharing for US leadership in Europe. By contributing to US global activities, the UK believed it could ensure consultation with Washington. For example, in 1983 and 1984, Britain sent a token military contribution of 100 personnel to the Multinational Force in Lebanon, that was led by the United States.[49] Similarly, during the Iran–Iraq war, Britain kept a naval presence of a destroyer and two frigates, the Armilla Patrol, in the Indian Ocean. When, in 1987, the US took the initiative of reflagging international oil tankers to accord them protection in the Persian Gulf,[50] Britain sent six minesweeping vessels in support as an expression of solidarity.[51]

The conceptual framework in which these activities were pursued was a relatively straightforward one: amidst a system in which there was an overarching strategic competition with the USSR, Britain regarded itself as contributing to a western conception of order. Yet this had to be fundamentally reappraised when in 1989 the Cold War was swept away. Henceforth the challenges to the western view of order became less easy to define. It was an opportune moment for the UK to conduct a wide-ranging debate about the implications of the new strategic environment for a middle-ranking power such as itself.

It is striking, however, the way in which the UK has faced the post-Cold War world with basically the same assumptions that guided its attitudes in the past. Admittedly, the UK has acknowledged that 'security' is now a more multifaceted concept, involving a broader range of political and economic factors than ever before. It has, for example, added the concept of 'defence diplomacy' to its military tasks; a recognition that influence flows from using the model of its own armed forces to convince other countries of the need to restructure their militaries and ensure tight civilian control. It has also been willing to employ its armed forces for quasi-military tasks – the deployment of Royal Navy frigates to the Caribbean for anti-drugs running operations, for instance. But at core, Britain's view about the nature of military power and its own position in the world remains unchanged. Britain still sees the use of military power as a responsibility that it must exercise in the world and something that it does well.

The actual employment of military power in the 1990s has varied, reflecting the complex and unpredictable post-Cold War strategic landscape. At one end of the spectrum, Britain has found itself involved in highly demanding military operations. For example, in the 1990–91 Gulf War, the UK took a leading role in a sustained aerial bombardment of Iraq and its military forces occupying Kuwait.[52] It proceeded to employ a full armoured division in the ground invasion that encircled Iraqi forces and liberated Kuwait City. It was a telling indication of the small size of Britain's armed services that almost the whole of its mechanised forces in Germany had to be cannibalised in order to provide such a divisional contribution. Similarly, in the case of Bosnia, Britain played a leading role in deploying a heavily armed Rapid Deployment Force as part of Operation Deliberate Force in the summer of 1995. In all these situations, the UK was required to deploy military forces that were capable of engaging in high intensity warfare. Military planners might be forgiven for expressing surprise that the sorts of military tasks they had prepared for during the Cold War actually became a reality once the East–West confrontation had ended.

At the other end of the spectrum, the UK has played a leading role in humanitarian operations and peacekeeping activities in which complex political issues have been at stake. The creation of 'Safe Havens' for Kurdish and Shi'ite refugees in northern and southern Iraq, as well as the policing of 'No Fly Zones' over Bosnia provide examples of the variable requirements for post-Cold War military operations.[53] In the case of the Bosnian conflict, the UK was one of the two main contributors of forces, with the French, to the United Nations Protection Force (UNPROFOR)[54] and has subsequently taken a full part in the Implementation (IFOR) and the Stabilisation (SFOR) forces. The British government has regarded its membership of the UN Security Council as conferring the responsibility to act as a major player in response to international peacekeeping duties. Such activities have attracted little domestic opposition in the press or in Parliament, demonstrating that they enjoy widespread popular support. What little criticism that has emerged has been aimed more at the weight of commitments that have been imposed upon the armed services, rather than the nature of the tasks they have been called upon to perform.

The sense in which British forces are overstretched by the breadth of commitments at the turn of the millennium, echoes a familiar refrain from the past. Britain has sought to undertake these missions as part of a defence structure that was conceived within a hesitant defence review of July 1990.[55] As part of this review the Army was reduced from a figure of 165,000 to a target figure of 120,000 – even though in practice it has not proved possible to recruit up to this level. There have been strong feelings within the armed services that they possessed insufficient strength to execute all the missions that have been asked of them. The withdrawal of troops from peace-keeping duties under SFOR and KFOR and a Gurkha battalion in East Timor has been evidence that the government has attempted to assuage these concerns and slim down the range of its overseas commitments when circumstances allow.[56]

It was partly in answer to this overstretch and partly to establish clearer strategic guidelines for the next decade that led the Labour government to conduct a Strategic Defence Review (SDR) in 1998.[57] The SDR reaffirms the need for Britain to be capable of fulfilling its international responsibilities and playing an activist role on the international stage. Despite the fact that no immediate security threats to the UK are identified, the SDR concludes a multitude of risks could impinge on UK interests and these might necessitate a military response.[58] An array of military tasks are identified in which the UK may have to act, ranging from regional conflicts outside of NATO, to UN peace support and humanitarian roles and even the employment of the armed services against organised crime.[59] The scale on which such deployments might occur are estimated to vary between a short but significant international crisis, such as the Gulf War, to a more prolonged but lower scale of involvement.[60]

Consistent with such potential tasks, the government has committed the UK to enhance those military capabilities that would enable it to intervene in situations at long distances from the home base. Unlike the 1980s when the outside interventionary role was drawn from residual military capacity, plans have been formulated to develop specifically global capabilities. A Joint Forces Headquarters and a Joint Rapid Deployment Force was announced. Emphasis has been placed on all the services being capable of flexible operations and being welded together in the necessary packages for force projection purposes. Renewed attention is being paid to the logistical needs of the services; something that had been acknowledged to have been neglected in the past, due to attention on the fighting 'teeth' units. New transport ships and heavy transport planes will be procured and two new conventionally powered aircraft carriers, designed to carry up to fifty aircraft, will form the backbone of the Royal Navy's long-range strike capability. This signals a major change in thinking; that an ability to undertake global interventions should become a central role for Britain's armed services.[61]

This renewed emphasis on 'internationalism'[62] has resonated in the rhetoric of the Labour government. Much was made of the fact that the Strategic Defence Review was shaped by foreign policy concerns and both ministers charged with elaborating its conceptual underpinnings, Defence Secretary George Robertson and Foreign Secretary Robin Cook, emphasised the special role that Britain played in the world. George Robertson declared the UK to be a force for good in the world and stated that 'the British are, by instinct an internationalist people'.[63] This was complemented by Robin Cook's repeated statements that Britain was adhering to an ethical dimension to its foreign policy. This ethical dimension, with its focus on human rights and international solidarity, was heavily trumpeted during the Kosovo conflict when Britain was at the forefront of those states arguing for the use of force against Serbia. The justification for the Kosovo campaign by the Prime Minister was ambitious: the need to uphold the moral values of world order against the threat of barbarism.[64] However, the ethics of Britain's international position is an issue that has returned to haunt the Labour government in relation to such issues as its arms sale to Indonesia and the activities of the mercenary company Sandline in the restoration of the government of Sierra Leone in West Africa.

Conclusion

Throughout the postwar period, ideas about international order and security were inextricably mixed with concern for national interests in British minds. Critics have bemoaned the fact that Britain had no strategic plan to manage her post-imperial decline, no formula for the relinquishing of the Empire. Yet this was symptomatic of a belief that Britain's presence abroad was vital both to deter Soviet-inspired aggression and to the maintenance of international peace and stability. In addition, Britain's own claim to the status of a front-ranking power rested on fulfilling such a role. In relation to alliance commitments, much of what Britain was expected to do would have proved to be hollow if put to the test. Yet to have admitted as much was unacceptable to Britain's image and status abroad. To have given up obligations risked a change to the established order and a gradual draining away of Britain's international position.

When change did occur, it has been the contention of this chapter that the ideational was an important factor in determining Britain's policies. A diminishing resource base and rising defence costs were factors that were faced by successive British governments. Pickering has shown that from as early as 1959 representatives of the Treasury and the Foreign Office were arguing for the termination of the East of Suez role.[65] In order to understand why change took place at a particular moment, it is necessary to understand the complex interplay of political factors that contributed to changing British perceptions. The assessments of political and strategic elites eventually overrode both material considerations and the powerful emotional attachments that the country held towards its overseas responsibilities. This was evident in the 1968 decision to withdraw forces from the Far East. Similarly, it was evident in 1982 when the Thatcher government decided to use force to recover the Falkland Islands and thereby perpetuate one of Britain's colonial legacies.

Even after the diminution of its worldwide military presence, Britain did not stop seeing itself as a global actor and its sense of international obligations continued. While Prime Minister Harold Wilson declared in the 1960s that Britain was nothing if not a world power, so in the 1990s Foreign Secretary Douglas Hurd stated with equal determination that it remained Britain's objective to be able to punch above its weight in international affairs. At the end of the century Britain still regarded itself as a major actor on the world stage – not on the scale of the 1940s and 1950s with its forces in numerous overseas bases – but in the sense that Britain should have a voice in all major international issues, a seat on the UN Security Council and military forces capable of global intervention alongside allies. The Strategic Defence Review reaffirmed these intentions and set a high priority on developing more muscular means 'to go to the crisis',[66] wherever in the world that it might take place.

Operationalising this global role for Britain in the future will present many challenges. One particular challenge will lie in determining alongside which partners the British role will be pursued? Hitherto, Britain's sense of global mission has been conducted alongside the US. This has continued to be evident in the 1990s: Britain has been highly visible alongside the US in using military force against Iraq to prevent it from developing weapons of mass destruction.[67] But few commentators would deny that the shared interests between the US and UK have diminished since the Cold War ended. This was starkly exposed in crises such as in Bosnia and Kosovo when Anglo-American attitudes towards resolving the problems have fundamentally diverged. The British have been forced to confront the fact that the US is less likely to share its political priorities in the future.

The alternative for Britain lies in seeking to enhance its own capacity to act globally in concert with its European allies. This is not to suggest that the Europeans will quickly come to rival the United States as a unitary actor upon the world stage. But the US is increasingly looking to Europe to either do more for its own defence or to contribute more actively to global military tasks. Britain will need to be capable of acting in concert with its European partners in the future. If European organisations can be enhanced and the necessary political will can be created, then the US is likely to welcome a European partner that can share international responsibilities. Developing such a relationship with its European allies will require a long-term reorientation in thinking from the UK. The prospect for this developing will be one of the themes analysed in the subsequent chapter.

Notes

1. Denis Healey, *The Time of My Life*, London: Penguin, 1989, p. 299.
2. *Statement Relating to Defence*, Cmnd. 7,327, London: HMSO, 1948.
3. Public Records Office, CAB 139/1929, FP (60) 1, 'Future Policy Study' 24 February 1960, p. 12.
4. *Statement Relating to the Defence Estimates*, Cmnd. 5,231, London: HMSO, 1973.
5. Quoted in H. Young, *This Blessed Plot: Britain and Europe from Churchill to Blair*, London: Macmillan, 1998, p. 24.
6. Oil was described by military planners in 1956 as the 'principal object of [the UK's] Middle East policy'. See PRO, DEFE 4/87 JP (56) 7, Discussed in COS (56) 55th Meeting, UK Requirements in the Middle East, 31/5/1956.
7. C. Bartlett, *The Long Retreat: A Short History of British Defence Policy, 1945–70*, London: Macmillan, 1972, p. 13.
8. Darby describes India as the 'keystone of the arch of defence'; see P. Darby, *British Defence Policy East of Suez, 1947–68*, Oxford: Oxford University Press, 1973, p. 4.
9. Ibid., p. 152.
10. The Baghdad Pact was renamed CENTO in August 1959 after the military coup in Iraq. The Baghdad Pact of 1955 committed Britain to defence cooperation with Iran, Pakistan and Turkey.
11. SEATO comprised cooperation with Pakistan, Philippines and Thailand.

12. C. Bartlett, op. cit., pp. 167–8.
13. PRO, DEFE 5/88 COS (59) 17, Brief for the 6th Meeting of the Military Committee of the Baghdad Pact, 22/1/1959.
14. PRO, DEFE 4/117 COS (59) 18th Meeting of the Baghdad Pact, 12/3/1959.
15. PRO, DEFE 5/84 COS (58) 155, Definition of Terms, 13/6/1958.
16. For details see F. Kitson, *Low Intensity Operations*, London: Faber and Faber, 1971.
17. PRO, DEFE 6/51 COS (58) 110 (Final) Baghdad Pact: Review of Existing Plans and Studies, 22/8/1958.
18. H. Kissinger, *The Times*, 23 March 1984.
19. For details see J. Newhouse, *The Nuclear Age: From Hiroshima to Star Wars*, London: Michael Joseph, 1989, pp. 102–6, 125–7.
20. PRO, CAB 139/1929, FP (60) 1, 'Future Policy Study' 24/2/1960, p. 24.
21. R. Dawson, and R. Rosencrance, 'Theory and Reality in the Anglo-American Alliance', *World Politics*, 19 (1) October 1966, p. 34.
22. PRO, DEFE 5/72 COS (56) 428, 'Relations Between ANZAM and SEATO', 4/12/1956.
23. The Thatcher government felt that they had been inadequately consulted about the US decision to invade the Commonwealth island of Grenada in 1983. Shortly before the invasion, the British Foreign Secretary Geoffrey Howe had told the House of Commons that he was unaware of an American intention to invade. G. Howe, *Conflict of Loyalty*, Basingstoke: Macmillan, 1994, p. 328.
24. PRO, CAB 148/30, OPD (67) 17th Meeting, Defence and Overseas Policy Committee, 21/4/1967.
25. D. Devereux, *The Formulation of British Policy Towards the Middle East, 1948–56*, Basingstoke: Macmillan, 1990, p. 105.
26. See W. R. Louis and R. Owen (eds), *The Suez Crisis and its Consequences*, Oxford: Clarendon Press, 1988.
27. M. Carver, *Tightrope Walking: British Defence Policy since 1945*, London: Hutchinson, 1992, p. 65.
28. Quoted in P. Darby, op. cit., p. 214.
29. CAB 130/213, MISC 17/1st, 'Defence Review 1964–5' 21/11/64.
30. D. Healey, op. cit., p. 293.
31. Before the Suez experience the Royal Navy had justified its carrier force as a contribution to 'broken-backed' fighting in a global war after an initial nuclear exchange had taken place.
32. H. Macmillan, *Pointing the Way, 1959–61*, London: Macmillan, 1972.
33. PRO, CAB 148/18, OPD (65) 29th Meeting, 16/6/1965.
34. PRO, CAB 139/1929, FP (60) 1, 'Future Policy Study' 24/2/1964.
35. W. Rees, 'The 1957 Sandys White Paper: New Priorities in British Defence Policy', in *Journal of Strategic Studies*, 12 (2), June 1989, p. 221.
36. P. Darby, op. cit., p. 155.
37. Australia was mooted as a base after the decision was taken to withdraw from Singapore and Aden. See D. Healey, op. cit., p. 290.
38. PRO, DEFE 4/94, Annex to JP (57) 8 (Final) 'Long Term Defence Policy', 24/1/1957.

39. This is agreed upon by most of the authors writing on this period. See, for example, C. Coker, *A Nation in Retreat?*, London: Brassey's, 1986. Also, J. Baylis, *British Defence Policy: Striking the Right Balance*, Basingstoke: Macmillan, 1989.

40. J. Pickering, *Britain's Withdrawal from East of Suez: The Politics of Retrenchment*, Basingstoke: Macmillan in association with the Institute of Contemporary British History, 1998.

41. Quoted in R. Ovendale, *British Defence Policy Since 1945*, Manchester: Manchester University Press, 1994, p. 133.

42. J. Pickering, op. cit., p. 150.

43. C. Bartlett, op. cit., p. 224.

44. D. Healey, op. cit., pp. 270–1.

45. P. Carrington, *Reflect on Things Past*, London: Fontana, 1989, p. 218. In her memoirs, former Prime Minister Margaret Thatcher expresses dismay at the decision of the Heath government not to reverse the policy of the previous government. See M. Thatcher, *The Downing Street Years*, London: HarperCollins, 1993, p. 162.

46. *The United Kingdom Defence Programme: The Way Forward*, Cmnd. 8,288, London: HMSO, 1981.

47. See, for example, L. Freedman, *The Politics of British Defence, 1979–98*, Basingstoke: Macmillan, 1999.

48. M. Thatcher, op. cit., p. 253.

49. G. Howe, op. cit., p. 327.

50. See G. Shultz, *Turmoil and Triumph: My Years as Secretary of State*, New York: Macmillan, 1993, and C. Weinberger, *Fighting for Peace: Seven Critical Years at the Pentagon*, London: Michael Joseph, 1990.

51. D. Sander, *Losing an Empire, Finding a Role: British Foreign Policy since 1945*, Basingstoke: Macmillan, 1990, p. 185.

52. There are several good accounts of the Gulf War. See, for example, K. Mathews, *The Gulf Conflict and International Relations*, London: Routledge, 1993.

53. L. Freedman, 'Bosnia: Does Peace Support Make any Sense?', *NATO Review*, 43 (6) November 1995, pp. 19–23.

54. D. Leurdijk, *The United Nations and NATO in Former Yugoslavia: Partners in International Cooperation*, The Hague: Netherlands Atlantic Commission and the Netherlands Institute of International Relations, 1994.

55. Editorial on the 'Options for Change Review', *The Independent*, 26 July 1990.

56. Bagehot, 'Who Hoon Is. And Why He Matters', *The Economist*, 11 March 2000, p. 45.

57. *The Strategic Defence Review*, Cmnd. 3,999, London: The Stationery Office, July 1998.

58. Centre for Defence Studies, *The Strategic Defence Review: How Strategic? How Much of a Review?*, London: Brassey's, July 1998, p. 6.

59. Cmnd. 3,999, op. cit., pp. 5, 15.

60. Ibid., p. 23.

61. Dodd and Oakes note the irony that it was a Labour government that cut the Royal Navy's aircraft carriers in 1966. T. Dodd and M. Oakes, *The Strategic*

Defence Review White Paper, Research Paper 98/91, House of Commons Library, 15 October 1998, London.

62. McInnes comments that the Labour government is 'internationalist by inclination'. Colin McInnes, 'Labour's Strategic Defence Review', *International Affairs*, 74 (4) October 1998, p. 384.

63. Cmnd. 3,999, op. cit., Introduction by the Secretary of State for Defence, G. Robertson, p. 4.

64. Speech of Prime Minister Tony Blair, www.fco.gov.uk, March 1999.

65. J. Pickering, op. cit., pp. 112–13.

66. Cmnd. 3,999, op. cit., p. 2.

67. See 'Britain Survey: A Power in the World', *The Economist*, 6 November 1999, p. 16.

Chapter 3

Preserving the Security of Europe

Wyn Rees

Introduction

Throughout the postwar period, Britain's global and European roles in security have coexisted alongside each other. Europe has been the vital theatre for British interests: Britain has been consistent in seeking to preserve a balance of power on the continent and preventing the preponderance of any single state.[1] But the European role has never been the sole focus of Britain's defence effort because the UK continued to regard itself as more than just a European power. Consistent with this, the UK expected its European allies to give it credit for the broader security obligations that it sustained during the Cold War, claiming as it did that it bore these burdens for the benefit of the West.

Britain has differed with some of its leading continental partners about the type of 'Europe' that it has wanted to see develop. Many of its allies, albeit to differing degrees, have grown to want a politically and economically integrated Europe. This vision of Europe would be capable of subsuming historical tensions between its members, ensuring its own security and projecting itself as a powerful and influential actor on the international stage. By contrast, a highly integrated, proto-federalist model has been anathema to Britain, a country traditionally sceptical of grand visions. Becoming a party to such an aspiration was once feared to put at risk Britain's special relationship with the Commonwealth and above all its transatlantic ally. Although Britain eventually acceded to the European Community, it has been a reluctant participant in the process of 'constructing Europe'. The UK has championed the cause of intergovernmental cooperation rather than integration, while domestic concerns about the loss of national identity and sovereignty have led policy-makers to proceed with caution.

As for defence, postwar British governments were reluctant to be tied too tightly into European security arrangements. With Imperial considerations and desires for partnership with the US uppermost in policy-makers' minds, the UK was content to remain on the sidelines as its European allies fashioned a credible defence of their own. Only when the evident lack of cohesion amongst the Europeans threatened to leave the continent without a credible defence structure was the UK prepared to intervene in the situation. From that point in the 1950s onwards, the UK supported a transatlantic defence structure in which America has provided the leadership and the Europeans have sought to prove that they bear a proportionate share of the burden. Not until the 1990s, with the demise of the Warsaw Pact, has this model been seriously questioned in the UK. Now at the end of the century there is a growing appreciation that a more balanced framework for continental security must be developed: one in which Europe is capable of acting, in some circumstances, autonomously. For reasons that will be explored towards the end of this chapter, the Blair government has come to envisage a more equitably balanced defence arrangement in which transatlantic structures are matched by more capable European ones.

This chapter will begin by analysing the creation of the Cold War institutions for the defence of the continent and the resulting military strategies. It will proceed to investigate the priority the UK accorded to American protection of Europe. The chapter will close by discussing the concentration of British security efforts on Europe from the early 1970s and the extent to which British policy has been reassessed in the post-Cold War period.

The institutions of Cold War defence

In the light of the postwar threats to Europe and the extent of the weakness of the principal continental powers, a debate arose about the most appropriate structures for ensuring its security. British policy-makers faced a fundamental dilemma: whether to seek to build a coalition of European countries that could resist the suspected military prowess of the Soviet Union, or to attempt to anchor the United States into undertaking a long-term presence on the continent. The UK had enjoyed an intimate relationship with the US during the war years[2] but it seemed inevitable that the Americans would eventually disengage from Europe – after all, at Yalta Roosevelt had stated that the US occupation in Germany would only last for two years after victory had been achieved.[3] On these grounds it seemed sensible to build up the indigenous military capabilities of the European states. Yet the uncertain position of Germany and the fears that it engendered in neigbouring France, risked undermining a strategy predicated on the reassertion of European power.

Thus, there have been different interpretations among analysts about the aims of British policy in the late 1940s. Some have seen in the signing of the Brussels Treaty of 1948 and the creation of a 'Western Union', an attempt by the British to fashion a bloc of western countries that could stand between the two superpowers. Certainly, for a period of time, Foreign Secretary Ernest Bevin expressed a desire to build a coalition, to be allied with the resources of a reinvigorated British Empire, that could provide a power base of western strength independent of the United States.[4] However, for other analysts, Western Union should be interpreted as an attempt to organise a western bloc for the purpose of convincing the US that the Europeans were worth defending.[5] According to this latter perspective, British efforts to galvanise their European partners were really designed to draw the United States into a more permanent role in the defence and leadership of the continent.

What can be agreed upon, however, is that the resulting Western Union Defence Organisation (WUDO) was an insubstantial answer to a very demanding task. Although Britain was given the honour of appointing Field Marshal Montgomery to the post of Chairman of the Commanders in Chief Committee, the WUDO remained a defence structure of limited means. Montgomery was highly critical of its capabilities and, regardless of opposition in Whitehall, advocated that Britain station around two divisions permanently on the continent.[6] The British government ultimately decided to remain silent as to the size of forces it would contribute to the defence of Europe. The UK was more preoccupied with protecting its global interests and it was only later that increased fears of Soviet aggression led it to consider more urgently the offer of forces to its European allies.[7]

It was not until the mid-1950s that a transatlantic structure emerged as the dominant framework for European defence. In October 1950 the French Prime Minister René Pleven proposed the creation of a 'European Defence Community' (EDC) which would form one half of an Atlantic security framework. It was envisaged that EDC would be supranational in nature: it would include a European army of 100,000 personnel, a defence minister with appropriate structures to ensure accountability and a common weapon procurement system.[8] This was to prove the high water point of attempts from within the continent to provide for its own defence. The British welcomed the EDC initiative as a positive contribution to security and as a mechanism to integrate German military strength of up to twelve divisions into the West. But the British declared their intention to remain outside the structure. In so doing they provided a telling insight into their attitude to European defence cooperation; namely to make only the minimum contribution possible. They argued that their own global obligations precluded involvement in the EDC and that the integration of a European effort within a broader transatlantic relationship was not an appropriate project for UK involvement.[9] Churchill's private view was hostile to the EDC. He believed that it would represent a 'sludgy amalgam' of European military capacities.[10]

Only when the French failed to ratify the EDC Treaty[11] and the nascent transatlantic structure appeared to be at risk of breaking up amid mutual recrimination, did the British government take the lead in orchestrating continental defence. Through the London Nine Power Conference and modifications to the 1948 Brussels Treaty, the Western European Union (WEU) was established. The WEU facilitated the rearmament of West Germany and its entry into NATO. Through the accompanying Paris Agreements the size of national contributions to continental defence were also determined. As part of these arrangements the UK committed itself to maintain a force of four divisions, or an equivalent fighting capacity, in Europe for a period of fifty years. In the face of a threatened American reappraisal of its position in Europe and doubts about the security of the continent, Britain instigated a momentous policy shift that was to determine its defence relationship with the continent for the rest of the century.

Henceforth, the British became the staunchest supporter of the Atlantic Alliance as the dominant organisation for the provision of military security.[12] Britain was content with US leadership within the Alliance which was expressed through the appointment of a US Supreme Allied Commander and its control over the extended nuclear deterrent on which NATO strategy ultimately rested. Britain enjoyed the status of the second most influential country within NATO. Its officers occupied important subordinate commands; it protected a key stretch of NATO's frontline, the North German plain, and it developed an independent nuclear capability.

Although NATO became enshrined as the security framework during the Cold War, the debate about a European defence identity did not end with the demise of the EDC. Two sorts of pressures kept the issue alive. The first was the signing of the Treaty of Rome and the subsequent success of the European Economic Community (EEC). The issue of defence was kept separate from the Community but as economic cooperation prospered, it raised the inevitable question of whether political integration and security should follow. The founding of European Political Cooperation (EPC)[13] in 1969 demonstrated that there were foreign policy implications attendant on the European Community's position in world trade and its international political status. Furthermore, the signing of the Single European Act in 1987 marked a major leap forward in economic cohesion through the creation of a single market. By the time of the 1992 Treaty on European Union, the wheel had come full circle: a 'Common Foreign and Security Policy' was created and a common defence policy was declared to be an ambition for the European Union.

The other pressure was French dissatisfaction with what they perceived to be an 'Anglo-Saxon' duopoly of influence in NATO. President Charles de Gaulle called for a 'Tripartite Directorate' to be created in which France would be granted an equal status along with Britain and the US and, when he failed to achieve this, he withdrew France from the Alliance's Integrated Military Structure in 1966. France kept alive the aspiration of a stronger European identity in defence that would rebalance the Atlantic Alliance and decrease what it perceived to be the unnecessary Amerian domination of the Alliance. France launched two versions of its 'Fouchet Plan' which attempted to create a common defence and foreign policy, on an intergovernmental basis, amongst the six members of the European Community.[14] It failed both in this endeavour and in its aim to detach West Germany from the US embrace but the French did not abandon this long-term aim.

Britain has consistently resisted continental initiatives that it interpreted as seeking to compete with NATO; not least because it was sceptical that its European partners could find the requisite political will and common interests to provide an alternative to American leadership. While it was successful in blocking attempts to create rival defence structures to NATO, it nevertheless recognised that a stronger expression of a European security identity was necessary for the long-term durability of the transatlantic relationship. The UK was particularly alarmed by evidence of diverging interests between the two sides of the Atlantic, in the 1980s, over East–West relations, as exemplified by the differing reactions to the imposition of martial law in Poland in 1981[15] and the shooting down of the Korean airliner flight 007 over Sakhalin two years later. It was also sensitive to American dissatisfaction with perceived European weakness, which manifested itself in calls for Europe to bear a larger share of the burden within the Alliance. The UK grew to advocate the need for a more coherent European voice to be heard in Washington.

The vehicle that the British supported for addressing these problems was the WEU. They participated in the 1984 reactivation of the organisation, which followed decades of benign neglect.[16] In a similar way to their earlier sponsorship of the 'Eurogroup' forum within NATO, the British cultivation of the WEU was designed to bolster the cohesion of the transatlantic relationship. Although the British were anxious that America might see this as the emergence of a European defence caucus, they hoped that the reinvigoration of the WEU would reassure both sides of the Atlantic. The subsequent 'Hague Platform' of 1987 enabled the British to secure agreement that closer European cooperation in matters of defence would be compatible with continuing American leadership of NATO.[17] Thus, US fears of being excluded from European forums were calmed while at the same time, the ambitions of the most ardent 'Europeanists' were held in check.

Military strategy: from massive retaliation to flexible response

Britain played a consistently influential role in NATO's military strategy during the Cold War, an unsurprising fact considering the stature of the UK within the Alliance. The Soviet Union and its allies possessed an overwhelming superiority in conventional forces and, with its hostile ideology, it was perceived to represent an enormous threat to the security of Europe. It was the only power that could threaten the physical security and survival of the UK and was consequently accorded the highest priority in British military planning. Yet prioritising the Soviet threat to Europe did not provide easy guidelines as to the level of defence spending that would be sufficient to counter the danger. Determining the appropriate levels of resources to devote to this task was a constant headache for policy-makers.

Britain's adoption of a 'Ten Year Rule'[18] in 1947, reflected an underestimation of the Soviet Union's technological capabilities. This had to be drastically revised at the end of the decade when the Soviets exploded an atomic bomb and when the fall of China to the revolutionary forces of Mao Tse-tung and the outbreak of war in Korea appeared to presage an East–West conflict. The Attlee government, galvanised by the hard-line stance taken in the United States, authorised a three-year, £4.7 billion expansion in defence spending. This rearmament programme was quickly scaled down once it became clear that war was not imminent, but it convinced British policy-makers that attempts to match the conventional military prowess of the Soviets were misguided. The UK could not afford to undermine its economic strength in the search for absolute security. A Cabinet paper written some years later summed up the attitude of the British government towards the need to husband scarce resources: 'overall defence expenditure must be kept at a level which will give the members of the Alliance the necessary margin of economic strength to compete with the Soviet threat in all aspects, without endangering their economic stability'.[19]

It was principally for this reason that the UK came to be the firmest advocate of a nuclear-orientated strategy within the Atlantic Alliance. Strategic nuclear weapons, employed against the homeland of the adversary, were considered to be the decisive instruments in future conflicts. The enemy was to be dissuaded from using force by the threat of massive nuclear retaliation against its civilian population and industrial infrastructure. The 1952 Global Strategy Paper, guided by the thinking of Sir John Slessor, signalled this shift in British policy.[20] The conventional force goals of 96 divisions that had been calculated at NATO's Lisbon summit convinced the UK that attempting to match the military strength of the eastern bloc was hopelessly unrealistic. With the new emphasis on nuclear weapons, the actual threat to Europe was assessed to be low, providing that US nuclear superiority counterbalanced Soviet military strength.

The practical manifestations of this thinking brought Britain into tension with its NATO allies. The UK argued that the Alliance's conventional forces served only to identify Soviet aggression and act as a tripwire before nuclear retaliation ensued. It was a British assumption that amid a global war, the utility of conventional forces would be limited as they would be largely immaterial to the outcome. For example, a British Chiefs of Staff paper declared that, 'The result of the initial nuclear exchange is critical and will dictate the final outcome of a general war'.[21] Logic dictated that conventional forces should be kept small and that weapon and ammunition stockpiles should be kept to the minimum deemed necessary to precede a nuclear exchange. NATO should prepare for a war of short duration. The 1956 Defence White Paper placed the role of conventional forces in global war last in the list of priorities for defence spending, after contributions to the deterrent and forces for Cold War and limited war tasks.[22]

Britain's NATO allies, however, led by the United States, were unconvinced by these arguments. They envisaged that a war in Europe could last for a long time and might comprise periods of conflict of varying degrees of intensity. The US, and particularly a vested interest within its Navy, argued that a conventional phase of hostilities could occur after the use of nuclear weapons, as the combatants sought to resuscitate their damaged societies. In the light of these possibilities they argued that NATO required extensive conventional capabilities. There were elements within the Royal Navy that were convinced by these arguments and were fighting a rearguard action against the short-war scenario, with the result that the UK was constrained from benefiting from the economic logic of its position.[23]

In Military Command 70 (MC70),[24] NATO's force goal targets for the period 1957–63 were based on the assumption of a long phase of conventional warfare. The Supreme Allied Commander (SACEUR), General Norstad, argued for an Alliance ground force of 30 divisions, which was significantly above what currently existed. Norstad advocated a NATO capability that would enable a 'pause' to be exacted during the early phase of the conflict, before the ultimate release of nuclear weapons. Such a hiatus would provide the opportunity for negotiation between the warring parties and might allow the *status quo* to be restored. American nuclear doctrine was moving away from the 'all-or-nothing' posture of Massive Retaliation due to the fact that Soviet nuclear capabilities would result in nuclear retaliation against the US homeland. A British Joint Planning Staff report in September 1960 acknowledged, 'There are several fundamental aspects of the NATO strategic concept on which the UK's interpretation differs from that of the NATO military authorities'.[25]

Britain remained hostile to ideas of a major conventional defence build-up in NATO. It stated its belief in the deterrent effect of nuclear weapons and it was mindful of pressure from the other commitments it was seeking to uphold outside of Europe. The Chiefs of Staff in London were sceptical as to whether many of the NATO members could afford the force goals stipulated in MC70 and there was a fear that any ambiguity over NATO's determination to employ nuclear weapons might serve as an encouragement to the adversary. This British attitude was consistent with its earlier policy of trying to ensure that European defence was assured with minimum UK contribution. Nevertheless, for the sake of Alliance unity, the UK compromised its position and accepted that a sizeable force was needed to complement NATO's nuclear potential. The British were prepared to allow, in the words of Prime Minister Antony Eden, that conventional forces would be capable of 'deal[ing] with any local infiltration'[26] and that sufficient war stocks should be available to fight a conventional phase of war for a 30-day period.[27]

This capacity to compromise proved particularly useful for Britain in its role of obtaining Alliance agreement over changing the strategic concept in the 1960s. When the US came to press for the adoption of the strategy of Flexible Response,[28] this was interpreted by some European countries as the US trying to wriggle out of its commitment to use nuclear weapons in defence of the continent. The British perspective differed from that of their allies. They believed that the biggest threat to NATO was disunity rather than external aggression. Defence Secretary Denis Healey was of the opinion that the Soviet Union was adequately deterred by NATO's nuclear capacity: it was the lack of self-confidence among European countries that led them to seek endless reassurances from the US about the sincerity of their nuclear commitment.[29] Britain played an important role in helping to assuage European concerns by the creation of the Nuclear Planning Group, which accorded non-nuclear allies a voice in the nuclear decision-making process.

The fact that the UK could countenance changes in US strategy with such equanimity owed much to Britain's independent nuclear status within the Alliance. This provided the UK with an insurance policy against the vagaries of intra-Alliance relations. It also contributed to Britain's status within NATO as it could both contribute to the allied nuclear offensive and strike at those targets that would be a priority for the UK during a global war. The British justified their deterrent to their European allies as a second centre of decision-making that would complicate the planning assumptions of the adversary. To the US, the British argued that their deterrent contributed to the burden sharing of nuclear responsibilities.

The 'special relationship' and NATO

Britain's interaction with the United States, in relation to Europe, has been complex. This has been due to the fact that the UK was pursuing two separate but mutually reinforcing goals. The first goal was a special bilateral relationship between the UK and the US that gave the British the status of the second most influential state within NATO and contributed to Britain's sense of being a global power. This was a selfish objective but it was nevertheless a powerful motivation for British policy-makers. In 1954 Anthony Eden described Anglo-American cooperation as being of 'overriding priority' to the UK.[30] Solidarity between the US and the UK was presented to European allies as something that helped to underpin the unity of the West.

The importance that the UK attached to securing such an intimate relationship with America is difficult to exaggerate. Because it placed such a premium on cooperation and because America had shown through its abrupt postwar cessation of support that cooperation could not be taken for granted; the UK was willing to sacrifice in order to preserve its privileged status. For example, the US was granted the right to station nuclear-capable B-29 aircraft in East Anglia in 1948, during the Berlin blockade, even though the British government could exercise little control over their possible use.[31] Despite the fact that such bases made Britain a more important target for Soviet nuclear attack, the UK was willing to accept this risk. Similarly, in April 1986, when the US requested help from its NATO allies in staging air attacks upon Libya in response to that country's alleged links with terrorism, the UK was the only European state to respond positively.[32] All the other NATO members refused, including the denial of overflying rights of their territory. Britain agreed to the American request in order to preserve the maximum amount of influence in Washington.

Cooperation between the two governments has been mirrored by cooperation between the militaries of the United States and UK. Regular liaison between the Pentagon and the Ministry of Defence, joint exercises and shared procurement of equipment have ensured links at all levels within the respective military establishments and have culti-vated the closest ties of any NATO allies. The contacts between the US and Royal Navies have been especially strong. The growing 'blue water' capability of the Soviet Navy in the 1960s and 1970s presented a challenge to the US Navy, and the Royal Navy increasingly took on the role of an Anti-Submarine Warfare (ASW) force in support of its US counterpart.[33] When the US Navy, in the early 1980s, embraced the more aggressive mission assigned in the 'Maritime Doctrine'[34] for naval vessels to seek and destroy the enemy in its home waters, the Royal Navy was an enthusiastic supporter.

The second goal of British policy has been to bind the US into the defence of Europe. The UK has believed that without America, the Europeans would lack the strength or unity to resist the Soviet threat. This helped to justify the sense of self-sacrifice in the minds of British policy-makers. They were of the opinion that the defence of the continent was not a credible option without the power of the United States; only another superpower could offset the military might of the USSR on the Eurasian landmass. The US military presence was particularly important in the immediate post-Cold War period when western intelligence agencies regarded Soviet conventional military strength as overwhelming. Despite the fact that these assess-ments were modified in the 1960s, the unwillingness of the European states to increase substantially their defence spending ensured continued reliance on the protection of the US.

The British also believed that the US provided the cohesion that bound NATO together. In British eyes the US acted as a pacifier of tensions between the Europeans, helping them to overcome their historical differences. America's superpower status made it a natural leader, a role Britain believed that no other European state could fulfil. This helps to explain why the British were so negative towards the concept of a more muscular European defence identity being developed alongside NATO. They had no confidence that an alternative community of interest could be generated out-side of the Alliance and they feared that the US would be alienated in the process.

The UK sought to serve as an interlocutor between the US and the Europeans. It believed that it was uniquely well placed to understand the contrasting priorities of the Europeans and the United States and to reconcile the differences between them. Although Britain did not always agree with the US position, it preserved its influence by expressing its views in private and avoided airing differences in public. For example, during the Korean War when President Truman appeared to hint that America was considering the use of atomic weapons, Prime Minister Attlee journeyed to Washington to exert British influence in private. In the early 1980s, the Thatcher government was able to represent a European position in the US when it secured four conditions from the Reagan administration that would guide its attitude to the development of the Strategic Defence Initiative (SDI) project.[35] Similarly, the British were effective in explaining European concerns to the US after the superpower discussions at the 1986 Reykjavik summit, in which the US and Soviet leaders had discussed the abolition of ballistic missiles.[36] Clarke has made the point that British influence in the Alliance tended to be at its strongest when the Cold War was at its most intense and when the US was looking to its allies for expressions of support.[37]

But this back-channel role that the UK has played in Washington has not been without its critics at home. There have always been those within the political elite that have bemoaned the extent to which Britain has neglected its influence in Europe because of the emphasis it has placed on its relationship with the United States. This was particularly the case during the Thatcher years because of the priority the Prime Minister attached to maximising Britain's voice in Washington and the apparent disregard with which she treated relations with Europe. This led to notable tensions within the Cabinet during Mrs Thatcher's premiership: most notable of which were the resignations of Leon Brittan, the Trade Secretary, and Michael Heseltine, the Defence Secretary, over the issue of European defence procurement.[38]

For their part, the American attitude towards this special UK role within NATO has varied over time. In the 1960s, the US made clear that it saw the value of the UK increasingly as one among a group of European states, rather than as an independent power.[39] The desire of the British to be treated with special favour by Washington complicated America's dealings with its allies as a whole. The US expressed irritation at the British policy of standing apart from the continent and, with the ending of the Cold War, the Bush administration signalled that Germany would become its new 'partner in leadership'. However, at other times the US has welcomed the willingness of the UK to look beyond narrowly European interests and has been grateful when the UK has shown solidarity with American positions that were opposed by other European nations. For example, the US has welcomed and cultivated the UK's opposition to a European defence identity and its staunch support for the centrality of NATO. This British attitude has served America well, as it has been able to rely on its ally to advance its cause in relation to other European governments.

Focusing on Europe

Britain's contribution to the security of Europe was a heavy burden on its defence budget. The focus in Army thinking was directed inevitably towards its largest single commitment of preparing for armoured warfare in Germany; while the Royal Navy had to be ready to defend the sea lanes of the eastern Atlantic from Soviet submarines. An increasing proportion of forces were kept within the UK but earmarked for the Central Front – which stretched the understandings that had been reached in the 1954 Paris Agreements that Britain would commit four divisions to continental defence. Britain sought to offset criticism from her allies with two arguments. First, the fact that Britain devoted a higher proportion of per capita spending to defence than the European average. Second, the UK's commitments outside of Europe were declared to be a contribution to the overall western defence effort. The Chiefs of Staff stated in 1957, 'The UK . . . in addition to her allegiances to NATO . . . has special responsibilities in regard to the need to counter Communism on a worldwide basis'.[40]

Domestic criticism of the burden of European defence spending was not helped by the frosty relationship with its major NATO ally, West Germany, over offsets payments. The British government complained that it incurred significant costs by stationing permanent ground and air forces on the soil of the Federal Republic and that the damage to British balance of payments was compounded by the spending taking place outside of the sterling area. Up until the mid-1950s, the West German government

offset all of the UK's military costs but, with the onset of its own rearmament programme, German offsets began to decline. As a result, a very real source of friction
emerged between Bonn and London. By the late 1950s the foreign exchange costs of
BAOR had risen to about £50 million but Germany would only provide offset payments
of £12 million annually over three years.[41] A revised agreement was not put in place until
1965 when Bonn accepted to pay for two-thirds of British costs until the end of 1967.[42]
After that time the offsets were reduced and they were finally terminated in 1980.

In spite of the UK's commitment to the defence of Europe, periodic cuts were
exacted in the size of its contribution. In the face of considerable criticism from NATO
allies, Defence Minister Duncan Sandys reduced the size of BAOR from 77,000 to
64,000 in 1957; followed by a 9,000 reduction two years later. Even deeper cuts
were discussed in Whitehall at various times. For example, in June 1965 the Cabinet
considered proposals to cut BAOR and withdraw the Second Allied Tactical Air
Force,[43] although this was never implemented. In May Prime Minister Harold Wilson
indicated his willingness to see cuts in Europe take precedence over reductions in
Britain's forces deployed in other areas of the world. He stated that 'he would rather
pull half our troops out of Germany, than move any from the Far East'.[44]

Yet when Britain did undertake a major reorientation of its defence policy in 1968
it chose to preserve the *status quo* in Europe. A decisive shift took place in which
Britain's global defence role was cut back in favour of Europe. Amid the pressure for
cuts in defence spending, the argument that Britain had to retain its role in NATO in
order to preserve its influence, proved to be vital. A policy document affirmed that 'we
should never forget that the preservation of the Atlantic Alliance is . . . the most basic
of all our interests'.[45]

Three main factors explain the pre-eminence of Europe in British policy. First,
there was a growing recognition that the country's future prosperity lay in Europe.[46]
Although it had just been rejected in its second attempt to enter the European Community, increasing economic interdependence with the continent and Britain's slug-
gish competitiveness made its admission a priority objective.[47] The economist Peter
Oppenheimer calculated that all the countries of north-western Europe had surpassed
Britain in output per head of population by 1964.[48] Conversely, the diminishing
economic importance of the Commonwealth (as discussed in the previous chapter)
lent additional support to arguments that Britain had to reorientate its stance. Several
important figures within the Wilson Cabinet were sympathetic to the call for a closer
British relationship with Europe at the expense of the Commonwealth. Notable among
these were Roy Jenkins, Chancellor of the Exchequer, George Brown, Foreign Secretary, and Anthony Greenwood, Minister for Overseas Development. This change
in Britain's perception of its interests was confirmed in the 1969 Statement on the
Defence Estimates when it explained that the concentration of the UK's defence effort
on the continent reflected a recognition of new 'political and economic realities'.[49]
In this way both Britain's international economic priorities and the evolving views of
the governmental elite were important in changing the focus of defence policy.

A second factor was politico-military in nature. Pressures on the defence budget
were making a strong case for a choice to be made between Britain's global and
European military roles. Until the latter part of the 1960s, Britain had configured its
armed services to fight two types of wars; one focused on Europe against the Warsaw

Pact and the other, so-called 'brushfire' conflicts, overseas. As these types of tasks demanded different force structures, resources were constantly in competition between them. Britain had retained the right under the 1954 Modified Brussels Treaty to withdraw forces for national tasks and there was a tendency to denude units from Europe to carry out colonial obligations. The frequency of British involvement in conflicts outside of Europe resulted in such conflicts receiving priority attention and increased the overstretch for Britain's armed services. For example, both the NATO Secretary General and SACEUR, in March 1965, complained about the shortfall in British forces assigned to the Alliance because of their diversion to tasks in the Far East. Darby noted the 'increasing tendency of army leaders to look upon BAOR as a manpower reserve for the overseas role'.[50] By the latter part of the 1960s, cuts in service personnel had contributed to a sense in which it was becoming ever more impractical to maintain two separate defence capabilities.

The third factor was that maintaining British force levels in Europe was felt to be necessary to reassure allies. Indeed a Defence and Overseas Policy Committee paper stated that troop levels on the continent were 'more a matter of political than military necessity'.[51] There were fears that reductions in Britain's forces on the continent could trigger a hostile response from the US. It was a well known fact in the 1960s that the US was considering reductions in the size of the forces it based in Europe. In addition, the British were worried about the ramifications of cuts on the West German and French governments. Germany was evidently the Alliance's most vulnerable member and the withdrawal of forces from BAOR would have left a major gap in the posture of Forward Defence, to which the German government was firmly committed. This might have led to the danger that West Germany's commitment to the Alliance would weaken. France was considered to be in a sensitive situation because it had recently reassessed its role in NATO and the British were wary that reductions in their forces might lead France to withdraw into isolation and leave the Alliance altogether.[52] A radical change in British policy risked promoting closer Franco-German relations and stimulating the development of nuclear cooperation.

Henceforth, the broad framework for the UK's military priorities remained consistent right up until the ending of the Cold War and beyond. British defence policy became Eurocentric and focused upon the execution of three main tasks (other than the continuation of the strategic nuclear deterrent): namely, the guarding of the North German plains, the patrolling of the eastern Atlantic and, to a lesser extent, the protection of the UK home base. The resources that were allocated to these tasks still varied over time. In 1977, in response to pressure from the United States, NATO defence ministers agreed on a 3 per cent annual increase in spending to take place over the next five years.[53] The incoming Conservative government of 1979 inherited this commitment and, in light of their election promise to prioritise defence, implemented it in full up to 1985.

This is not to suggest that the concentration upon a NATO-orientated policy ended all debates about the UK's military activities. In the eyes of some on the left, NATO was a US-dominated alliance that was wedded to a nuclear posture that would lead to catastrophic consequences in war. Such critics argued either for Britain to change NATO's strategy or for Britain to unilaterally withdraw from the Alliance and redirect its military spending to peaceful purposes. For others, their criticism was that the UK was bearing too large a share of the burden in Germany. Baylis records some of the influential figures that supported reductions in Britain's commitments to BAOR, such as former Prime Minister James Callaghan and a former Chief of the Defence Staff Lord Hill-Norton.[54] Within this school of thought were echoes of a long-standing debate between a 'Maritime' lobby and 'Continentalists'. The maritime lobby advocated that Britain should place greater emphasis on its naval tradition and so allow it to reduce its spending on forces based in Germany. According to this view, the UK was placing its desire for alliance solidarity ahead of its own national interests.

Even among those committed to the defence of NATO's Central Front, there were debates over the most effective strategy for deterring Warsaw Pact aggression. One influential view was that the advent in new technology was permitting a change in the traditional superiority of the means of offence over defence. In concert with developments in US military thinking that emphasised technological improvements in the lethality of modern weapons, the British began to reassess their approach to military planning in BAOR. A greater emphasis upon manoeuvre became evident under General Sir Nigel Bagnall, as compared with the former strategy which envisaged a static defence of the inner German border.[55] It was foreseen that British forces might be able to absorb the first echelons of a Warsaw Pact armoured assault before delivering a counter-stroke, with the help of substantial reinforcements. This was complemented by the RAF's interest in 'deep strike': the capacity to employ air power to target enemy forces deep inside eastern Europe before they ever reached NATO's forward lines. This offered the opportunity to reassess the Alliance's traditional reliance on the early recourse to tactical and theatre nuclear weapons to offset the adversary's conventional military preponderance.

In the event, the end of the Cold War brought many of the debates about Britain's contribution to NATO to a sudden halt. As the Warsaw Pact imploded and Russian forces began to be withdrawn from Central Europe, the threat which had provided the foundation for UK planning had disappeared. If that threat were ever to be reconstituted, a considerable warning time would be available. The Alliance was able to dismantle its strategy of Flexible Response and nuclear weapons were removed from German territory. Britain, like its other NATO partners, secured significant reductions in its military spending and BAOR was effectively halved in size. By the latter years of the 1990s it was declared finally that a strategic attack on NATO was no longer a task for which the UK would allocate forces.

Britain and post-Cold War European security

Although the European situation was transformed after 1990, British policy-makers have continued to treat the continent as their foremost security concern. Although the threats to security have been substantially reduced, a broader array of 'risks' have taken their place that could lead to the destabilisation of the region. This assessment has been borne out by the plethora of localised conflicts that have occurred since the Cold War ended: predominantly intra-state and ethnic conflicts that have still demonstrated the capacity for large-scale loss of life and for the creation of refugee movements. Britain has found the need to be actively engaged, alongside its allies, in countering these problems and therefore the priority it has attached to Europe has not fundamentally changed.

A central objective of post-Cold War British policy has been to ensure that NATO retained its position as the continent's principal defence organisation. The utility of the Alliance in British eyes was beyond question. First, it provided continuity and reassurance to allies and former adversaries alike, in the midst of an unstable and transitional period. Second, NATO perpetuated an American role in Europe and provided insurance against residual security threats such as Russian military power. Lastly, it remained an issue in which the UK could wield influence; whereas in areas such as economics it was a secondary power to countries such as Germany. British influence in security had been hard won over a 40-year period and was not going to be relinquished easily. The UK signalled its determination to continue its leading role in the Alliance by securing the status of 'Framework Nation' in the Allied Rapid Reaction Corps at the end of 1991.

NATO had become more than a military alliance to Britain. It had come to represent a peaceful community of western states with a broadly similar ideology and a shared perception of security. The Alliance's core values, namely adherence to liberal democracy, market economics and the rule of law, as well as the growing interdependence among its members, accorded the organisation a sense of solidarity. This was vital for dealing with security problems now that the unifying 'glue' of a common external threat had been removed. NATO was not only a source of strength to the West but also of attraction to the East. It was recognised that the Alliance had a role to play in projecting stability towards the East, with the prospect of offering membership to former enemies.[56] The UK set a premium on protecting NATO's homogeneity and as a consequence was wary about the organisation's rapid enlargement into central and eastern Europe.[57]

Even Britain accepted, however, the need for NATO to adapt itself to the transformed European security environment. While the Alliance had hitherto been configured for dealing with collective defence tasks, it now had to reorientate itself to deal with new types of military tasks. These might include crisis management and peacekeeping missions, reflecting the new types of conflicts that were threatening the continent.[58] Such tasks were more varied and diverse than anything that was conceived during the Cold War and required more flexible military forces that could be deployed at short notice to crisis zones. It was acknowledged that the old distinctions of 'in' and 'outside' the NATO area were no longer meaningful if the Alliance was to retain a sense of purpose in the future.[59]

In the event, NATO has been judged to have adapted successfully to such challenges. The Alliance demonstrated its capacity to conduct sanctions monitoring missions in 'Operation Sharp Guard' off the coast of former Yugoslavia. From 1992 a NATO headquarters provided coordinated command arrangements for the UN-mandated troops distributing humanitarian relief in Bosnia, while in 1995 NATO employed military force to compel the Bosnian Serbs to enter into peace negotiations. This was followed by large-scale peacekeeping duties in the IFOR–SFOR missions in Bosnia and then in 1999, the Alliance used aerial bombardment to compel Serbia to withdraw its military forces from Kosovo. Particularly notable was the central role played by the British government in the Kosovo campaign. The Blair government was not only the most vociferous advocate of the use of force but went on to lead the peacekeeping mission, KFOR.

The primacy of the Alliance was thus assured by its actions in the Balkans – albeit late in the case of Bosnia and, some would argue, precipitate in the case of Kosovo. NATO's key position among European security organisations was acknowledged in the North Atlantic Council meeting in Berlin in June 1996, which agreed that NATO would have the right to choose whether to be the lead organisation in future crises.[60] Through the concept of 'Combined Joint Task Forces', European-led operations might be granted the ability to borrow Alliance military assets to conduct tasks if the US declines direct involvement.[61] Granting NATO the right to lead in future crises was complemented by efforts to 'Europeanise' the structures of the Alliance, in order to grant European states more influence in its decision-making structures. These achievements served to emphasise the durability and continuing relevance of NATO and reassure the United States that it was still the vital actor in continental security.

Part of the motivation for Britain's support for the Alliance during its adaptation process was the fear that a European defence framework could arise to fill a vacuum left by NATO. Proponents of a more muscular European defence identity had seen in the end of the Cold War an historic opportunity to advance their cause. The ghost of the EDC had reappeared in the 1990s, to evident British consternation, in the guise of a resuscitated Western European Union. At Maastricht the WEU was accorded the status of the defence arm of the European Union, despite US concerns. Britain set its face firmly against the WEU duplicating the Alliance's functions: not only was it sceptical of a European defence capability being viable, but it was also alarmed at the prospect of losing influence in NATO.[62] The UK's membership in both organisations enabled it to constrain the WEU's development in favour of the Alliance.[63] The Conservative government, under Prime Minister John Major, argued that the WEU should only be employed for low level, specialised tasks[64] and opposed the WEU being employed in either former-Yugoslavia or the 1996 crisis in Albania.[65] When it was proposed that the WEU might be integrated into the EU, the UK resisted, partly on the grounds that neutral states within the EU would gain a veto power over defence operations of the WEU's ten members and partly because it argued that defence had to remain an intergovernmental activity.

Ironically, the fact that NATO has reasserted its organisational primacy and that the European defence identity has languished, led the 1997 Labour government to reassess its strategy. Certain events during the 1990s caused British policy-makers to question whether the *status quo* adequately fulfilled the needs of the UK. In particular, several cases of transatlantic tension and divergence raised the issue of whether it was wise to be wholly reliant on US leadership in crises and whether a more muscular European capability might serve to strengthen, rather than detract from, the Alliance. The Bosnian experience, for example, witnessed a rift between European capitals and Washington over the Vance–Owen Peace Plan,[66] the maintenance of the United Nations Protection Force (UNPROFOR) and the lifting of the arms embargo against the Bosnian Muslims. In the case of Kosovo, the opposition of the Clinton Administration to consider the use of ground forces against Serbia risked the failure of the entire NATO operation with all the attendant danger of undermining the Alliance's unity. Such crises exposed the potential for disagreement that existed in the post-Cold War situation now that the common interests between Europe and the United States have become less predictable. The military weakness of the European allies offered no alternative courses of action independent of the United States.

The Labour manifesto of 1997 had stated the party's intention to take a leading role in Europe. Once in office, the government has been willing to show greater flexibility over the issue of a European defence capability. It was constrained neither by the ideological baggage nor the arithmetical pressures of the slim House of Commons majority of its predecessor. A recognition emerged that in spite of European states spending approximately two-thirds of the US budget on defence, their individual national programmes afforded only a tiny fraction of the American capacity to deploy military power overseas. The British could point to their own Strategic Defence Review[67] as a model for the type of military restructuring that all the European allies should undergo in order to configure their forces for more flexible and rapidly deployable operations. No longer can territorial defence be considered a sufficient planning scenario.

In the autumn of 1998 the British government took steps to enhance Europe's ability to act independently in military terms.[68] It sought to develop practical improvements in Europe's capacity to deploy forces as well as consider institutional arrangements.[69] At a Franco-British summit in St Malo in December 1998 the UK and France announced their intention to cooperate more extensively on military operations outside of western Europe.[70] The UK has seen France as its most important military partner in these endeavours: France has long embodied the desire for a more capable European defence identity and it is the most capable overseas military actor on the continent alongside the UK. As France has drawn closer to NATO during the Chirac Presidency, Britain has reciprocated by embracing some of France's goals for Europe.

Of even greater symbolic importance was the British government's decision to withdraw its long-standing opposition to the WEU being integrated into the European Union. At the Cologne and Helsinki European Council meetings in June and December 1999 it was agreed that the European Union would be endowed with the capacity for 'autonomous' military action.[71] Many of the military facets of the WEU would be transferred to the EU so that the latter would no longer have to task another organisation to act on its behalf. The EU would seek to develop the capability to carry out the Petersberg tasks that had hitherto been the domain of the WEU. In order to achieve this, a Rapid Reaction Corps of 50,000–60,000 troops will be assembled from among the European nations, by 2003, capable of being deployed within 60 days.

This initiative was of considerable significance for British attitudes towards Europe. It has demonstrated a willingness to begin to build a meaningful military capability within the framework of European integration, something that Britain has eschewed since the demise of the EDC. Its importance has not been lost on other actors. The United States expressed initial misgivings over these developments, with speeches from Secretary of State Madeline Albright and NATO Ambassador Alexander Vershbow.[72] These have now been largely allayed but the US remains wary of any development that could have the effect of excluding it from a voice on European defence decisions.

Thus at the end of the millennium Britain sought to find a way to reconcile the contrasting pressures to preserve the transatlantic defence relationship while simultaneously enabling a European defence identity to grow. British policy-makers have come to believe that the risk of the US becoming frustrated by the inability of the Europeans to act, outweighs American fears of European independence. Britain has insisted that

European defence capabilities must be enhanced in a manner that is compatible with NATO. Yet they are aware that allowing the EU to develop a defence competence has unleashed a powerful new dynamic in the European security debate. It will remain to be seen whether duplication and frictions can be avoided and what sorts of capabilities will be considered necessary to underpin the EU as a defence actor.

Conclusion

The security of Europe grew to be the foremost preoccupation of Britain in the postwar period. Although at the end of the Second World War it was not the focus of British attention, this attitude changed over time as the country's interests were re-evaluated and the implications of modern warfare were understood. By 1968, the Supplementary Statement on Defence could declare categorically that 'our security lies fundamentally in Europe and must be based on the North Atlantic Alliance',[73] while Defence Secretary, John Nott, could state in the 1980s that 'Europe . . . dwarfs every other British interest'.[74] The truth of these statements have been borne out by the fact that ever since the Cold War has ended, Europe has remained the primary concern of British policy-makers. While the size of the British presence on the continent has decreased, conflicts such as those in Bosnia and Kosovo have kept Europe uppermost in the minds of politicians and the military alike. In retrospect it is ironical that although Britain prepared for war in Europe for 43 years, it has been since the end of the Cold War that British forces have been called into action on the continent.

British policy towards Europe has been remarkable for its continuity. As Britain's military presence around the world decreased, so the European commitment became proportionally more significant. The 'declinist' thesis that British policy can be understood simply in terms of diminishing resources, provides an insufficient explanation. In the latter part of the 1960s, long-term military pressures, the growing political attraction of the continent and changing economic realities eventually led the UK to concentrate upon Europe. The power of ideas and perceptions was therefore vital in explaining this change of focus. At the same time Britain has continued to believe that it has a special contribution to make to preserving global order.

It could be argued over the longer term that the UK has failed to capitalise fully upon the military investments it has made in Europe. After all, Britain built up a stable relationship with West Germany through the stationing of the forces of BAOR and the Second Allied Tactical Air Force, yet it enjoyed little of the broader intimacy that a country like France experienced with its neighbour. This was partly because Britain refused to compromise its relationship with the United States when dealing with its European partners. Partly it was because a disjunction existed between the British role as a good ally within the Alliance and the semi-detached role that it pursued towards European political cooperation. It has been a perennial weakness of the British that they have been unable to turn their military influence in Europe into a broader degree of political influence. In effect Britain has borne the burden of a disproportionate level of defence spending among its European allies without ever reaping the potential political rewards.[75] What remains to be seen is whether the new policy inaugurated at the end of the 1990s, aimed at drawing Britain closer in military terms to its European partners, will provide the UK with broader political influence in the future.

Notes

1. See E. Barker, *The British Between the Superpowers, 1945–50*, London: Macmillan, 1983.
2. See, for example, A. Danchev, *Very Special Relationship: Field Marshal Sir John Dill and the Anglo-American Alliance 1941–44*, London: Brassey's, 1986.
3. M. Gilbert, *Churchill: A Life*, London: Heinemann, 1991, p. 818.
4. See J. Kent and J. Young, 'British Overseas Policy: The "Third Force" and the Origins of NATO – in Search of a New Perspective', in B. Heuser and R. O'Neill (eds), *Securing Peace in Europe 1945–62: Thoughts for the Post-Cold War Era*, Basingstoke: Macmillan, 1992, pp. 41–64.
5. See A. Bullock, *The Life and Times of Ernest Bevin. Volume III. Foreign Secretary, 1945–51*, London: Heinemann, 1983.
6. Public Record Office, DG 1/11/56 MD (50) 12 'Western Union Defence Organisation', 5/7/1950.
7. See Paul Cornish, *British Military Planning for the Defence of Germany 1945–50*, Basingstoke: Macmillan in association with King's College London, 1996.
8. E. Fursdon, *The European Defence Community: A History*, London: Macmillan, 1980.
9. A. Eden, *Full Circle*, London: Cassell, 1960, p. 36.
10. M. Gilbert, op. cit., p. 900.
11. The French failure to ratify the EDC Treaty was due to a perception that, without the UK involved as well, there would be insufficient counterweights within the framework to offset German power. In addition, the government was struggling to extricate France from its military disasters in Indochina.
12. The Article V territorial defence guarantees of the WEU were even operationalised through NATO.
13. EPC was a process of informal consultation between European foreign ministers on matters of mutual concern. For further details see S. Nuttall, *European Political Cooperation*, Oxford: Clarendon Press, 1992.
14. P. Winand, *Eisenhower, Kennedy and the United States of Europe*, New York: St Martin's Press, 1993, pp. 247–50.
15. F. Halliday, *The Making of the Second Cold War*, London: Verso, 1983, pp. 144–5.
16. W. Rees, *The Western European Union at the Crossroads: Between Trans-Atlantic Solidarity and European Integration*, Boulder, CO: Westview Press, 1998, Chapter 2.
17. A. Cahen, 'The Western European Union and NATO: Building a European Defence Identity Within the Context of Atlantic Solidarity', in *Brassey's Atlantic Commentaries*, No. 2, London, 1989, p. 15.
18. This assumed a low risk of war for the next five years and then only a marginally greater risk for the subsequent five years.
19. PRO, CAB 129/84 CP (56) 269, 'UK Forces in Germany', 28/11/1956.
20. J. Baylis and A. Macmillan, 'The British Global Strategy Paper of 1952', in *Journal of Strategic Studies*, 16 (2) 1993.

21. PRO, DEFE 5/80 COS (57) 280 Appendix, 'Minimum Essential Force Requirements for the Period up to 1963', 19/12/1957.
22. *Statement on Defence, 1956*, Cmnd. 9,691, London: HMSO, 1956.
23. J. Slessor, 'British Defence Policy', in *Foreign Affairs*, 35 (4) July 1957, p. 552.
24. MC 70 was NATO's 'Minimum Essential Force Requirements' which resulted from the Alliance's rethink on strategy in the late 1950s.
25. PRO, DEFE 4/129 COS (60) 55th Meeting, 'NATO Strategy', 13/9/1960.
26. A. Eden, op. cit., p. 372.
27. General Norstad wanted a 90 day fighting capability.
28. See J. Stromseth, *The Origins of Flexible Response: NATO's Debate over Strategy in the 1960s*, Basingstoke: Macmillan, 1988.
29. D. Healey, *The Time of My Life*, London: Penguin, 1989, p. 308.
30. A. Eden, op. cit., p. 135.
31. These were the famous 'Attlee–Truman Understandings'. For details see J. Baylis, *Ambiguity and Deterrence: British Nuclear Strategy, 1945–1964*, Oxford: Clarendon Press, 1995, p. 121.
32. For details see B. Davis, *Qaddafi, Terrorism and the Origins of the US Attack on Libya*, New York: Praeger, 1990.
33. For the rise of Soviet naval power see M. McGwire, K. Booth and J. Connell (eds), *Soviet Naval Policy: Objectives and Constraints*, New York: Praeger, 1975. For a study on the Royal Navy see E. Grove, *Vanguard to Trident*, London: Bodley Head, 1987.
34. The Maritime Doctrine was formulated during John Lehman's period as Secretary of the United States Navy.
35. G. Howe, *Conflict of Loyalty*, London: Pan, 1994, p. 390.
36. J. Newhouse, *The Nuclear Age: From Hiroshima to Star Wars*, London: Michael Joseph, 1989, p. 399.
37. M. Clarke, 'Britain' in M. Brenner (ed.), *NATO and Collective Security*, Basingstoke: Macmillan, 1997, p. 6.
38. L. Freedman, 'The Case of Westland and the Bias to Europe', *International Affairs*, 63 (1) 1986, pp. 19–23.
39. P. Winand, op. cit., p. 226.
40. PRO, DEFE 4/96 Annex to JP (57) 28 (Final) CPX 7, 22/3/1957.
41. P. Darby, *British Defence Policy East of Suez, 1947–68*, Oxford: Oxford University Press, 1973, p. 161.
42. PRO, CAB 128/41, CC 38 (66) 'Germany', 20/7/1966.
43. PRO, CAB 130/213 'Miscellaneous 17/5', 13 June 1965.
44. PRO, PREM 13/214 'Record of a conversation between the Prime Minister and Dean Rusk', May 1965.
45. PRO, CAB 139/1929, FP (60) 1, 'Future Policy Study', 24/2/1960.
46. R. Jenkins, *A Life at the Centre*, London: Macmillan, 1991, p. 212.
47. A Cabinet Committee in 1964 had warned against the dangers of Britain becoming isolated from the continent. The minutes record that: 'Such isolation will result in this country finding itself progressively of lesser importance in the determination of the great issues that have to be resolved between the United

States, the Soviet Union and the major powers of Continental Europe'. PRO, CAB 148/40, OPD (0) (64) 'Defence Policy', 30/10/1964.

48. Quoted in H. Young, *This Blessed Plot: Britain and Europe from Churchill to Blair*, London: Macmillan, 1998, p. 106.

49. *Statement on the Defence Estimates*, Cmnd. 3,390, London: HMSO, 1969.

50. P. Darby, op. cit., p. 275.

51. PRO, CAB 148/40, op. cit.

52. PRO, CAB 130/213, Misc 17/1st, 'Defence Review 1964–5', 21/11/1964.

53. G. Howe, op. cit., pp. 144–5.

54. J. Baylis, *British Defence Policy: Striking the Right Balance*, Basingstoke: Macmillan, 1989, pp. 69–70.

55. See C. McInnes, 'BAOR in the 1980s: Changes in Doctrine and Organisation', *Defense Analysis*, 4 (4) 1988, pp. 377–94.

56. For a discussion of enlargement issues see S. Croft, J. Redmond, W. Rees and M. Webber, *The Enlargement of Europe*, Manchester: Manchester University Press, 1999.

57. M. Clarke in M. Brenner, op. cit., p. 19.

58. See D. Yost, *NATO Transformed: The Alliance's New Roles in International Security*, Washington: United States Institute of Peace, 1998, ch. 4.

59. *Defending Our Future*, Cmnd. 2,270, London: HMSO, 1993.

60. M. Brenner, 'Terms of Engagement: The United States and the European Security Identity', *The Washington Papers*, CSIS, 1998, p. 41.

61. C. Barry, 'NATO's Combined Joint Task Forces in Theory and Practice', *Survival*, 38 (1) 1996, pp. 81–97.

62. The UK was also worried that the Article V guarantee would provide a backdoor route to NATO defence guarantees.

63. W. Rees, op. cit., pp. 120–1.

64. Namely the 'Petersberg' tasks of humanitarian operations, peacekeeping and the employment of combat forces in crisis management.

65. 'Operation Alba' in Albania was led by Italy, with the participation of France, Spain and Greece.

66. D. Owen, *Balkan Odyssey*, London: Indigo, 1995, ch. 3.

67. *The Strategic Defence Review*, Cmnd. 3,999, London: The Stationery Office, 1998. For an informed assessment see T. Dodd and M. Oakes, *The Strategic Defence Review White Paper*, Research Paper 98/91, House of Commons Library, London, October 1998.

68. Britain signalled its change of thinking on European defence issues at the informal European Council meeting at Pörtschach under the Austrian Presidency of the European Union.

69. The British initiative was undertaken in response to wider political considerations – European defence was the only area in which Britain could launch a major initiative.

70. 'Declaration on European Defense', St Malo, 3–4 December 1998, www.fco.gov.uk.

71. Presidency Conclusions, Helsinki European Council, 10–11 December 1999.

72. A. Vershbow, Speech at Wilton Park, England, 26 January 2000.
73. *Supplementary Statement on Defence Policy 1968*, Cmnd. 3,701, London: HMSO, July 1968.
74. J. Baylis, op. cit., p. 131.
75. Britain still spends more than the European average on defence, leading some commentators to propose that it should be reduced to the average of its allies. See M. Chalmers, *Biting the Bullet, European Defence Option for Britain*, London: Institute for Public Policy Research, 1992, p. 53.

Chapter 4

Britain's Nuclear Weapons Discourse

Stuart Croft

Introduction

It is possible to read the development of British defence policy from the end of the Second World War in terms of the nuclear question. Indeed, from before the defeat of Nazi Germany and Imperial Japan, Britain was working with the United States to produce nuclear forces that would enable the two states to develop deterrence of future global acts of aggression. The subsequent unfolding of events and policies could be seen as merely iterations on this fundamental position.

Such a reading would, however, be inappropriate. One can understand the nuclear debate in Britain at a variety of levels but perhaps most fundamentally, it has been about the interplay of identity and security. British nuclear policy coexisted with other national nuclear policies, but the UK interpreted these material realities (nuclear weapons) ideationally: *Soviet* nuclear weapons threatened the existence of Britain; but *American* nuclear weapons promised to help preserve the UK from this cataclysmic threat.[1]

So the British nuclear debate must be read in terms of this relationship between identity and security, which in turn can be understood only in terms of the relationship between the material and the ideational. But in what sense was there a *debate*? The validity of British nuclear forces has been subject to two perspectives, propounded by those who in this chapter will be referred to as the orthodox and the alternative thinkers.[2] The orthodox thinkers included virtually all of those responsible for British government policy in the security field since the late 1940s, as well as the majority of those in the 'strategic community'. They came to dominate the military, defence journalism and the defence industry. In contrast, the alternative thinkers have tended to comprise members of protest organisations, sections of academia and the churches, and the opposition backbenches.

There are two problems with a conventional understanding of the British nuclear debate. The first is the assumption that it was always clear to the postwar British leadership that the UK had to become a nuclear weapons state. The historical record questions this. Prime Minister Attlee's initial reaction to the dawning of the nuclear age was to argue against national control of nuclear forces and in favour of international control.[3] As Smith and Zametica noted, 'What he [Attlee] wanted was nothing less that a drastic revision of the principles governing British foreign and defence policy; and he believed that the implications of the newly formed United Nations Organisation . . . was an overwhelming justification for such a revision.'[4] In this, Attlee was supported by some in Cabinet: at the Cabinet Meeting on 8 November 1945, 'Some ministers thought it would be wiser to make an immediate offer to disclose this [atomic] information to the Soviet government.'[5] For some, confrontation with the Soviet Union was unavoidable, while others sought to pursue consensus among the major powers.[6] Gowing noted that they had argued that 'If it was our policy to build world peace on moral foundations rather than on the balance of power we should be prepared to apply that principle at once to the atomic bomb.'[7] Of course, all of this changed when the decision was taken in January 1947 to pursue a British bomb programme, but it is ahistorical to ignore the early period.

The second problem with the conventional reading is that it suggests that the British defence consensus has twice collapsed over nuclear weapons. The first was during the late 1950s and the early 1960s when mass protest met the development of the British bomb. However, the momentum began to run out of the anti-nuclear protest movement, and this led to the regeneration of the British defence consensus along traditionally accepted lines. The second breakdown in the consensus occurred from the early 1980s until, arguably, as late as 1990.[8] Once more, the challenge to the predominant security view lessened in intensity over time, as East–West relations improved and major arms control agreements were signed. But this characterisation – the fractured consensus, the rebuilding of the consensus, re-fracturing and rebuilding – does not hold if one focuses on the *intellectual* debate. It was certainly true that voluble argument and public dissent rose and fell over time; but this was based on an intellectual substructure that was – and still is – consistent.

Throughout the two major challenges to British nuclear policy, it has been the orthodox perspective that has predominated in terms of British defence policy. And in the periods of low public controversy, the orthodox thinkers were able to completely ignore the alternative thinkers. So why should it be worthwhile to examine the 'failed' propositions of the alternative thinkers? Because this chapter attempts accurately to reproduce the debate over British defence. It would not be useful to reproduce a purely 'material' analysis, focusing simply on deployments and tests because perhaps more than any other area of British defence examined in this book, the nuclear question raised central questions of identity, of notions of threat and amity which cannot be understood through an examination of hardware, but only by the ideational construction of the meaning of that material hardware. This will become more apparent over the course of this chapter.

This chapter will elaborate the perspectives of the orthodox thinkers, and then the alternative thinkers along the lines of their central assumptions and arguments. It will then assess the degree to which both perspectives were affected by the end of the Cold War. The conclusion will examine four myths in the British nuclear debate and will then compare the views of the orthodox with those of the alternative thinkers. However, it will be argued later that these two perspectives have been incommensurable; that is, there have been no independent grounds for evaluating between them and that therefore the proponents of the two views have simply been talking past each other.

Establishing and entrenching orthodoxy ——————————

The establishment of the orthodox position in Britain over nuclear weapons is usually dated from the end of the Second World War. During the mid-1940s, the British struggled with the problems of deciding how to come to terms with the postwar world. But by the time of the Berlin blockade of 1948, the British official attitude towards the postwar world had apparently been set. This view continued to dominate orthodox thinking and set the framework for considering nuclear relations during the Cold War. That framework had three parts, and each of these will be examined in turn.

The primary assumption for the orthodox thinkers was that the international system was an anarchic one. The classic reflection of this in nuclear terms was expressed by the Maud Committee, set up in 1940 to investigate the possibility of manufacturing an atomic weapon. The Committee concluded that 'no nation would care to be caught without a weapon of such decisive possibilities'.[9] Fundamentally, no other state could be trusted – this has important implications for Anglo-American relations, which will be addressed next – and so Britain had to develop and maintain its own nuclear force.

Clearly, in such a world it was vital to recognise the identity of the chief adversary. From the late 1940s onwards, there was never any doubt in the orthodox view about Soviet hostility. Geopolitically, the USSR was seen to threaten to control the whole of continental Europe, and a desire to avoid unipolar domination of the continent had been a constant in British foreign policy going back at least to the Napoleonic wars. In addition, communism seemed to threaten the British way of life. A classic statement of this was made in 1947 by the Permanent Under Secretary at the Foreign Office. Sir Orme Sargent commented that 'the only real danger to peace is now the Soviet Union. If the Soviet Union disappeared, or Russia were under a different ideology, the world could soon settle down to peace.'[10] Hostility to Soviet communism was as much a feature of the Attlee governments as of any subsequent Conservative government in Britain.[11] This meant that Soviet policy would always be viewed through the lens of worst case thinking; Margaret Thatcher's government was to disagree with the West Germans over the reaction to Gorbachev's reforms in the late 1980s, with Britain operating on worst case analysis (Gorbachev sought to divide NATO), and the West Germans arguing that Gorbachev heralded fundamental changes in East–West relations.[12]

The orthodox thinkers therefore viewed the world as anarchic, the chief threat as the USSR, and utilised worst case analysis. These assumptions led to a desire to work with the United States, the second part of the framework. British policy before the twentieth century had been concerned with keeping the balance between groups of states. From the 1940s, the perception was that the Soviet Union was the predominant European power, one that could not be matched by any grouping of European states: hence, on purely 'rational' grounds, separated from any feelings about the 'naturalness' or otherwise of the special relationship, there had to be an alliance with the United States.

Following this logic, the United States was therefore seen as a much more important ally than, say, France or (West) Germany. This was because it was only the United States on the Western side that could have brought about changes to the strategic situation, by providing counterbalancing power against pressure from the East through its nuclear and industrial power, thereby bringing stability to Europe. It was of great importance to the orthodox view for Britain to be able to influence the actions and attitudes of the United States: the special relationship was consequently of overwhelming importance.[13] That relationship was special because the British strategic community claimed to have a relationship with the American community that the latter did not share with any other. That privilege was used to maintain an American commitment to European security, but also to restrain any destabilising impulses on the American side. The British felt that, to quote Attlee, they would be 'unequal no doubt in power but equal in counsel'.[14] This related, above all, to nuclear strategy.

The most obvious aspect of this relationship related to the provision of American nuclear delivery vehicles for the British bomb.[15] Why did policy-makers insist on purchasing delivery systems for the British independent deterrent from the United States, first Polaris and subsequently Trident, instead of producing them indigenously, as did the French?[16] Clearly, purchasing weapons systems from Washington made the British deterrent force an easy target for political opponents, repeating, in a variety of terms, Harold Wilson's original condemnation of the 'the so-called British, so-called independent, so-called deterrent'.[17] Although costs and technological capabilities were important elements in this reliance, for the orthodox thinkers other reasons were political. One conventional wisdom has been that the British have maintained an independent nuclear deterrent to enhance prestige and international standing. Perhaps a more persuasive argument is that, certainly in the early period, nuclear weapons were sought not to enhance prestige, but rather because the pursuit of nuclear weaponry was seen to reflect the status that the United Kingdom already possessed. From the early 1960s, when the British began to rely on the American delivery systems of Polaris and Trident, it might be suggested that this reflected a concomitant lessening of status for the United Kingdom. However, this development was in some ways actually the culmination of British efforts to work more closely with the Americans, and this can be seen by examining the rationale for the British bomb.

The first clear public rationale for the British bomb was developed by Defence Secretary Denis Healey in the 1960s. Healey reportedly argued that 'if you are inside an alliance you increase the deterrent to the other side enormously if there is more than one centre of decisions for first use of nuclear weapons'.[18] This approach became institutionalised among the public rationales of the orthodox thinkers. In 1980, Defence Secretary Francis Pym explained that the decision to use nuclear force 'would be a decision of a separate and independent Power, and a Power whose survival in freedom might be more directly and closely threatened by aggression in Europe than that of the United States. This is where the fact of having to face two decision-makers instead of one is of such significance.'[19] The 1987 Statement on the Defence Estimates, produced just before the General Election, explained that, 'Although the mainstay of the Atlantic Alliance's deterrent forces is provided by the United States, the presence of an independent nuclear deterrent under absolute British control greatly complicates the calculations that would have to be made by anyone contemplating an attack.'[20]

The orthodox thinkers have never wanted to argue that Britain possesses the bomb because it does not trust the United States, as the French argued, for this would both undermine Britain's privileged position in the special relationship, and also undermine deterrence.[21] Hence, the British independent force was in part an investment to gain influence over American nuclear strategy. Purchases of American delivery systems, initially through Polaris, was seen as British weakness; but in retrospect it represented in some senses a success, for by moving to Polaris the United Kingdom was able to maintain a force that was operationally independent, while deepening a whole range of collaborative contacts with the United States, which offered the possibility of enhancing British influence over American policy.

But tensions always remained. The British sought influence in Washington; in order to achieve that, there was joint Anglo-American targeting, and a stress on the commitment of the British force to NATO. On the other hand, given the independence of the British force, final decisions about use and targets had to be taken by the British government for strategic and national ends.[22] This dilemma was acutely demonstrated in the terms of the Nassau agreement of 1962, when the United States agreed to sell Polaris to Britain. Prime Minister Harold Macmillan agreed that 'these British forces will be used for the purposes of international defense of the Western Alliance in all circumstances' except 'where Her Majesty's Government may decide that supreme national interests are at stake.'[23] Thus, there has been a tension between alliance and national roles, between the demands of possession and the requirements of threat. A nation would only consider the use of nuclear force should supreme national interests be at stake.

The third part of the framework could be called the belief in the nuclear order. The orthodox thinkers' case could be summarised as follows. In an anarchic world, states would fundamentally have to rely upon their own efforts for security, and so it was important for Britain to develop nuclear forces, particularly given the threatening nature and power of the Soviet Union, which required a reliance on the United States as a balancer. And Britain was to develop its nuclear forces as a means of influencing Washington to buy a privileged position while not compromising on an ability to maintain British nuclear deterrence. Thus, for the orthodox thinkers, it was better to live in a nuclear world than in a post-nuclear (i.e., full nuclear disarmament) world.

British nuclear weapons had a crucial role to play but so did the entire nuclear order. A nuclear deterrence system made all war inconceivable. As a consequence, nuclear weapons were inherently seen to be an international good. As the 1987 Statement on the Defence Estimates put it,

> it is easy to forget that in the first half of this century the world was twice plunged into immensely destructive global conventional war.... In the last century Europe was torn asunder by several major wars. By contrast, in the ... 40 years of nuclear deterrence – there has been no war in western Europe, either conventional or nuclear, in spite of deep ideological hostility between East and West.[24]

In the starkest contrast to the alternative thinkers, as will be seen below, the nuclear order was seen to be stable and positive. As Margaret Thatcher put it, 'Conventional weapons alone do not deter, and two world wars in Europe have already proved that. We want a war free Europe, and we need to keep nuclear weapons to achieve that.'[25]

For the orthodox thinkers, nuclear deterrence and British possession of nuclear weapons were the key ingredients of security. They simply could not have agreed to either British or NATO complete nuclear disarmament, regardless of Soviet policy. The orthodox view was that nuclear deterrence was stable, and infinitely preferable to any other conceivable world. The alternative thinkers, however, made precisely opposite assumptions, and focused upon ways to bring the East–West confrontation and the nuclear order to a peaceful end.

Alternative thinkers and international security

This section will examine the case of the alternative thinkers focusing on four specific issues which contrast strongly with the case set out by the orthodox thinkers. However, in order to set some context, it will begin with an examination of the intellectual roots developed in the 1940s and 1950s.

The category labelled here as 'alternative thinkers' became firmly associated with those outside the decision-making structures of the British state, but this was not always so. In November 1945, P. M. S. Blackett, a key government adviser, argued against any moves towards embarking upon a nuclear bomb programme. Development of a British bomb would waste resources, could not in any case produce a large enough stockpile to be effective, and would invite a Soviet pre-emptive attack.[26] He was not convinced about the deterrent abilities of nuclear weapons, since nuclear war would not be short. Given the use of three million tons of bombs dropped by air by the allied forces during the war, and that one atomic bomb produced destruction equivalent to 2,000 tons of those bombs, 'it is certain that a very large number of atomic bombs would be needed to defeat a great nation by bombing alone'.[27] Blackett's unconventional views meant that he became 'suspect as an adviser in Whitehall – or at least in the ministry of defence'.[28]

But by the early 1950s opposition to the British bomb became increasingly public. The Hydrogen Bomb National Campaign sought an international conference to control the development and testing of what at the time was called the 'superbomb'. The Peace Pledge Union began to organise sit down protests, seeking the end of Britain's nuclear programme, the closure of American bases in the United Kingdom, and the withdrawal of Britain from NATO.[29] In 1955 the Committee for the Abolition of Nuclear Weapons Tests was formed, developing into a national organisation within eighteen months.[30] Finally, on 15 January 1958, the Campaign for Nuclear Disarmament (CND) was formed in the office of Canon John Collins, who had been an important figure in the opposition to 'Bomber' Harris' bombardment of German cities during the war.

By the time of the establishment of CND, three important and mutually supporting arguments were developed in the case against the British bomb: that the threat and consequences of nuclear war were greater than the threat and consequences of Soviet invasion; that the continuation of the policies then being implemented could only lead to destructive and catastrophic warfare; and that neutralism was the only way of breaking out of the Cold War cycle.

The first argument related to the great threat of nuclear weapons compared with the threat of the Soviet Union. In the late 1950s Sir Stephen King-Hall developed a critique of nuclear weapons from the standpoint of 'better red than dead'. King-Hall argued that the use of any nuclear weapon would lead to an uncontrollable escalation to the use of all strategic weapons, and thus Britain had to eliminate its own nuclear force and its connection with American nuclear forces. In his classic statement, for 'between Britain occupied by the Russian army and a Britain as a smoking radioactive charnel house the former is the lesser of the two great evils'.[31] Such an argument gained credibility through the belief in the importance of systematic non-violent resistance. British defence policy would be reoriented away from nuclear and conventional arms into an ability to withstand blockade and occupation. Whereas not all agreed with this logic, many agreed with the sentiments, which seemed wholly in line with moral reasoning. Much of the moral argument at this time was dominated by the writings of church men and women.[32] For example, the Bishop of Exeter argued that 'It would be immoral and unchristian if Britain were to use the hydrogen bomb, either offensively or in retaliation after attack. . . . It can have no conceivable moral warrant, and it would be directed against the helpless.'[33]

The second argument, therefore, suggested that continuation of current policies threatened complete disaster. For Bertrand Russell, probably the best known figure amongst the nuclear dissenters of the 1950s and 1960s, 'Our planet cannot persist on its present course. There may be war, as a result of which all or nearly all will perish.'[34] Should a nuclear war not occur, 'it will only be because the Great Powers adopt new policies'.[35] However, perhaps the most significant proponent of this perspective was Philip Noel-Baker, in particular through his highly influential book *The Arms Race*.[36]

The third and final argument stressed the value of neutralism, and the creation of a new world order through destroying the bloc system: 'By seeking to abolish nuclear weapons and the alliances which depend on them we are opening up an area of freedom in which peaceful change is possible for all people.'[37] Stuart Hall argued that 'Since the dissolution of the two camps can be effected only through negotiation, Britain's role must be to prepare the West to negotiate. . . . She cannot do this from a position of neutrality in Europe; and she cannot afford to leave NATO to its own devices.'[38] But how long should Britain continue in this role? At what point should morality, as opposed to pragmatism, dictate abandonment of the effort and the move to neutralism?

By the mid-1960s, the public visibility of the alternative thinkers' anti-nuclear campaign began to decline; however, thinking was continuing during the late 1960s and into the 1970s, refining and developing ideas, so that by the early 1980s, the alternative thinkers had a clear case to articulate. Much of that case was based on the lines set out in the 1950s; however, it was all deeply imbued with an anti-Americanism that had been developed during the anti-Vietnam war protests of the 1960s and 1970s. Four central ideas were enunciated, that will form the basis for the rest of this section: a reduced perception of any Soviet threat; disengagement from the United States; dealignment and a desire to change the nature of international relations; and fierce opposition to nuclear weapons and nuclear deterrence.

Firstly, the alternative thinkers began to develop what in many senses was a radical argument; that threats to national security were not the predominant issues in global or British politics. A starting point for all nuclear dissenters in the 1980s was the inadequacy of the dominant security paradigm which concentrated on state threats to survival, and in particular stressed the threatening nature of the Soviet Union. The alternative thinkers, echoing the analysis of earlier writers such as Sir Stephen King-Hall, argued that the threat of nuclear war was much greater than the threat of Soviet invasion. For Ken Booth, 'At the start of the 1980s . . . [people] had in fact come to fear nuclear weapons more than the Soviet Union itself.'[39] More explicitly, Booth argued that 'War is the threat, not the Soviet Union.'[40] Paul Oestreicher, at the time Assistant General Secretary of the British Council of Churches and Vice-President of CND, argued that Soviet domination '*is* preferable to annihilation'.

Fundamental reappraisals were central to the alternative thinkers' case. As Michael Clarke put it, 'all alternative thinking tries to go back to first principles to address the question, what is security? In particular, what is to be defended, and from whom or what does it need to be defended?'[41] For the alternative thinkers, it was impossible to defend against nuclear weapons, and nuclear deterrence was inherently unstable and therefore threatening. The Alternative Defence Commission, a loose organisation set up in 1980 comprising over a dozen alternative thinkers who shared a commitment to denuclearising security policy, believed that 'The notion that there can be a sufficiently reliable stability in any form of nuclear deterrence is, in our view, an illusion.'[42]

One of the leading structuralist thinkers amongst the alternative thinkers was Mary Kaldor. She argued that the central problem in the debate over nuclear weapons was the role of war itself. For Kaldor, warfare is 'located at the centre of the capitalist crisis. Capitalism needs the state, needs non-economic forms of coercion, and, as long as states are divided by geography, needs warfare.'[43] Thus the system was at fault, and it was the system to which the Soviet Union reacted:

> The Soviet system was developed in opposition to capitalism and that is its *raison d'être*. The role of warfare is defensive, against capitalism. . . . Where warfare has been used in the East, in Hungary, Czechoslovakia or Afghanistan, the aim has been to secure buffer states.[44]

For Kaldor, the nature of capitalism in the West was the root problem, which showed itself in the nuclear policies of the West.

A similar structural perspective was that it was the nature of the Cold War that was responsible for the nuclear danger. For Edward Thompson, the Cold War dominated politics and created a new category of thinking: 'exterminism'.[45] For Fred Halliday, various factors such as nuclear parity, third world revolutions, rising American militarism, and the sharpening of contradictions within the capitalist world had, by the early 1980s, given rise to a new Cold War: 'If unchecked, their momentum could lead towards a Third World War that would realise the exterminist potential of the present arms race.'[46]

Following these arguments it is clear that orthodox ways of thinking about security policy were inadequate. Ken Booth argued that, 'much of our thinking about "defence" rests on stale and inaccurate images of the Soviet Union. . . . The need for a revised picture of the Soviet Union predated the arrival of Mr. Gorbachev.'[47] Thompson wrote that, 'I find it objectionable to refer to the Soviet Union as "the enemy".'[48] Differences in the assumptions of the alternative thinkers and the orthodox thinkers were fundamental. The latter calculated the large Soviet capabilities for attack. Using worst case analysis, they argued that capabilities had to be translated into intentions. Since the USSR had the capability to attack the West, it also had the intention. This was a line of reasoning that, to the alternative thinkers, was appallingly weak and dangerous. Kaldor argued that 'the technological dynamic in the Soviet military system . . . stem[s] from the West'.[49] It was a case of the Soviets striving to match western developments, rather than preparing for invasion. Malcolm Dando and Paul

Rogers argued that the West 'are, as usual, leading this phase of the nuclear arms race . . . we have to recognise *their* real fears of us'.[50] In order to do this, the alternative thinkers sought a fundamental reappraisal of the role of the United States, and of the Anglo-American relationship.

This led to the second issue, which might be termed the American problem. If nuclear war rather than the USSR was the main threat, then this coloured the view taken of the United States. The Alternative Defence Commission called for the decoupling of the United States and Europe.[51] The danger, they argued, was that the United States had been developing nuclear strategies likely to lead to war. The orthodox thinkers stressed the influence that the United Kingdom had in Washington through the special relationship; all alternative thinkers argued that no such special relationship existed. Ken Booth, for example, suggested that 'it will be just a matter of time before the "special relationship" is fully revealed to be special only in its one-sidedness'.[52] For Duncan Campbell, 'The British political leadership has often deluded itself about the "special relationship" it believes we enjoy, based on a common language and liberal-democratic capitalist societies.'[53]

The alternative thinkers were perhaps predisposed towards anti-Americanism, following the campaigns against US involvement in Vietnam, but they argued that the role of the United States in world politics was becoming even more dangerous, with terrifying changes in nuclear policy. The alternative thinkers were certainly not friendly towards the concept of mutually assured destruction, whereby nuclear deterrence would be maintained by the threat of total national (and, indeed, global) annihilation. However, for many alternative thinkers, the United States, under the Reagan administration, had moved away from this distasteful approach towards even worse strategies based on concepts of nuclear war-fighting. Thus, Britain had to escape the linkage with the Americans, for 'our ties entail an unacceptable risk that Britain might be dragged into a war between the superpowers.'[54] The orthodox thinkers sought a close Anglo-American relationship so that British policy-makers could influence and restrain American thoughts and actions. For the alternative thinkers, close Anglo-American relations made the Americans more confident and more prone to unilateral action, which in turn made Britain more of a nuclear target: 'Put in simple terms, the damage that the United Kingdom may suffer in war arises in significant measure from the presence of US bases here.'[55] The United States was largely seen to be irresponsible, and a nation that the British could not influence. Therefore, 'US disengagement would enhance British security in the first instance simply by removing many major targets of likely attack, and some possible centres of confrontation in a crisis.'[56]

The third set of issues revolved around moving beyond alliances. The alternative thinkers sought not only to eliminate nuclear weapons but also to abolish militarised institutions and militarised thinking. Thus, the end of alignments, the end of the bloc system, was a shared goal. E. P. Thompson, for example, articulated a view of a liberated, independent Europe.[57] However, strong and important differences existed among the alternative thinkers. Three approaches could be identified. Some sought immediate dealignment, a withdrawal of the United Kingdom from NATO. Others argued that Britain could reform NATO, but should set deadlines so that if no adequate reform measures were brought about, Britain would still withdraw. The third, and most moderate view, was that if the United Kingdom withdrew from NATO, it would lose all influence over the organisation; therefore, Britain had to stay within NATO, while continually arguing for change.

Of these approaches, the first was in many ways the purist, to withdraw from NATO immediately, and adopt either a neutral or a non-aligned position. Peter Johnson in *Neutrality: A Policy for Britain*, set out arguments for immediate moves towards dealignment.[58] In the influential *Protest and Survive*, E. P. Thompson had argued that Britain must 'detach ourselves from the nuclear strategies of NATO'.[59] Thompson was later to explain that nuclear disarmament would strike at the Cold War confrontation, 'by initiating a counter-thrust, a logic of process leading towards the dissolution of both blocs, the demystification of exterminism's ideological mythology, and thence permitting nations in both eastern and western Europe to resume autonomy and political mobility.'[60] Despite Thompson's tactical concern about the immediate political effect of adopting a policy calling for the withdrawal of Britain from NATO, this was adopted by CND at its conference in Sheffield in 1982. Thompson's concern was that 'we cannot allow our enemies to paint us into a corner. The slogan "NATO out of Britain, Britain out of NATO" is a good one, but it must be taken with a nuclear free zone in Europe, and the break-up of both blocs.'[61]

The desire for a compromise lay behind the second approach, which was to argue for changes in NATO strategy, but to withdraw from NATO within a certain time period if no changes occurred. For the Alternative Defence Commission, 'a British government with fundamental objections to nuclear deterrence policies would have an obligation either to work to remove NATO's reliance on nuclear weapons or to leave the Alliance.'[62] The Commission advocated setting deadlines:

> [A]n anti-nuclear British government should seek to change NATO policy by making its membership of the Alliance conditional upon the implementation of the following set of measures: the adoption of a no first use policy [within two years] . . . ; the establishment of a NWFZ [nuclear weapons free zone] at least 100 kilometres wide in the FRG along the East–West German border . . . [within three years]; the withdrawal of most US battlefield nuclear weapons from Europe within about four years.[63]

In another example, Dan Smith argued for a partial withdrawal from NATO, while attempting to change NATO strategy. For Smith, partial withdrawal meant unilaterally adopting a non-nuclear defence policy, rejecting the strategic assumptions of NATO particularly with regard to the Soviet threat, and withdrawing all British forces from Germany and the rest of Europe.[64]

The third and final approach rejected the compromise view as impractical. Policy should have been to stay within NATO, and work for a change within the Alliance. As Booth put it, 'NATO should continue to provide the framework for British strategy. Unilateralists should not throw out our security baby with the dirty nuclear bath water.'[65] This was the policy of the Labour Party, which was to cause one of the most significant differences between Labour and CND. In the June 1987 General Election manifesto, the Party stated that 'Labour's defence policy is based squarely and firmly on Britain's membership of NATO'.[66]

The fourth and final part of the alternative thinkers' case was to stress the primacy of denuclearisation. Of course there were many that opposed nuclear weapons on purely moral grounds, but the mainstream amongst the alternative thinkers did so on the grounds of political logic. For these alternative thinkers, all of the above intellectual strands came together in the central proposition of the alternative thinkers: nuclear weapons, and nuclear thinking, had to be eliminated. Tactics varied, but this goal remained firm. The thrust of the work of the alternative thinkers was on changing the nature of international relations, which meant an end to the Cold War. Nuclear deterrence, it was argued, was a mechanism that kept the Cold War functioning: only by eliminating nuclear weapons could the nations of the world overcome division. This not only meant the division of Europe and the East–West ideological divide: it also related to North–South relations.[67] One of the most dreadful by-products of nuclearised politics was the cost of the arms race: 'the waste of resources in the face of our local as well as global poverty is monstrous'.[68]

In the view of the orthodox thinkers in a war the possession of British strategic nuclear forces offered some possibility of sanctuarising the United Kingdom and American nuclear bases from Soviet theatre nuclear attack. Were the Soviet Union to attack anyway, the strategic use of British nuclear weapons could have triggered the use of the much larger American force. These possibilities – sanctuary and trigger – would enhance deterrence. The alterative thinkers, however, argued that this approach was deeply flawed. The presence of British and American nuclear weapons on British soil made the United Kingdom a target of such importance that were war to break out, the Soviet Union would have had no option but to attack. Whereas the orthodox thinkers saw the British strategic force as offering a possibility for acting as a pivot between controllable and uncontrollable nuclear war, the alternative thinkers argued that there was no possibility of control. In any case, any use of Britain's nuclear force would bring down a full Soviet response, destroying that which it was supposed to protect: 'the catalytic or trigger rationale for Britain's independent nuclear weapons . . . is fundamentally irrational. Sparking off a general nuclear war by catalytic independent action makes no sense as either a war-fighting or war-terminating strategy.'[69]

The alternative thinkers were strongly condemned by the orthodox thinkers in their arguments against British nuclear strategy. However, in their criticism of NATO nuclear strategy, flexible response, the alternative thinkers received support from a most unexpected direction. Their critiques of flexible response and early nuclear first use were supported and developed by a group of analysts who may perhaps best be termed 'disenchanted orthodox thinkers'. These most uncomfortable people shared many of the orthodox thinkers' assumptions, yet agreed with the alternative thinkers on the need to change NATO strategy by reducing reliance on nuclear response. For example, Lord Mountbatten expressed his hostility to tactical nuclear weapons (a central and vital element in flexible response), while Lord Zuckerman argued that 'If the NATO policy of "flexible response" were regarded as a means of waging actual war, then the concept would be equivalent to a game of "chicken" with nuclear weapons.'[70] Later, in 1984, the British Atlantic Committee published *Diminishing the Nuclear Threat*, a report written by a number of distinguished former military officers who argued that a central concept in flexible response, controlled escalation, was impractical.[71]

Yet no really strong alliance developed between the alternative thinkers and the 'disenchanted orthodox thinkers'. Partly this was because there was a significant cultural difference between the two. The 'disenchanted orthodox thinkers' sought to bring about reform within the existing parameters of security policy. Many of the alternative thinkers were strongly influenced by anti-militarism and pacifism. Some, like Dan Smith, were explicit: 'I come to the consideration of alternative defence policy with an anti-militarist bias.'[72] Others, such as Mary Kaldor, were more fundamentally critical than any of the disenchanted orthodox thinkers. She argued that alternative thinkers should develop an anti-war strategy: 'An anti-war strategy is an act of faith. For it presupposes the possibility that class society does not degenerate into barbarism at the point of most acute conflict.'[73] Thus, although there were points of similarity between alternative thinking and the disenchanted orthodox view, the gap between them still proved to be too large.

The impact of the end of the Cold War

The analysis so far has concentrated on the two perspectives as they affected the debate during the Cold War. It might be expected that with the collapse of the Soviet Union and the Warsaw Pact, those two perspectives would have been fundamentally challenged. But this has not been the case. Indeed, the effect of the most dramatic changes in international relations for 50 years has actually not led to any fundamental re-evaluations. Both the orthodox and alternative thinkers rest secure in their assumptions.

The orthodox thinkers still argue that the United Kingdom needs to continue with developing its nuclear capability in the form of the Trident system. Although the Soviet Union may have disappeared, the threat of Soviet nuclear weapons has not. As the 1992 Defence Estimates put it:

> uncertainties and risks remain. The massive nuclear arsenal of the former Soviet Union still exists. . . . Planned reductions will . . . take years to implement, and the residual holdings will have colossal destructive potential. . . . Russia remains the largest single military power in Europe.[74]

The emphasis on worst-case thinking remains, and hence there is nothing to be said for British nuclear disarmament in such uncertain times. Subsequent political and economic turmoil in Russia has not lead to a change in the essence of this perspective: weapons remain and, in the hands of a dictator could again threaten Britain and Europe.

There is an additional strand to the orthodox thinkers' post-Cold War perspective. They put emphasis on newly emerging threats, which might also in turn require deterrence through the possession of nuclear forces. As the 1992 Statement put it, 'Outside Europe, the proliferation of ballistic missiles and weapons of mass destruction and of sophisticated conventional weapons could pose a threat to our dependencies, our allies and the United Kingdom itself.'[75]

These two themes were key in the new Labour government's Strategic Defence Review. In the section of the SDR that dealt with deterrence and disarmament, the SDR explains that 'while large nuclear arsenals [i.e. Russia] and risks of proliferation [i.e. Iraq and others] remain, our minimum [nuclear] deterrent remains a necessary element of our security'.[76] Of course, this is not to argue that British nuclear policy has not changed with the end of the Cold War, for it has. After 1992, Britain gave up its role in nuclear artillery, its air-launched nuclear weapons, and the Royal Navy (minus the strategic nuclear submarines) has given up any nuclear weapons role. In the SDR further reductions in nuclear weapons were announced.[77] However, although more 'radical' measures were considered ('taking submarines off deterrent patrol, and removing warheads from their missiles and storing them separately ashore'), abolishing Britain's remaining nuclear forces was not.[78]

The end of the Cold War has, therefore, not ended the nuclear relationship of the United Kingdom with the government in Moscow. Further, there are possibilities that new relations will develop with states in the South developing ballistic missile and nuclear capability. Such 'business as usual' prescriptions are widely condemned by the alternative thinkers, for whom the orthodox thinkers are too caught up in their nuclear mindset to realise the greater opportunities available in the aftermath of the Cold War.[79] Their basic challenge is to bring about greater measures of disarmament now. The alternative thinkers do recognise that some steps have been taken in Britain, but the central issue – reliance on a policy of threatening the use of weapons of mass destruction for political purposes – remains.

In contrast to the orthodox view, the alternative thinkers argue that the time of reduced tensions should be grasped not only to reduce excess levels of weapons, but also to abolish the nuclear mindset. An excellent example of this was given by Ken Booth in 1992 in reviewing a study on controlling nuclear weapons in the former Soviet Union. Booth argued that:

> It seems entirely sensible, when confronted by a group of independent states which are trying to bind themselves together in some as yet undetermined way, that outsiders attempt to encourage either complete nuclear abolition or, second best, encourage the centralization of nuclear weapons in the hands of only one member. . . . But if the proposition is so self-evident, why should it not also be applied to other evolving communities of independent state (such as in western Europe)? Would it not make equal sense – for anti-proliferation purposes – for the European Community to pursue complete nuclear abolition or, second best, the centralization of its nuclear weapons into the custodianship of the most powerful and economically effective member, Germany?[80]

The apparent point that Booth made was of double standards, but the deeper point is that an obsession with nuclear issues prevents security from being enhanced. Thus, as Paul Rogers and Malcolm Dando have argued, 'there is a need for new political thinking in the West. Now is the time to seize the opportunity to reverse the arms race.'[81] Rogers has been one of the leading alternative thinkers in Britain, and in a seminal article of his position published in *International Affairs* he argued that the

> much broader approach to security is radically different from traditional attitudes in which international security is seen primarily in terms of state-centred defence postures. . . . The counter argument is that we are entering an era of genuinely global insecurity which will give rise to problems that require approaches which will need to transcend previous concepts of national, or even alliance, security.[82]

Events following the fall of the Berlin Wall have strengthened the perception of the cases for both the orthodox and alternative thinkers. For the former, the dangers of nuclear proliferation are greater in the post-Soviet world, while they refuse to accept that the great nuclear power of Russia can yet be ignored. Nuclear deterrence, then, has wider utility in the post-Cold War world. For the alternative thinkers, a time of reduced international tension is the ideal moment to bring about a movement away from the reliance on nuclear deterrence which, they still hold, is dangerous. While this might not have the urgency of earlier times, it is still an important policy goal.

Conclusion

This chapter has sought to set the development of British nuclear policy into the intellectual context of the debate between two strong factions in the UK over the course of the past 50 years. The argument is that British nuclear thinking has emerged from the dynamic of the debate between the two perspectives. This is not to suggest that some synthesis has emerged for, as will shortly be suggested, the two are incommensurable, but rather that the arguments on both sides have been sharpened by the existence of the other. Indeed, one cannot conceive of an orthodox view without an alternative one; 'Self' is meaningless without a concept of 'Other'. Thus, to understand the nature of British thinking about nuclear weapons one must consider the entire debate, not simply focus on the policies of governments.

It remains the task of the conclusion to compare and contrast these views. However, first it would be useful to recap four myths regarding the nuclear debate in Britain that do not merit close examination.

The first myth is that British governments have always been committed to a British nuclear programme. As was argued in the introduction to this chapter, that perspective is simply ahistorical, as the Attlee government agonised over the decision. Second, it is not helpful to characterise the British debate over nuclear weapons in terms of breakdowns of consensus for, as this chapter has sought to demonstrate, at the level of ideas and argument there has never been a consensus. Third, is perhaps a half-myth; that alternative thinkers have always been outsiders. As shown earlier, P. M. S. Blackett was one of the most important of the early alternative thinkers, but was certainly not an outsider. However, it is true that no one on the 'expert panel' constructing the Labour government's SD Review in 1998 could be described as an alternative thinker.[83] The final myth is that Britain has sought nuclear weapons for largely status reasons. As the section on the orthodox thinkers illustrates, the core was security, not status.[84]

The views of the two perspectives are fundamentally different in a variety of ways, but there are perhaps three grounds for comparison. First, rather than focusing on the emphasis on status in the views of the orthodox thinkers (security was, as already argued, more important), it is important to consider how significant status has been in much alternative thought. As Christopher Driver put it, the leaders of CND 'mostly believed and said that the policy which they proposed would leave Britain not only safer and more independent but in a sense greater than before'.[85] This chapter began by suggesting that the British debate over nuclear weapons could and should be understood in terms of identity, or identities. Both perspectives had different notions of British identity at the core. The orthodox thinkers' conception of British identity has been a narrow one; that is, they have focused on the notion of a Britain challenged and threatened by other identities in an anarchic international system. By contrast, the alternative thinkers' conception has been that British identity could not be separated from the international, for nuclear weapons threatened the whole world and Britain needed to give a lead to the world to move away from that which Thompson described as the 'logic of exterminism'. The domestic–international division thus has had a much more fundamental meaning to the orthodox thinkers. And this goes wider than nuclear issues, for it reflects a dichotomy between those who argue that military force can contain global threat to the UK, and those who argue that those military responses are part of the threat. As Paul Rogers has put it:

> There is a pronounced tendency in [British] defence circles to see the post-Cold War world as one that is increasingly disorderly, and to take the view that Britain will need to maintain forces . . . to maintain stability and the security of Western interests. . . . [However,] seeking military solutions will be not only inadequate but quite probably counterproductive.[86]

Second, both orthodox and alternative thinkers have used history to try to bolster their positions, particularly the world wars. The orthodox thinkers have argued that the alternative view is akin to appeasement that brought about the Second World War, while the orthodox view is criticised by the alternative thinkers as being analogous to that which brought about the First World War.

Third, the two views are incommensurable – that is, orthodox and alternative thinkers have spent 50 years talking past each other. There is no analytical framework that is common to both that can be used in order to evaluate between the rival claims. It is not possible to look at the two views and, using logic, evaluate the correct one for the two perspectives use different 'logics' and there are no grounds for privileging one over the other. This means that the intellectual disagreement over nuclear weapons cannot be resolved by debate.

The British nuclear debate has been divided and divisive, and the questions above all discursively constructed. Due to the incommensurable nature of the perspectives of the orthodox and alternative thinkers, this is likely to continue into the future.

Notes

1. The same point is made in a different way by A. Wendt, 'Constructing International Politics', *International Security*, 20 (1) 1995, p. 73.
2. See S. Croft, 'Continuity and Change in British Thinking about Nuclear Weapons', *Political Studies*, 42 (2) 1994, pp. 228–42.
3. For example, Attlee wrote a letter to President Truman on 25 September 1945 in which he argued that the destructive capabilities of nuclear weapons meant that sovereignty was no longer a valid concept and, therefore, that the Soviet Union, United Kingdom and United States should work together to internationalise the atom bomb. For the text, see British Public Record Reference PREM 8/116.
4. R. Smith and J. Zametica, 'The Cold Warrior: Clement Attlee Reconsidered, 1945–7', *International Affairs*, 61 (2) Spring 1985, p. 243.
5. Idem.
6. See A. Bullock, *Ernest Bevin Foreign Secretary*, Oxford: Oxford University Press, 1985; and A. Deighton, *The Impossible Peace*, Oxford: Clarendon, 1990. The nature of this disagreement is examined in S. Croft, *The End of a Superpower*, Aldershot: Dartmouth, 1994.
7. M. Gowing, *Independence and Deterrence*, London: Macmillan, 1974, p. 70.

8. A reason for a date as late as this is that in their Policy Review Document, the Labour Party accepted for the first time since the early 1980s that they would not make 'a commitment to getting rid of all nuclear weapons for as long as others have them'. *Opportunity Britain*, London: The Labour Party, 1991.

9. M. Gowing, *Britain and Atomic Energy 1939–45*, London: Macmillan, 1964, p. 394.

10. Sargent's updating of the VE Day stocktaking memorandum: Public record office reference FO 371/66546.

11. On Bevin's hostility, see A. Bullock, op. cit.

12. On this see Stuart Croft and David H. Dunn, 'Anglo-German Disagreement over CFE', in S. Croft (ed.), *The Conventional Armed Forces in Europe Treaty: The Cold War Endgame*, Aldershot: Dartmouth, 1994, pp. 106–35.

13. As shown by the essays in W. R. Louis and H. Bull (eds), *The Special Relationship: Anglo-American Relations Since 1945*, Oxford: Clarendon Press, 1986, the special relationship related to many aspects of Anglo-American relations. But for the orthodox thinkers, the core was security policy.

14. A letter from Attlee to Bevin, date 10 December 1950: FO 800/517.

15. See J. Simpson, *The Independent Nuclear State: Britain, the United States and the Military Atom*, London: Macmillan, 1986; and P. Malone, *The British Nuclear Deterrent*, London and New York: Croom Helm and St Martin's Press, 1984, especially pp. 58–74.

16. For further details, see Chapter 1 in this book. In essence, problems with the Blue Streak and Blue Steel missile programmes led the UK to turn to the US to share its systems, firstly with Polaris, and then subsequently with the Trident missile system.

17. Yet when Wilson came to power, Labour broadly continued existing policy. See C. Ponting, *Breach of Promise: Labour in Power 1964–70*, London: Hamish Hamilton, 1989, especially Chapter 6.

18. B. Reed and G. Williams, *Denis Healey and the Policies of Power*, London: Sidgwick and Jackson, 1971, p. 169.

19. Hansard, Vol. 977, Col. 679, 24 January 1980.

20. *Statement on the Defence Estimates 1987*, London: HMSO, 1987, p. 39.

21. US Secretary of Defense Robert McNamara famously warned that 'limited nuclear capabilities, operating independently [i.e., the British], are dangerous, expensive, prone to obsolescence and lacking in credibility as a deterrent'. Quoted in L. Freedman, *The Evolution of Nuclear Strategy*, London: Macmillan, 1981, p. 307.

22. See L. Freedman, *Britain and Nuclear Weapons*, London: Macmillan for the Royal Institute for International Affairs, 1980, p. 130.

23. 'The Nassau Agreement' reproduced in A. Pierre, *Nuclear Politics*, London: Oxford University Press, 1972, pp. 346–7.

24. *Statement on the Defence Estimates 1987*, op. cit., p. 13.

25. *Hansard*, Vol. 128, Col. 1,294, 4 March 1988.

26. See M. Gowing, *Independence and Deterrence*, op. cit., pp. 194–206.

27. See P. M. S. Blackett's, *Fear, War and the Bomb: Military and Political Consequences of Atomic Energy*, London: Turnstile Press, 1948, pp. 4–5. Blackett carefully managed not to directly address the question of British nuclear weapons. He was

never fully immersed in the 'strategic community' following his departure from government (he was to return, in technological education, in 1964), focusing on science, and thus his writings on policy issues were not that extensive. However, he was to write two more important books: *Atomic Weapons and East–West Relations*, Cambridge: Cambridge University Press, 1956; and *Studies of War, Nuclear and Conventional*, Edinburgh: Oliver & Boyd, 1962. See also his article 'Steps Towards Disarmament', *Scientific American*, 206 (4) April 1962.

28. See Michael Howard, 'P. M. S. Blackett', in J. Baylis and J. Garnett (eds), *The Makers of Nuclear Strategy*, London: Pinter Publishers, 1991, p. 155.

29. See A. J. R. Groom, *British Thinking About Nuclear Weapons*, London: Pinter, 1974, pp. 169–71.

30. See C. Driver, *The Disarmers*, London: Hodder & Stoughton, 1964, pp. 30–3.

31. S. King-Hall, *Defence in the Nuclear Age*, London: Gollancz, 1958, p. 13.

32. See, for example, J. Vincent, *Christ in a Nuclear World*, Manchester: Crux Press, 1962.

33. At a speech at the Church of England Convocation of Canterbury on 11 May 1954; cited in C. Driver, *The Disarmers*, op. cit., p. 198. The Bishop was one of the most respected theologians in the Church.

34. B. Russell, *Common Sense and Nuclear Warfare*, London: George Allen & Unwin, 1959, p. 20.

35. Ibid., p. 21.

36. P. Noel-Baker, *The Arms Race*, London: Calder, 1960.

37. John Rex, 'Britain without the Bomb', in *New Left Pamphlet*, 1960, p. 16. Cited in Groom, *British Thinking About Nuclear Weapons*, op. cit., p. 409.

38. S. Hall, *Breakthrough*, London: Combined Universities CND, 1958, p. 16.

39. Ken Booth, 'Unilateralism: A Clausewitzian Reform', in N. Blake and K. Pole (eds), *Dangers of Deterrence: Philosophers on Nuclear Strategy*, London: Routledge and Kegan Paul, 1983, p. 42.

40. Ken Booth, 'Part One: Alternative Defence', in K. Booth and J. Baylis, *Britain, NATO and Nuclear Weapons: Alternative Defence Versus Alliance Reform*, London: Macmillan, 1989, p. 267.

41. M. Clarke, 'The Alternative Defence Debate: Non-Nuclear Defence Policies for Europe', in *ADIU Occasional Paper*, Number 3, Science Policy Research Unit, University of Sussex, August 1985, p. 3.

42. The Alternative Defence Commission, *The Politics of Alternative Defence*, London: Paladin, 1987, p. 24.

43. Mary Kaldor, 'Warfare and Capitalism', in E. Thompson, M. David, R. Williams, R. Bahro, L. Magri, E. Balibar, R. and Z. Medvedev, J. Cox, S. Kugai, M. Raskin, N. Chomsky, A. Wolfe, M. Kaldor and F. Halliday, *Exterminism and the Cold War*, London: Verso for New Left Review, 1982, p. 282.

44. Ibid., p. 280.

45. See E. Thompson, 'Notes on Exterminism: the Last Stage of Civilisation', in ibid., pp. 1–35.

46. F. Halliday, 'The Sources of the New Cold War', in ibid., p. 318.

47. K. Booth, *Britain, NATO and Nuclear Weapons: Alternative Defence Versus Alliance Reform*, op. cit., p. 125.

48. E. P. Thompson, 'A Mid-Atlantic Moderate', in M. Clarke and M. Mowlam (eds), *Debate on Disarmament*, London: Routledge and Kegan Paul, 1982, p. 123.

49. M. Kaldor, 'Is there a Soviet Military Threat?', in ibid., p. 43.

50. M. Dando and P. Rogers, *The Death of Deterrence*, London: CND Publications, 1984, pp. 83–4.

51. See, for example, *The Politics of Alternative Defence*, op. cit., p. 53.

52. K. Booth, *Britain, NATO and Nuclear Weapons: Alternative Defence Versus Alliance Reform*, op. cit., p. 61.

53. D. Campbell, *The Unsinkable Aircraft Carrier*, London: Paladin, 1986, p. 91.

54. K. Booth, *Britain, NATO and Nuclear Weapons: Alternative Defence Versus Alliance Reform*, op. cit., p. 96.

55. D. Campbell, op. cit., p. 17; also see M. Dando and P. Rogers, *The Death of Deterrence*, op. cit., pp. 61–2; and P. Rogers, M. Dando and P. van der Dungen, *As Lambs to the Slaughter*, London: Arrow Books, 1981, especially ch. 5 'Target Britain'.

56. D. Campbell, op. cit., p. 334.

57. See, for example, in E. P. Thompson, *Zero Option*, London: The Merlin Press, 1982.

58. P. Johnson, *Neutrality: A Policy for Britain*, London: Temple Smith, 1985.

59. E. P. Thompson, *Protest and Survive*, London: Penguin Books, 1980. The title mocked that of the Home Office civil defence booklet, *Protect and Survive*.

60. E. P. Thompson, 'Notes on Exterminism, the Last Stage of Civilization', in op. cit., p. 28.

61. Thompson, in a letter to *The Times*, cited in C. Rose, *Campaigns Against Western Defence*, London: Macmillan for the RUSI, 1986, p. 145.

62. The Alternative Defence Commission, op. cit., p. 138.

63. These are just examples of a longer list: ibid., pp. 150–1. This analysis was very much in line with the Alternative Defence Commission's first report: *Defence Without the Bomb*, London: Taylor and Francis, 1983.

64. D. Smith, 'Non-Nuclear Military Options for Britain', *Peace Studies Papers*, Number 6, Bradford University School of Peace Studies: Housemans, April 1982.

65. K. Booth, 'Unilateralism: A Clausewitzian Reform?', op. cit., p. 58.

66. *Modern Britain in a Modern World*, London: The Labour Party, 1987, p. 15. At the 1987 Labour Party Conference, resolution Composite 30 was adopted, through which 'Conference reaffirms Labour's commitment to remain a member of NATO'.

67. This was an important theme in the work of the Alternative Defence Commission.

68. D. Jenkins, 'Simplicity of Death, Complexities of Life', in D. Martin and P. Mullen (eds), *Unholy Warfare: The Church and the Bomb*, Oxford: Basil Blockwell, 1991, p. 234.

69. K. Booth, 'Unilateralism: A Clausewitzian Reform?', in op. cit., p. 56. Also see J. MacMahan, *British Nuclear Weapons For and Against*, London: Junction Books, 1981.

70. See Earl Mountbatten, 'The Final Abyss?', especially pp. 13–14, and Lord Zuckerman 'Defence is Indivisible', p. 21 in *Apocalypse Now?*, Nottingham:

Spokesman for the Atlantic Peace Foundation in support of the World Disarmament Campaign, 1980.

71. *Diminishing the Nuclear Threat*, London: British Atlantic Committee Report, 1984. The authors were General Sir Hugh Beach, Lord Cameron, Sir Frank Cooper, Sir Douglas Dodds-Parker, General Sir Anthony Farrar-Hockley, Hugh Hanning, Brigadier Kenneth Hunt, Professor Sir Ronald Mason and Major-General Christopher Popham.

72. D. Smith, 'Non-Nuclear Military Options for Britain', op. cit., p. 9.

73. M. Kaldor, 'Warfare and Capitalism', op. cit., p. 286.

74. *Statement on the Defence Estimates 1992*, Cmnd. 1,981, London: HMSO 1992, para. 104, p. 7.

75. Ibid., para. 4, p. 8.

76. *Strategic Defence Review*, London: The Stationery Office, 1998, ch. 4, para. 60, p. 17.

77. Fewer than 200 operationally available warheads will be held; each Trident submarine will only carry 48 warheads (down from 96); only 58 Trident missiles will be held; and the Trident submarine system will perform both strategic and sub-strategic functions: see *SDR*, op. cit., paras. 9–11, section 5-2, 'supporting essays' section.

78. *SDR*, op. cit., para. 13, section 5-5, 'supporting essays'.

79. See K. Booth, *New Thinking about Strategy and International Security*, London: HarperCollins, 1991, pp. 10–20.

80. K. Booth, ' "Loose Nukes" and the Nuclear Mirror', *Arms Control: Contemporary Security Policy*, 13 (1) 1992, p. 140.

81. P. Rogers and M. Dando, *A Violent Peace: Global Security after the Cold War*, London: Brassey's, 1992, p. 179.

82. P. Rogers, 'Reviewing Britain's Security', *International Affairs*, 73 (4) 1997, p. 668.

83. An exception could be made for Patricia Lewis. Other members included Lawrence Freedman, Colin Gray and Sir Michael Quinlan. A full list is published in the *SDR*, op. cit., pp. 1-11, 1-12, 'supporting essays'.

84. On this question of status, see Stuart Croft and Phil Williams, 'The United Kingdom', in R. C. Karp (ed.), *Security with Nuclear Weapons? Different Perspectives on National Security*, Oxford: Oxford University Press for SIPRI, 1991, especially pp. 145–7.

85. C. Driver, op. cit., pp. 72–3.

86. P. Rogers, 'Reviewing Britain's Security', op. cit., p. 656.

Chapter 5

The Management of UK Defence

Matthew Uttley

Introduction

In the extensive literature on post-1945 British defence the term 'management' has been applied loosely to cover such diverse topics as the administrative and bureaucratic structures within which defence decisions have been formulated,[1] the performance of postwar British defence reviews[2] and the management of major military equipment projects.[3] In the context of debates about Britain's relative post-1945 decline, attention has tended to focus on attempts by successive governments to manage the balance between defence resources and commitments. This emphasis reflects the 'affordability' constraint that has plagued policy-makers as the postwar costs of defence commitments have risen at higher rates than defence budgets. At issue in this debate has been the efficacy of government attempts to implement 'economies', or reductions in military commitments in response to declining resources.[4]

In parallel, however, policy-makers have also sought to reconcile financial dilemmas by applying two further concepts to the management of defence resources. The first has been the quest for 'efficiency': optimising the use of defence inputs to maximise required defence outputs. The second has been the objective of maximising defence 'effectiveness', or ensuring that scarce defence resources are channelled to meet key objectives. This chapter focuses on two discrete management areas where British governments have sought to enhance efficiency and effectiveness. The first is the post-war trend towards increased organisational, functional and operational integration between the individual armed services which culminated in the late 1990s in the concept of 'jointery'. The second is the impact of 'managerialism', introduced most extensively by the post-1979 Conservative administrations, which has formed a 'crusade against bureaucratic waste, belief in the superiority of private sector managerial techniques and drive towards value for money'[5] in the allocation and use of defence resources.

Service autonomy versus 'jointery' in UK defence management

Commentators have characterised the debate about post-1945 central organisations of defence as a dialectic between two contrasting models:

On the one hand, were advocates of the so-called 'Hankey' model, who argued the case for separate and independent departments of government responsible for each of the three armed services; on the other were supporters of the 'Mountbatten' school, who looked to a single Ministry of Defence with functional responsibility, a single chief of Defence Staff with functional responsibilities across the board for operational matters, and *in toto* a system of total centralisation.[6]

At issue in this debate has been the appropriate balance between the individual armed services bringing their own unique and specialist expertise to the content and direction of defence policy with forms of centralised control, functional organisation and tri-service planning.[7]

Before the outbreak of the Second World War the first significant attempt to institutionalise coordination between the three armed services and their respective Ministerial Departments of State was the creation of the Minister for Coordination of Defence in 1936. Wartime planning and coordination between the armed services operated effectively, largely because Prime Minister Churchill acted as a *de facto* Minister for Defence. However, the period between 1939 and 1945 demonstrated the integrated nature of modern warfare and the pressing need for future plans and operational contingencies to be dealt with on an integrated and tri-service basis.

The Attlee government addressed these wartime lessons in the 1946 White Paper on Central Organisation for Defence.[8] A notable achievement was the creation of a new Ministry of Defence (MoD) which had areas of executive authority over the three service departments and the Ministry of Supply. Correspondingly, in other respects the Attlee government's reforms had only a limited impact in reducing the independence and influence of the single service chiefs in the planning and execution of defence policy. First, the MoD lacked a Central Staff to conduct its major functions. Instead, this was left to a single service based Chiefs of Staff Committee and a joint system for operational planning and coordination. Second, the MoD had only limited responsibility for the coordination of weapon development and procurement which left a major role for the individual service ministries in formulating requirements for and funding their own equipment requirements.

Between 1946 and 1958, the limited early postwar rationalisation of the higher organisation of defence and the considerable autonomy still enjoyed by the single services had two adverse effects. First, there was intense inter-service rivalry for roles and missions during a period where defence resources were under strain.[9] Second, evidence suggests that the absence of strong and centralised control led to inefficient 'budget decisions which were viewed not from an overall but from a single service perspective'.[10] In 1958, Defence Minister Sandys attempted to ameliorate these problems in the White Paper Central Organisation for Defence[11] by providing the Chairman of the Chiefs of Staff Committee with a defence planning staff and a title change to the Chief of Defence Staff (CDS).

However, it was the appointment of Mountbatten to the post of CDS in 1958 that was to affect more significant organisational change. Mountbatten was wedded to the idea of abolishing the separate service departments and the unification of their functions in a single Ministry of Defence. Mountbatten also argued the need for a single Secretary of State for Defence with two functional ministers, a junior minister for each of the single services and a Defence Staff to support the CDS. By July 1963, when

Mountbatten's plan was presented to Parliament all of the key recommendations were endorsed with the exception of an enhanced role for the CDS. The 1963 reforms served to increase the relative importance of the MoD in relation to the individual armed services.[12]

Under Healey's tenure as Defence Secretary, the emphasis in organisational change was to enhance 'functionalism' – or the compartmentalisation of discrete areas of defence activities which cut across the remits of the individual armed services – through further reorganisation and rationalisation of the higher management of defence. Functionalism was seen as the route to increased efficiency within the defence organisation because it offered scope to remove unnecessary duplication in the structures and activities of the individual services. In addition, during February 1968 a single defence budget was introduced putting an end to the tri-service system, the separate service planning staffs were combined in a single defence planning staff and a single Minster of State for the Armed Forces was established. As Edmonds points out, the situation by 1967 'could be described as a hybrid of the old (Hankey) federal model with some new (Mountbatten) functional provisions'.[13]

Following the election of the Conservative administration in 1979, the pendulum swung further towards the Mountbatten model. In July 1984, as part of a policy to increase functionalism and introduce new management structures, Defence Secretary Heseltine strengthened further the functional staffs and downgraded the relative import-ance of the individual service Chiefs of Staff.[14] The most radical change was that the CDS and his MoD civil service equivalent, the Permanent Under Secretary (PUS), became the Secretary of State for Defence's principal advisers on military operations and strategy, and political and financial policy, respectively. Assisting CDS were four functional departments – accountable to a new post of Vice CDS – with four Defence Staffs, each under a Deputy CDS for Personnel, Systems, Commitments, and Strategy and Policy. The PUS became responsible for an Office of Management and Budget, long-term financial and budgetary control, administration, civilian manpower, and for the work of the Chief of Defence Procurement and respective staff.

The period between 1945 and the end of the Cold War ushered in significant changes to the higher management of UK defence which were manifested in a gradual transition from the 'Hankey' to the 'Mountbatten' model of organisation. This was reflected in the strengthened role of the MoD and the Defence Staff at the expense of the autonomy of the three armed services: a trend in response, *inter alia*, to the growing complexity of military planning, the need for coordination in areas including weapon acquisition and the imperative of reducing scope for inter-service rivalries for defence roles and missions. In parallel, the trend was for increased functionalism as discrete defence activities which cut across the remits of the individual armed services were compartmentalised on tri-service lines.

Since the Cold War, initiatives have further consolidated the level and nature of cooperation between the armed services. The trend has been towards greater and more systematic integration of national forces and planning, or as the current terminology has it, 'jointery': planning for 'military operations in which elements of more than one service participate'.[15] The primary drivers for jointery have been twofold. The first is financial, and stems from the downward trend in post-Cold War defence budgets. As Edmonds points out, the:

new preoccupation [with jointery] only happened when the Ministry of Defence, in response to almost unrelenting pressure from the Treasury to find further savings in the defence budget over and above the steady reductions in defence expenditure after 1989, found that further economies were to be achieved by bringing the three armed services together in joint commands, combat support and support functions.[16]

The second driver for jointery has reflected changing British threat perceptions. By the mid-1990s, British policy-makers concluded that the demise of the bipolar system and the diminished military threat posed by the former Soviet Union served to eliminate the short warning risk of a large-scale offensive in central Europe.[17] At the same time, British defence planners recognised that the Cold War certainties provided by bipolar stability had been replaced by a more diffuse set of risks on a global scale.[18] This reappraisal of threats and risks has had fundamental implications for British force planning. During the Cold War, the British armed services were structured to deal with the Soviet threat and were configured primarily for collective security through the NATO alliance on the assumption of high intensity conflict. Since the Cold War, the response has been to look for ways to configure forces in terms of capabilities and intend their use in expeditionary warfare through flexible force packages capable of projecting power to meet the spectrum of new global risks.

This shift in thinking has had an important impact on relations between the three armed services. During the Cold War 'a distinction between the institutional and operational arrangements for the armed services made some sense'[19] because of the functional roles of each service within NATO's overall force posture. Since the Cold War, however, the requirement to project military power has created an operational imperative for enhanced 'jointery'. The primary operational drivers have been the perceived need to project power from the sea in littoral areas and the deployment of expeditionary forces which are supported by air elements, as a means to meet contingencies on a global scale.[20] In practical terms, jointery has been reflected in a range of initiatives adopted throughout the 1990s, and which were consolidated in the 1998 SDR. These include the formation of a Permanent Joint Headquarters (PJHQ), the Joint Rapid Deployment Force (JRDF) and the Joint Services Command and Staff College (JSCSC). As a consequence, 'jointery' has become the orthodoxy.

However, some commentators have expressed concerns about the practical implications of joint solutions to the management of defence resources. From an economics perspective, Hartley, for example, observes that jointery 'resembles cartel and monopoly' which may enable the armed services to collude or entrench inefficient practices that do little to enhance operational capabilities.[21] Moreover, Hartley argues that current policies may have other adverse implications. The first is that jointery may not facilitate closer cooperation between the services but, rather, displace inter-service rivalries to other areas. The second is the risk of 'minimalist jointery', whereby a tri-service approach is only adopted in peripheral military functions rather than applied to those activities that affect the core organisational interests of the individual services. Finally, Hartley points to the danger that the services may use the mantra of jointery to obscure the flow of information to policy-makers on the costs and benefits of individual service procurement proposals that has traditionally been generated by overt inter-service competition.

At a more general level, the postwar trends towards centralisation, functionalism and jointery continue to raise the fundamental question of 'how joint is enough?' On the one hand, as a former First Sea Lord points out, 'those who believe that military matters can easily be categorised into land, sea and air, in our modern technologically agile world, are making a facile and anachronistic judgement'.[22] On the other hand, important questions remain concerning the appropriate balance between those areas most effectively conducted on a single-service basis with those activities which can be achieved more effectively through 'joint solutions'.[23] Consequently, for the contemporary analyst of UK defence management the practical impact of current British joint initiatives – and their implications for operational and financial efficiency and effectiveness in the employment of scarce defence resources – remains an important area for case study research, empirical analysis and international comparative evaluation.

Hierarchies versus markets in UK defence management

Between 1945 and 1979, successive British governments adopted initiatives intended to reduce waste, duplication and maximise managerial efficiency within the MoD and armed services. Given the proportion of the defence budget spent on equipment, weapons procurement was an area exposed to a series of management reforms designed to enhance cost effectiveness.[24] During the late 1960s, reforms to UK central government departments as a whole emphasised, in part, the application of private sector management practices to public bureaucracies. The 1968 Fulton Report, for example, recommended that departments should encourage two-way transfer of personnel between the public and private sectors, and create accountable units of management in government ministries.[25]

On the one hand, against a backdrop of financial pressures and tight defence budgets, the 1945–79 period was characterised by 'a [government] predisposition to resort to organisational reform, procedural change and the espousal of managerial principles as responses to recurring and persistent difficulties and dilemmas'.[26] On the other hand, these reforms either had a limited impact, or perpetuated a postwar consensus over how defence should be managed. In the case of the Fulton recommendations, they were accepted by government but implementation was hindered because the recommendations were administered by senior civil servants who had considerable discretion about what to introduce and what to ignore.[27] Equally, despite government reforms, the internal management of the MoD and the armed services retained three fundamental characteristics. First, lines of budgetary authority in the MoD and the armed services were configured on strictly hierarchical lines on the assumption that this arrangement ensured clear lines of political and financial accountability. Second, though the use of private contractors by the MoD and the armed services was well established for the development and production of military equipment, the MoD and the armed services maintained an 'in-house' capability across the spectrum of frontline and defence support functions. This approach assumed that a comprehensive in-house capability provided cohesion within the defence establishment in peacetime and enhanced preparation for conflict. Correspondingly, UK defence was largely immune from private sector involvement or competition in the provision of support functions. Third, the MoD and the armed services remained largely insulated from private sector business practices and management techniques.

The election of the Thatcher government in 1979 marked a significant postwar watershed in UK defence management. The new government and subsequent Conservative administrations pursued three discrete sets of initiatives. First, policies were adopted which introduced private sector methods of organisation and budgetary control within the MoD and services to replace the traditional hierarchical model. Second, new policies emphasised a major role for the private sector in the provision of defence support services. Third, measures were introduced which exposed the MoD and services to competition from the private sector.

The drivers behind the post-1979 Conservative reforms were twofold. The first was economic and financial considerations. During the early 1980s, government was anxious about a 'funding gap' between the resources allocated to defence and Britain's stated military commitments.[28] At the same time, government was reluctant to address this 'funding gap' through a major structural review of defence commitments. Instead, the Defence Secretary Heseltine 'preached more effective management as the solution to the budgetary predicament' through 'cutting the MoD's own bureaucracy down to size'.[29] Heseltine's assumption was that efficiency savings from the MoD and armed services' running costs could reduce the funding gap – a perception that was fuelled, in part, by post-1979 efficiency scrutinies undertaken by Sir Derek Rayner which indicated scope for significant savings if commercial practices were applied in defence support areas.[30]

Budgetary considerations explain the quest for economies. However, they do not provide a sufficient explanation for the tranche of new defence management initiatives subsequently adopted. The second driver which accounts for this was the Conservative administration's diagnosis of deficiencies in UK public sector administration and its blueprint for reform.[31] Reflecting 'New Right' ideology, the government's belief was that the optimal mechanism for allocating goods is the market.[32] The Conservative critique was that existing public sector bureaucracies were inherently inefficient because – as monopoly providers of goods and services – they were immune from the efficiency incentives affecting private firms in competitive markets. The government's 'solution' to the ills of the public sector had three central tenets. The first was 'managerialism': bringing management techniques to defence that had been successfully applied to private business. The second tenet was to change the 'market structure' of defence support provision by exposing activities traditionally conducted in-house by servicemen and civilians under monopoly conditions to external competition. The third tenet was to change the 'organisational status' away from public towards private sector forms of defence support provision. The administration assumed that an efficiency programme based on these premises would generate sufficiently large savings for the UK to meet stated defence commitments without a substantial reduction in operational effectiveness.[33]

Policies of 'managerialism' were applied to those areas of MoD activity 'that could not be privatised or subjected to the sanitising forces of the market'[34] because of operational considerations. Here, 'the Thatcher government's general approach [was] to couple the application within the public sector of those private managerial techniques perceived as most conducive to value for money – notably objective setting and performance measurement'.[35] Over the course of the 1980s and 1990s, this was reflected in three major initiatives: the Management Information System for Ministers (MINIS), the New Management Strategy (NMS) and the Defence Agency programme.

During his tenure as Defence Secretary, Michael Heseltine's focus was on the management of resources. Investigations he commissioned into the workings of the MoD during 1984 revealed that 'the organisation could be more economical in senior management posts, that lines of accountability were blurred and that compromise was the central component in giving advice and taking decisions'.[36] In response, Defence Secretary Heseltine introduced MINIS – a management system which involved three stages. First, each section within the MoD was required to prepare a statement of activities, staff numbers and achievements, developing performance indicators where possible. Second, these statements were considered and evaluated by ministers and MoD top management. Third, decisions arising from these evaluations were then implemented within the ministry's various sections.[37] The MINIS initiative presupposed that the MoD needed to adopt a more business-like approach and aimed at improving the management of the defence budget.

In 1991, policies to commercialise the internal workings of the MoD and the armed services were consolidated in the NMS.[38] Under the NMS, the ethos of grafting 'private sector best practice' onto the defence establishment was reflected in three areas. First, the MoD was required to allocate the defence budget to 23 'top-level budget holders' who were then responsible for delegating to a series of lower-level budget holders. The aim here was to 'put responsibility, accountability, authority and cash in the hands of those who actually [ran] the business – in other words delegating management away from the centre and down the chain of command'.[39] Second, NMS formalised a system of management plans which defined what budget holders were expected to deliver from their allocated resources. Third, these initiatives were accompanied by performance reviews intended to measure the achievements of budget holders and provide a basis for future resource allocation.

Building on the NMS principles, attempts to commercialise the MoD and armed services were extended in the Defence Agency programme. During 1988, 'The Next Steps' report produced by the government's Efficiency Unit concluded, *inter alia*, that management throughout central government departments was characterised by insufficient attention to service delivery, short termism and a shortage of commercial skills.[40] The report recommended the establishment of semi-autonomous agencies to carry out the executive – or service delivery functions – of government departments. The new organisations were to be given well-defined frameworks by the parent department setting out the policy, budget, targets and the degree of authority delegated to the agencies. Consequently, strategic control remained with Ministers but once the policy and framework were set agency chief executives would have as much independence as possible in deciding how those objectives were to be met.[41]

In a number of respects, agency creation reflected the distinct ideological agenda of the Conservative administration and the perception that less money could be spent delivering the same capability in terms of defence and security. The first assumption was that by divorcing defence policy from service delivery, agency creation would enable chief executives in the new organisations to pursue their objectives using private sector management techniques. Second, it was assumed that agencies would provide a means of subdividing the monolithic MoD structure into more manageable units. Finally, by creating semi-autonomous 'business' units within the defence sector, agency policy was seen as a mechanism to import or second private sector personnel from industry, so augmenting commercial management expertise in the delivery of defence support services.[42]

By late 1997, almost all the defence service support, personnel and budgetary areas had been absorbed into 48 Next Steps Agencies which employed over 100,000 service and civilian personnel. The creation of the Defence Procurement Agency (DPA) which was announced in the 1998 Strategic Defence Review has brought over half of the total defence budget under the control of defence agencies. In addition to the Next Steps Agencies which remain within the overall command and management structure of the MoD, the Conservative administration created three 'trading fund agencies' – the Defence Evaluation and Research Agency (DERA), the Meteorological Office and the Hydrographic Office – which fall outside the direct control of the MoD and rely instead on direct cash payments for their services.

Policies to introduce competition and alter the market structure of support provision were also a major theme in post-1979 conservative defence management reform. In May 1980, Prime Minister Thatcher declared that 'in the past, governments have progressively increased the number of tasks the civil service is asked to do without paying sufficient attention to economy and efficiency'.[43] The government's response was a planned phased reduction of civil service personnel of 14 per cent from 705,000 to 630,000 by 1985.[44] Required to streamline UK based civilian staff by 48,000, amongst other measures the MoD was forced to consider 'the possibility, either of greater involvement of non-civil service organisations in the provision of services, or putting work out to contract'.[45]

By 1983, early MoD initiatives had demonstrated efficiency gains but also limitations. Contracting out contributed 'significantly' to a 39,000 reduction in personnel and annual savings of £5.8 million (1981/82 prices).[46] Correspondingly, however, the focus on civilian manpower targets ignored potential savings from competition in military support areas (equipment maintenance, training, etc.). In certain cases manpower ceilings also led to 'inflexibilities and sub-optimisation':[47] the National Audit Office, for example, identified eight contracts which had been let at additional cost to the MoD of almost £200,000 to save 52 civilian posts.[48] Moreover, in the absence of a Ministry-wide bureaucratic structure to monitor its introduction, policy was implemented by departments on an *ad hoc* basis.[49]

During 1983, a more systematic competition policy emerged. Announcing a major defence efficiency review, Defence Secretary Heseltine stated that henceforth:

> the only work which is carried out within our own defence support organisation should be that which is essential for clearly proven operational reasons, or where there is financial advantage for the taxpayer.[50]

Where neither condition obtained, policy was to transfer the activity to the private sector. Average cost-savings of 30 per cent were anticipated, as well as further incidental manpower economies. By 1985, five activities had been selected as 'mandatory' areas for competition: catering, cleaning, laundry, security guarding and minor maintenance. The new imperative of achieving cost-savings as well as manpower reductions meant that contracting out was extended to 'non-mandatory' functions undertaken by uniformed service personnel.

Policy entered a more intensive phase during 1986 after the publication of the influential Treasury report, *Using Private Enterprise in Government*.[51] Recommending measures which would 'essentially save money, but incidentally help to achieve man-power targets', the report advocated that 'competition should become a regular part of every Department's efficiency drive . . . [and] . . . Departments should review all their activities to see if they offer scope for contracting-out'.[52] The MoD's response was market testing: periodic assessment of the efficiency of all in-house support units against tenders from industry.

The framework established in 1986 underpinned MoD policy during the subse-quent Conservative administrations. Over the four years to 1990, contracts for over 120 functions were established and the MoD tested activities worth £103 million. The commitment to competition was reaffirmed in the 1991 White Paper Competing for Quality[53] which led to an expansion of 'multi-activity' contracts covering a range of technical and managerial functions on one site. Examples of the 'facilities manage-ment' approach included the contractorisation of the Ballistic Missile Early Warning System, RAF Fylingdales, and several major stores depots.[54]

Between 1979 and 1997, market testing and contracting out had a major impact on defence support services in two respects. First, policy evolved from *ad hoc* experi-ments with private sector provision to a systematic competition policy which affected the spectrum of support functions. Second, the trend was for the encroachment of competition to include military support functions traditionally undertaken by uni-formed personnel.

In parallel with measures to expose activities to competition, the Conservatives also introduced policies which were designed to encourage the private sector to finance and run defence support activities. Treasury interest in the use of private capital to fund the UK public sector emerged during the early 1980s against the backdrop of debates over how then nationalised industries could access private capital for investment.[55] By the late 1980s, however, the Treasury measures that emerged had become redundant as a result of the extensive privatisation programme and the lack of incentives for public bodies to seek private capital because, under existing Treasury rules, any income generated was simply offset by commensurate reductions in public expenditure. By November 1992, the government had revisited the concept that activities traditionally undertaken by the public sector could be financed and run by private firms under arrangements whereby the firm could be remunerated by government through a series of 'user charges' for the services provided. In policy terms, what emerged from these deliberations was the Private Finance Initiative (PFI).

Underpinning PFI policy was the assumption that economies would accrue through the transfer of risk to the private sector. Moreover, PFI presupposed that incentives for private sector efficiency were generated because contractors are paid by the MoD only when they meet specific performance targets. Finally, an attraction of reliance on private rather than public funding, was that it allowed the MoD to proceed with major capital projects for which there was no provision in the defence budget. In effect, therefore, PFI was seen as a way for the MoD to obtain services that would otherwise have not materialised. A measure of the importance government attached to PFI projects in the defence sector was that by 1999, the MoD had completed 24 major programmes with a value of £1.1 billion.

Throughout the 1980s and 1990s, initiatives to increasing managerialism, competition, private sector provision in the UK defence sector remained controversial. A succession of government reports have claimed the Conservative reforms generated efficiency gains and ameliorated the funding gap between defence resources and commitments. Correspondingly, the 'privatisation' of defence has been criticised on two fronts: by those who argued that the MoD has done 'too little' in terms of exploiting the potential of competition and private sector best practice; and those who claim that government has gone 'too far' in 'commercialising' defence.

Not surprisingly, official government publications have been keen to point out the success of new management initiatives in the allocation and employment of defence resources. Scrutinies into the performance of MINIS[56] and the NMS[57] have pointed to manpower economies, increased financial delegation, cost awareness and flexibility at all levels of the defence establishment, as well as the perception of effective incentive structures among civilian and military staff employed in defence agencies.[58] In areas exposed to the 'Competing for Quality' initiative, government figures indicate that over 112 defence support activities with a combined annual operating cost of £1 billion were reviewed by the MoD after 1992. After market testing, private firms were successful in winning contracts worth approximately £450 million which provided the MoD with a 20 per cent reduction in operating costs. Moreover, government statistics point to 27 per cent savings in costs that were acquired through successful in-house bids and internal efficiencies.

However, the scope and success of the reform process has been challenged by influential economists and commentators who argued that the MoD and the armed services have done 'too little' in exploiting potential cost-savings and efficiency gains that genuine market forces could provide. According to this critique, the MoD has done little to change the market structure of service provision leading to a continuation of in-house monopoly provision. One example of this tendency frequently cited is the case of defence support agencies, which have remained within the military chain of command and thus largely immune from private sector business practices or competition.[59] A second criticism is that in areas where competition has been introduced its application has tended to be limited in scope. Hartley, for example, questions why only £1 billion of activities from a total support budget of approximately £8 billion has been exposed to market testing. Given MoD claims that market testing and contracting-out have generated savings of approximately 20 per cent, Hartley's argument is that applying competition to include the entire defence support budget could yield far more significant economies.[60] A further area of concern is that of the lack of adequate reward structures for competition policy because efficiency savings by individual budget-holders have been 'clawed-back' by the central MoD.[61] Critics also point out that though relatively junior civilian and military personnel have been affected by the reform process, these initiatives have had little impact on the behaviour of service chiefs and Whitehall decision-makers.[62]

At the opposite extreme, other critics argue that the commercialisation of defence during the 1980s and 1990s went 'too far'. The first strand of this critique is the claim that except for a small range of exclusively civilian activities, market testing and contracting-out run the risk of adversely affecting the operational capability of the armed services in maintaining adequate national defence. A distinction is drawn between 'efficiency' (the relation of inputs to outputs) and defence 'effectiveness' (the quality of outputs in terms of their impact on national defence). Illustrative is Air Vice Marshal Palin's observation that: 'economic principles and commercial practices are not sufficient in themselves to determine what we [the armed services] should buy or how we should carry out a particular function. Cheaper substitutes do not necessarily give value for money.'[63] Instead, critics argue that 'value for money' assessments should not be limited to cost-based criteria alone. The case against contractorisation surrounds the mechanism for ensuring that 'moving the task to the private sector [does] not affect the Services' operational capability'.[64] General concerns have included: less direct control and flexibility in the use of staff; the risk of contractor exploitation when in-house units were disbanded; and the long-term effects of 'de-skilling' in areas contracted out.[65] Additional operational concerns cited include the danger of contractorising support functions 'to the point where [there are] insufficient people to fill the wartime establishment'[66] and secrecy requirements for defence-related activities.

The second strand of the 'too far' critique is the argument that 'managerialism', notably the delegation and decentralisation accompanying defence agency creation, risks undermining traditional models of parliamentary accountability.[67] Under traditional notions of ministerial responsibility the minister is responsible for the actions of the department. However, within defence agencies chief executives have been responsible for the delivery of services – a separation of policy and operations which demolishes 'the myth that a minister can be responsible for everything'.[68] According to critics, the practical difficulty of maintaining the distinction between policy and operational matters has led to confusion as to where ministerial responsibility and accountability to Parliament actually lies.[69]

A third strand of the 'too far' critique has been the claim that purported efficiency gains from competition have been outweighed or significantly reduced by 'hidden costs'. Theoretically, the benefits of market testing result from the periodic contestability of markets: the threat of substitution by rival organisations and consequent incentives for efficiency. In reality, according to critics the additional administrative costs – overheads incurred in organising competitions and monitoring contractor performance – have significantly reduced savings.[70]

Despite the controversies surrounding managerialism, competition and private sector involvement in defence provision, the Conservative reforms were inherited and extended following the election of the Blair government. The 1998 Strategic Defence Review and associated policy statements include explicit commitments to extend agency creation and PFI projects (renamed 'Public/Private Partnerships' (PPP) during 1998) in the defence sector. Indicators of the Blair government's enthusiasm for the PFI/PPP concept are recent statements indicating there are no 'no-go' areas for private sector provision, and the assertion that PFI/PPP can reach close to the frontline and contribute to operational capability.

Consequently, the Conservative defence efficiency reforms introduced during the 1980s and 1990s have fundamentally altered the landscape of UK defence management. Moreover, the Blair government's acceptance and extension of these reforms indicate broad cross-party consensus on the value of managerialism, competition and private sector provision in the defence sector. However, for the analyst of UK defence policy important issues remain to be resolved. One issue is the absence of systematic data on the financial impact of the reform process. In the past, governments have presented selective examples or global estimates of cost savings with no explanation of how the figures were derived. Until comprehensive data enter the public domain, questions remain about the extent to which defence commercialisation has generated economies. Secondly, given the ongoing commitment to defence reform, there are outstanding questions about the scope and limitations of competition and private provision in the defence sector. At issue here is just how far defence activity can be exposed to market forces before operational capability becomes impaired. Finally, questions remain about the transaction costs incurred in the management reform process, and the extent to which these costs of organisational change reduced the MoD's overall savings. Only when these issues are addressed will a comprehensive picture of the impact of post-1979 defence management reform emerge.

Conclusion

The context of postwar British defence management initiatives has been the search for economies as a means to reconcile resources and commitments. An important subset of this activity has been attempts to increase financial and operational efficiency and effectiveness with those resources assigned to defence. This chapter has focused on two areas of reform intended to meet these objectives: policies to rationalise the relationships between the three armed services and initiatives to 'commercialise' defence provision.

A comparison of reform in these areas points to diversity in the quest for management 'solutions'. On the one hand, postwar reform of the higher management of defence and inter-service relations has been an incremental process. On the other hand, the Thatcher government's injection of managerialism and commercial practices into the defence sector formed a distinct turning point because it marked a fundamental challenge to a wider postwar consensus concerning public sector management as a whole. However, these reforms also share common characteristics. Each highlights a tendency for British defence policy-makers to assume that management change can provide comprehensive solutions to long-standing problems and constraints. The 'efficiency programme' implemented by the Conservative governments of the 1980s and 1990s was presented not only as a source of value-for-money *per se*, but also as a 'solution' to the perceived gap between defence commitments and resources. Similarly, the 'jointery' concept implemented since the Cold War has acquired the status of an orthodoxy in organisational and operational terms.

Consequently, postwar developments in British defence management suggest a pattern: a series of managerial orthodoxies which, when challenged by prevailing constraints, have been rejected or revised and replaced by new orthodoxies. In effect, therefore, the management of postwar British defence has been an iterative process. Given the trends towards 'jointery' and managerialism in the UK defence sector two ongoing questions are likely to confront the policy-makers of today and tomorrow. First, how joint is enough? And second, what are the scope and limitations of market forces and private sector involvement in the provision of national defence?

Notes

1. See, for example, M. D. Hobkirk, *The Politics of Defence Budgeting: A Study of Resource Allocation in the United Kingdom and the United States*, London: Macmillan, 1984; and M. Howard, *The Central Organisation for Defence*, London: RUSI, 1970.

2. See, for example, I. Bellany, *Reviewing Britain's Defence*, Aldershot: Dartmouth, 1994.

3. See, for example, G. M. Dillon, *Dependence and Deterrence: Success and Civility in the Anglo-American Special Nuclear Relationship, 1962–82*, Aldershot: Gower Press, 1983; and P. Nailor, 'British Defence Policy in the 1960s', in F. Gregory, M. Imber and J. Simpson (eds), *Perspectives upon British Defence Policy*, Southampton: Southampton University Press, 1978, pp. 62–7.

4. See Chapter 1 of this volume.

5. J. Greenwood and D. Wilson, *Public Administration Today*, London: Unwin Hyman, 1989, p. 122.

6. M. Edmonds, 'Central Organizations of Defence in Great Britain', in M. Edmonds (ed.), *Central Organizations of Defence*, London: Frances Pinter, 1985, p. 85. This section paraphrases the key developments outlined in 'Central Organizations of Defence in Great Britain', and M. Edmonds, 'The Higher Organisation of Defence in Britain, 1945–85: the Federal–Unification Debate', in M. Edmonds (ed.), *The Defence Equation*, London: Brassey's, 1986, pp. 57–78.

7. See M. Howard, *The Central Organisation for Defence*, London: RUSI, 1970.

8. *Central Organisation for Defence*, Cmnd. 6923, London: HMSO, 1946.

9. See for example B. Holden Reid, 'Civil War Between Services', in *Military History*, January 1984, pp. 1–7; and W. P. Snyder, *The Politics of British Defense Policy, 1945–1962*, Ohio: Ohio University Press, 1964.

10. Edmonds, 1985, op. cit., p. 61.

11. *Central Organisation for Defence*, Cmnd. 476, London: HMSO, 1958.

12. *Central Organisation for Defence*, Cmnd. 2097, London: HMSO, 1963.

13. Edmonds, 1985, op. cit., p. 71.

14. *Central Organisation for Defence*, Cmnd. 9315, London: HMSO, 1984.

15. Ministry of Defence, *United Kingdom Doctrine for Joint and Combined Operations*, Joint Warfare Publication 0-10, 3rd Study Draft, 1997, p. 1-1.

16. M. Edmonds, 'Defense Management and the Impact of Jointery', *Defense Analysis*, 14 (1), 1998, p. 14.

17. For a more detailed analysis of this point, see A. Dorman, M. L. Smith and M. R. H. Uttley, 'Jointery and Combined Operations in an Expeditionary Era: Defining the Issues', *Defense Analysis*, 14 (1), 1998, pp. 1–8; and, S. E. Airey, 'Does Russian Seapower Have a Future?', *RUSI Journal*, 140 (6) 1995, pp. 15–22.

18. See, for example, V. Gray, 'Beyond Bosnia: Ethno-National Diasporas and Security in Europe', *Contemporary Security Policy*, 17 (1) April 1996, pp. 146–73.

19. J. R. Stocker, 'Canadian Joint Operations', *RUSI Journal*, 141 (3) 1996, p. 36.

20. Dorman, Smith and Uttley, op. cit., p. 3.

21. K. Hartley, 'Jointery – Just Another Panacea? An Economist's Perspective', *Defense Analysis*, 14 (1), pp. 79–86.

22. Admiral of the Fleet Sir Jock Slater, 'A Fleet for the 90s', in *RUSI Journal*, 138 (1) 1993, p. 8.

23. For a discussion, see Dorman, Smith and Uttley, op. cit., pp. 4–5.

24. See, *Report of The Management Committee on the Management and Control of Research and Development*, London: HMSO, 1961; Ministry of Technology, *Report of the Steering Group on Development Cost Estimating*, London: HMSO, 1969; and D. Miller, 'Planning Programme Budgeting Systems and the Case of Rational Decision-Making in Britain's Ministry of Defense', in *Defense Analysis*, January 1990, pp. 131–45.

25. See M. Dillon, 'Recurring Dilemmas and Decision-Making for Defence', in J. Baylis (ed.), *British Defence Policy in a Changing World*, London: Croom Helm, 1977, p. 222.

26. Ibid., p. 212.

27. Greenwood and Wilson, op. cit.

28. For a discussion, see: K. Hartley, *The Economics of Defence Policy*, London: Brassey's, 1991, ch. 1; and, D. Greenwood, 'Expenditure and Management', in P. Byrd (ed.), *British Defence Policy: Thatcher and Beyond*, London: Philip Allan, 1991, pp. 36–66.

29. Greenwood, op. cit., p. 38.

30. Ministry of Defence *Statement on the Defence Estimates 1981*, Cmnd. 8212-I, London: HMSO, 1981, p. 68. For a detailed analysis of the Rayner scrutinies see B. Collins, 'The Rayner Scrutinies', in A. Harrison and J. Gretton (eds), *Reshaping Central Government*, Oxford: Policy Journals, 1987, pp. 11–22.

31. For a general discussion see K. Ascher, *The Politics of Privatisation: Contracting Out Public Services*, London: Macmillan, 1987.

32. For an overview of 'New Right' assumptions, see M. Pirie, *Micropolitics*, London: Wildwood House, 1988; and D. King, *The New Right*, London: Macmillan, 1987.

33. See Hartley, 1991, op. cit., pp. 18–19.

34. Greenwood and Wilson, op. cit., p. 122.

35. Ibid., p. 121.

36. M. McIntosh, *Managing Britain's Defence*, London: Macmillan, 1990, p. 146.

37. For a more detailed discussion, see J. Greenwood and D. Wilson, op. cit., pp. 125–30; and, R. Tonge, 'Financial Management', in D. Farnham and S. Horton (eds), *Managing the New Public Services*, London: Macmillan, 1993, pp. 78–98.

38. For an extended discussion, see for example, M. Stewart, 'Future Resource Management in Defence', *RUSI Journal*, 138 (2) 1993, pp. 73–6.

39. Ibid., p. 73.

40. Efficiency Unit, *Improving Management in Government: The Next Steps*, London: HMSO, 1988.

41. See P. Kemp, 'Can the Civil Service Adapt to Managing by Contract?', *Public Money & Management*, 10 (3) 1990, pp. 25–32.

42. See L. Metcalfe and S. Richards, *Improving Public Management*, London: Sage, 1990, pp. 228–38.

43. Hansard, 13 May 1980, p. 1050.

44.	*The Economist*, 17 May 1980, p. 49.
45.	*Statement on the Defence Estimates 1981*, Cmnd. 8212-I, London: HMSO, 1981, p. 68.
46.	House of Commons Defence Committee, *Seventh Report, Statement on the Defence Estimates 1988*, HCP 495, London: HMSO, 1988, p. 82.
47.	House of Commons Committee of Public Accounts, *Forty-First Report, Ministry of Defence: Control and Use of Manpower*, Session 1988–89, HCP 397, London: HMSO, Q. 3924.
48.	National Audit Office, *Ministry of Defence: Control and Use of Manpower*, London: HMSO, 27 April 1989.
49.	Ibid., p. xii.
50.	*Statement on the Defence Estimates 1984*, Cmnd. 9227-I, London: HMSO, 1984, p. 18.
51.	HM Treasury, *Using Private Enterprise in Government*, London: HMSO, 1986, p. 15.
52.	Ibid., pp. 6–7.
53.	HM Treasury, *Competing for Quality: Buying Better Public Services*, Cmnd. 1730, London: HMSO, 1991.
54.	Ibid., p. 28.
55.	Extracts from Minutes of the Treasury and Civil Service Committee, *Private Finance for Public Projects*, London: HMSO, 1993, p. 18.
56.	F. Cooper, 'Ministry of Defence', in J. Gretton and A. Harrison (eds), *Reshaping Central Government*, Oxford: Policy Journals, 1987, pp. 115–17.
57.	National Audit Office Report by the Comptroller and Auditor General, *The New Management Strategy in the Ministry of Defence*, London: HMSO, 1994.
58.	Kemp, op. cit., pp. 59–60.
59.	See, for example, E. Mellon, 'Executive Agencies: Leading Change from the Outside-in', *Public Money & Management*, 13 (2) 1993, pp. 5–11.
60.	K. Hartley, 'Defence', in A. Harrison (ed.), *From Hierarchy to Contract*, London: Policy Journals, 1992, p. 13.
61.	For a discussion, see M. R. H. Uttley, 'Competition in the Provision of Defense Support Services: The UK Experience', *Defense Analysis*, 9 (3) 1993, p. 277.
62.	See K. Dowding, *The Civil Service*, London: Routledge, 1995.
63.	R. Palin, 'A Military Perspective', in P. Sabin (ed.), *The Future of UK Air Power*, London: Brassey's, 1988, p. 140.
64.	*Statement on the Defence Estimates, 1989*, Cmnd. 675-I, London: HMSO, 1989, p. 35.
65.	See, for example, Audit Commission, *Competitiveness and Contracting Out of Local Authorities' Services*, Occasional Paper No. 3, London: HMSO, 1987, p. 5.
66.	Palin, op. cit., p. 140.
67.	See Dowding, op. cit., pp. 254–6.
68.	M. J. Smith, 'Reconceptualizing the British State: Theoretical and Empirical Challenges to Central Government', *Public Administration*, 76 (1) 1998, p. 63.
69.	Ibid.
70.	See, for example, Centre for Public Services, *Monitoring Public Services*, Sheffield: CPS, 1991.

Chapter 6

The Politics of Defence

Andrew Dorman

Introduction

Defence has always been deeply ingrained with political sensitivities. Past administrations have often been bracketed by their most notable defence failures or the wars they have fought. Anthony Eden is remembered for the Suez débâcle and Margaret Thatcher for the Falklands War and Westland Saga. While this might appear to be a relatively crude justification for the role of politics in defence, at a deeper level defence has a far more significant impact. Margaret Thatcher would include the reduction in the size of the Civil Service and the wide-scale privatisation of state-owned industry among her long-term achievements, both of which had a significant impact upon defence.[1] More significantly, in an age of finite resources, the cost of defence precludes or alters spending in other areas which also have political implications.

A number of reasons for the political sensitivity of defence can be identified. Firstly, in the debate about high and low politics defence remains at heart a minimalist view of government. This tension has, in part, been reflected in the respective approaches of the political parties to defence. For the Conservatives defence has traditionally been 'the cut of last resort',[2] very much in line with the minimalist view. The early years of the first Thatcher government sought to make a virtue out of its commitment to defence spending while the country was in a deep recession and other areas of government expenditure were significantly reduced.[3] For Labour defence has remained one of the many areas competing for government resources, and has thus been a limiting factor on its social programmes.[4] Moreover, defence has also been an area in which Labour has been able to follow their 'internationalist' leanings, with defence diplomacy being only the most recent example of this.[5]

Secondly, defence has an international context, whether it be in threat assessment, alliance membership or the procurement of major weapons programmes.[6] Defence agreements carry with them assumptions, obligations and risks for those undertaking them which have a significant impact upon other states and non-state actors. Poland, the Czech Republic and Hungary all found themselves committed to an air war in the Balkans, less than a month after joining NATO.[7] Procurement from abroad, whether through direct supply, license production or collaboration, impacts upon government policy at a variety of levels, ranging from employment patterns to military capability. The American decision to abandon the Skybolt air launch ballistic missile programme plunged British defence policy into crisis.[8]

Thirdly, defence has a significant impact upon domestic politics. As the subsequent procurement chapter will make clear, the issue of manufacturing employment and research and development expenditure in the defence sector are major concerns that successive governments have sought to make judgements on. Moreover, the size, technical requirements and status, mean that defence has frequently become a political football. The original decision taken by the then Labour government to develop the Nimrod AEW3 system, rather than purchase the American Boeing E-3A system, revolved around the issues of research and development, and employment in Britain.[9]

Fourthly, defence raises the moral dilemma about the use of force and role of armed forces. From the United Kingdom's perspective this has traditionally been most evident in the opposition to the maintenance of a strategic nuclear deterrent and the stationing of American nuclear weapons on British territory.[10] However, it is also apparent in a number of other areas since defence policy centres upon the potential use of force by a state within the international arena. The House of Commons Defence Committee concluded that Britain's position in the world was reliant on its defence expertise.[11] The Blair government has referred to Britain's involvement in terms of 'Forces for Good' and emphasised the moral agenda through an ethical dimension to foreign policy.[12] In these moralistic debates the issue of the sale of defence equipment overseas remains an area of major political contention.

This chapter will consider the politics of defence at a number of levels, which reflect the four dimensions given above. Firstly, it will examine the role of defence in inter-party politics and argue that notions of a defence consensus can, at best, only be temporary because of the political dimension of defence. Secondly, it will consider the role defence has played within the two major parties. Thirdly, the chapter will consider the politics of procurement, drawing together both the domestic and international strands, by examining a number of case studies. Finally, the chapter will pull together some conclusions, reflecting the broader questions set out in the introductory chapter.

Defence and inter-party politics: the myth of a defence consensus?

Many commentators have pointed to the consensus on defence issues that character-ised the first three decades of the Cold War.[13] This has been largely attributed to the similarity in viewpoint of the opposing front benches. However, this view is a little generous. While overall policy remained consistent, there were a number of disagree-ments over specific policy issues and events. For example, while in opposition during the 1950s the Labour Party not only opposed the Anglo-French invasion of Egypt in 1956 but also went through its first unilateralist phase in relation to nuclear weapons.[14] While in opposition in the mid–late 1960s the Conservatives fundamentally disagreed with a number of the defence decisions of the Labour government, most notably the cancellation of the TSR-2 and the decision to withdraw from East of Suez. It was noticeable that in the case of the latter once in power the Conservatives slowed the pace of the withdrawal of British forces stationed East of Suez begun under Labour, but they did not fundamentally alter their predecessor's policy.[15] Thus it is clear that one must be careful with the assumption of a consensus prior to the late 1970s. There were a number of divisions, but these were issue driven. However, from 1979 onwards, defence became an issue of continued and explicit disagreement.

The divisions between the parties began to become more pronounced from the early-1970s onwards, reflecting the impact of the left wing in the Labour Party,[16] and the 'New Right' within the Conservative Party, pulling their parties in opposite directions.[17] Within the Labour Party defence had always been a sensitive issue and as the era of détente began to be replaced by that of the Second Cold War, the issue of defence became increasingly fraught within the party as internal support for unilateralism was renewed.[18] This resurgence culminated in the election of Michael Foot, a noted unilateralist, as leader of the Labour Party, ahead of the multilateralist Denis Healey, and the level of support for Tony Benn in the deputy-leadership contest.[19] This schism contributed to the creation of the Social Democratic Party (SDP) which rapidly gained the allegiance of the majority of Labour's experienced defence speakers. Those from the multilateralist right wing who remained found themselves marginalised as the shadow defence portfolio was temporarily passing to Tribunite control.[20] The result was a severe weakening of Labour's front bench defence team. These divisions within the Labour Party would not have been so significant if it were not for two other interlinked factors. Firstly, the deep-seated unpopularity of the Conservative government caused them to look for areas which they could use to divert public opinion away from politically damaging issues such as high unemployment. Secondly, the outbreak and successful completion of the Falklands War in the space of three months unleashed what became known as the 'Falklands factor', and rapidly turned public opinion in favour of the Conservatives.[21] These factors provided an important lesson for the Conservatives which they were not slow to utilise to their full advantage in the 1983 general election. As a result, for the first time since the end of the Second World War, defence became a major party political issue at a general election, second only to unemployment.[22]

Aware of the success that the issue of defence had brought them in the 1983 election the Conservatives aimed to avoid making any decisions on defence issues which the other parties could exploit. Thus, while they ensured that the parliamentary defence debates focused on the nuclear question, they sought to maintain the impression that Britain's conventional forces were not adversely affected by the Trident decision. However, there had been a cost. During the period 1983–87 the Conservatives had delayed making a number of politically damaging decisions on defence programmes, such as the failed Nimrod AEW aircraft. Instead, they placed emphasis on maintaining frontline numbers and continuing to search for remedies to allow these projects to be completed. The result was the steady rundown in the fighting capacity of the frontline units as the shortage of manpower and lack of the necessary spares worsened. Frontline units became increasingly unable to sustain themselves in combat and grew ever more dependent on untrained Army reserves to make up their numbers in war time. As a result, the Conservative election strategy for 1987 involved a total focus on the nuclear issue, and a consequent questioning of the trustworthiness of their opponents. This led defence to became the litmus test of good governance which undermined the election campaigns of Labour and the SDP/Liberal Alliance.[23]

As a consequence, the Labour Party was forced to reconsider its unilateralist defence policy in the aftermath of the election defeat in 1987 and, by the time of the next election in 1992, return to a more traditional multilateralist defence policy. By then both main parties sought to avoid defence as an electoral issue for differing reasons. The Labour leadership's complete shift away from a unilateralist defence policy had only occurred post-1987 and was, therefore, vulnerable to criticism.[24] Equally the Conservatives sought to avoid defence as a campaign issue because of the cuts they had undertaken as part of the Options for Change exercise.[25] As a result, a consensus of sorts existed based on the need to preserve the strategic nuclear deterrent and effect a peace dividend in the wake of the end of the Cold War.

However, by the time of the 1997 general election, the situation had altered. In the run up to the election the new Labour leadership sought to seize the initiative in a number of areas traditionally considered Conservative strongholds. They committed themselves, therefore, to a foreign policy led defence review.[26] The language used was very conservative in nature to avoid criticism, which led them to ring-fence certain key areas, such as Trident. The outgoing Conservative administration denied the need for a defence review and unsuccessfully tried to use defence to discredit Labour during the election campaign.

As a result, it was of no great surprise that the Blair government sought to carefully manage the whole review process and avoid any suggestion that they were any less supportive of defence. The government continued to contend that foreign policy, rather than Treasury constraints, governed its conduct, and it was noticeable that the reductions planned for were significantly less than the Treasury had hoped for.[27] Moreover, it was also clear that certain areas really were ring-fenced, which severely limited the review's ability to be radical. It therefore did not leave itself open to criticism from the Conservative opposition.

Defence and intra-party politics

Defence has been an important factor in the intra-party politics of Britain's two major parties. For the Conservatives it has traditionally been viewed as the cut of last resort. With the exception of the 1957 Defence Review,[28] there were no official Conservative defence reviews that involved a significant cutback in defence expenditure during the Cold War. Even the notorious 1981 Nott Review revolved around the redistribution of existing defence expenditure.[29] As a result, the gap between the resources allocated to defence by the Conservatives and the programmes they committed themselves to frequently led to large deficits that subsequent Labour governments were forced to address. For example, the funding gap steadily rose between 1957 and 1964 so that the incoming Labour government was forced to undertake a series of reviews once it had decided not to increase defence spending significantly.[30] The same situation occurred in the period 1970–74 which led to the 1975 review.[31] There were a number of reasons for this. Firstly, traditional Conservative policy has been to preserve Britain's place in the world with defence playing a key role. There was a general view that Britain had a world role to fulfil in the postwar world. Traditional Conservative ideology saw defence as one of the fundamental responsibilities of government, and, therefore, significant reductions to defence in the light of the threat posed by the Soviet Union was assumed to be irresponsible.

However, this picture was complicated by the emergence of the New Right within the Conservative Party during the 1970s. Although Margaret Thatcher emphasised defence spending there was not a major shift in policy *per se* because of her other policy goal – the arrest of Britain's long-term economic decline. This led one observer to refer to the 'Thatcher Schizophrenia' in which she could never decide whether she wanted to be remembered in history as the 'Iron Lady' or the 'Iron Chancellor'.[32] This inherent tension was reflected in what Jordan and Richardson have referred to as her 'clear policy *theory*'.[33] This reinforced her emphasis upon the reduction in government expenditure, while at the same time requiring significant fiscal support for defence. Moreover, this 'policy *theory*', with its reduction in public expenditure matched to less regulation and greater entrepreneurship linked into the policies of privatisation of state industries, reducing civil service numbers, management reforms of the civil service, changes in industrial policy and trade union reform. Through all this the MoD 'as both the largest Department in central government and the biggest employer of Civil Service manpower . . . was in the forefront of such studies and pressures'.[34] It was, therefore, hardly surprising that the defence budget has remained a battlefield for the competing wings of the Conservative Party. The result was a fierce division between the monetarists and the traditional wing of the Conservative Party about Britain's place in the world and the management of defence policy in support of this. The latter was most evident in the management and procurement reforms of the 1980s, while the former was revealed during John Nott's time as Secretary of State for Defence.[35] His 1981 defence review, with its European focus, reflected the peak of monetarist control of declaratory policy.

Post-Cold War this division manifested itself in the early 1990s in the difference between the security policy promulgated by the Foreign and Commonwealth Office and the Ministry of Defence. The end of the Cold War and the collapse of the Soviet Union found Britain with what William Wallace described as: '[a] Government which has no clear sense of its place in the world or its foreign policy priorities'.[36] This was primarily due to internal conflicts within the Conservative government. At a time when many argued that defence policy would return to its position as the servant of foreign and economic policy, in Britain defence policy evolved in a foreign policy vacuum.[37]

Secondly, no Conservative government, and more importantly, no Conservative defence minister wanted to be remembered for abandoning particular roles. Eden's fall following the Suez disaster, and Nott's after the Falklands, only served to reinforce this. Partly this was due to notions of ministerial success faced by successive ministers. As Madgwick puts it:

> Ministers feel, indeed are, exposed and vulnerable. They need and want public success and to stand well with their colleagues; they struggle to avoid failure, blame and humiliation. Avoiding blame and seeking credit are major concerns for ministers, more attractive than power itself, which is a means to credit, status and comfort. These concerns, added to department concern for status and territory, are basic forces in British government.[38]

Not surprisingly there is a tendency for ministers to have a strong departmental focus, especially since they often feel judged by their ability to promote their department's policies and increase its budget. When put in charge of a spending department, such as the MoD, Ministers tend to feel that they have a justifiable case for an increase in the expenditure of their department. In this view they have the ready support of their department. Those seeking to scale the ministerial ladder to higher office have little time in which to make a positive impact in their department and defence reductions have generally been negatively received. Moreover, the Conservative back bench Committee on Defence has traditionally undertaken a watching brief over successive defence ministers, reinforcing this tendency.

Thirdly, the inevitability of cutbacks led to defence increasingly being seen to be a poison chalice, especially after the furore over the Nott review. This is a relatively new phenomenon. In 1957 Macmillan gave the defence portfolio to a trustee, Duncan Sandys, in order that the post-Suez review could be overseen. Likewise, Thatcher gave Nott the task of managing a defence ministry whose costs appeared to her to be spiralling out of control. However, she and her successor John Major used the department to muzzle potential leadership challengers. The complexity and scale of the defence portfolio make it a particularly time-consuming post which keeps any minister preoccupied, while its Cabinet status ensures that an individual's views remained muffled by Cabinet collective responsibility. Moreover, it generally presents ministers with difficult decisions about defence priorities that do not help the individual to court popularity within the party or wider public opinion. Examples of this phenomenon include the appointments of Francis Pym, Michael Heseltine and Michael Portillo to defence.

For the Labour Party, defence has raised a number of different but no less contentious issues. These can be subdivided into three main areas. Firstly, the Labour Party was divided over Britain's place in the world, and Britain's relations with the other major powers. The internationalist leanings of some encouraged them to follow the traditional Conservative line of emphasising the importance of a British military presence overseas, but to de-emphasise the national interest in favour of the common good. This, in part, explains the internal turmoil within the Cabinet about the decision to largely withdraw from East of Suez in 1968, following the devaluation of the pound.[39] When it entered office in 1964 the Wilson government never intended to abandon a world role. In fact on the nuclear front it initially saw the requirement for a fifth Polaris submarine as a means of providing a nuclear umbrella for India against China, in order to discourage India from developing its own nuclear programme. However, the economic position confronting the government forced it to largely abandon the world role and withdraw further in the 1970s.[40]

The issue was again raised with the first post-Cold War Labour government. The origins of Defence Diplomacy can be traced to the changes in the strategic context brought about by the end of the Cold War. During the Cold War British foreign and defence policy concentrated upon dealing with the perceived threat posed by the Soviet Union. This led successive governments to emphasise Britain's membership of NATO, to preserve the special relationship with the United States and to retain a strategic nuclear deterrent.[41] The end of the Cold War freed the government of many of the constraints that the Cold War had imposed. A much broader view of security was adopted by the new Labour government through its proclamation of a new ethical dimension to foreign policy[42] and the emergence of the Department for International

Development from within the shadows of the Foreign and Commonwealth Office (FCO).[43]

The second area of contention within the Labour Party has concerned weapons of mass destruction and, in particular, nuclear weapons. The creation and subsequent retention of a nuclear deterrent, together with the basing of American nuclear weapons in or around Britain, and Britain's membership of a nuclear alliance led to much soul searching within the party. For two periods, the late 1950s–early 1960s and for much of the 1980s opponents of these weapons held sway within the party and, according to conventional wisdom, were one of the principal reasons for Labour's defeat in both the 1983 and 1987 general elections.[44] Even outside these periods successive Labour leaders have had to be careful. The initial decision to develop a British atom bomb was undertaken without the full Labour Cabinet being consulted.[45] This ruse was subsequently adopted by James Callaghan in the late 1970s to oversee the Polaris improvement programme and commence initial studies into the replacement of the Polaris system via a Cabinet subcommittee.[46]

The third area of contention has lain in the relative priority that the defence budget should receive compared with other areas of government. On first appearance it would seem that Labour governments are more willing to undertake defence reductions as part of a reapportionment of government expenditure, and this has certainly been the argument from within the left wing of the party. Many have viewed defence as just another element of government which has to compete for resources. This view has certainly been reflected in attitudes towards what is deemed success for defence teams. Unlike the Conservatives, successive Labour defence ministers have not had their level of success measured in terms of overall defence spending. They have, therefore, been far freer than their Conservative counterparts to undertake the financially-driven defence reviews required of successive postwar governments. However, the argument is more complicated than this and it was noticeable that it was a Labour government that sought to significantly increase defence expenditure in the early 1950s in the light of the Korean War. Perhaps a truer picture would be that Labour defence teams have been generally freer to change the relative amounts spent on defence depending upon which part of the party has ascendancy within the government.

Politics of procurement

The purchasing of equipment for the armed forces cannot avoid infringing upon domestic and international politics. The scale of British defence spending means that it will inevitably have an impact on the domestic economy. The 1957 Defence Review pointed this out with some stark statistics:

> Over the last five years, defence has on average absorbed 10 per cent of Britain's gross national product. Some 7 per cent of the working population are either in the Services or supporting them. One-eighth of the output of the metal-using industries, upon which the export trade so largely depends, is devoted to defence. An undue proportion of qualified scientists and engineers are engaged on military work. In addition, the retention of such large forces abroad gives rise to heavy charges which place a severe strain upon the balance of payments.[47]

Moreover, procurement involves not just the physical purchase of hardware but also the commitment to fielding and maintaining units in the field. Not surprisingly this is a significant political minefield. Firstly, manufacturing jobs in general and the preservation of the defence industrial base are politically important. The decision about the replacement of the army's FV-432 armoured personnel carrier in 1980 was a good example of this.[48] The Chief Scientific Adviser had argued for the acceptance of the American Bradley because it had TOW anti-tank missiles, while the British-made Warrior, only had a gun which was not even stabilised, so the vehicle had to stop to fire accurately. The decision went before the Minister for Defence Procurement, Lord Strathcona, who opted for Warrior, justifying his decision on the need to preserve jobs in Wolverhampton.[49]

Secondly, defence decisions can have a strong impact on regional policy whether this be where troops are stationed or from where equipment is purchased. This can present government with dilemmas that it does not want. For example, Michael Heseltine decided to divide an order for two new frigates. In the Commons he readily admitted that:

> [t]he cheapest solution from the point of defence procurement would be to place the order for both ships with one yard, but, in the light of the wider and relevant factors involved, I have decided that an order for one type 22 frigate will be placed with Cammell Laird and for the second with Swan Hunter. . . . This offers the prospect of survival of Cammell Laird as a major warship builder; without such a contract the yard would have closed.

Thirdly, defence procurement is frequently affected by the proximity of general elections and the need to influence key marginal seats. The naval programme has traditionally built in some slack to allow additional orders to be placed with key shipyards. During the six week run up to the 1979 general election three Type 42 destroyers and two Type 22 frigates were ordered, all from marginal constituencies.[50]

The fourth area of sensitivity lies in Britain's involvement in a number of defence agreements and alliances. This has imposed a number of restrictions on Britain's defence policy. As the financial gap between the long-term costings and the likely defence budget increased during the late 1980s the Services began to look for areas that could be cutback or abandoned. The army suggested that the UK Mobile Force (UKMF), centred on one Infantry Brigade, was a good candidate for reduction as it represented a poor return for the level of resources committed and was a classic case of political tokenism.[51] The storm broke with John Stanley's confirmation that the future of UKMF was being reconsidered. In Denmark, the most likely recipient of the UKMF in wartime, the opposition Foreign Affairs spokesman suggested that if the commitment were withdrawn the whole basis of Denmark's commitment to NATO would have to be reconsidered.[52] To George Younger, the then Secretary of State for Defence, there was the wider question of support for Lord Carrington, the NATO Secretary-General, and his efforts to prevent other nations backsliding. Younger, therefore, blocked the army's decision because of its likely impact upon Denmark and NATO in general.

It is clear that procurement is inherently political in nature, with the result that all the decisions taken have a political subcontext. This situation is complicated further by the domestic and international context in which procurement decisions are taken. Procurement is also one area of the defence portfolio in which ministers can have a significant impact in the short term. It is, therefore, an area subject to considerable ministerial involvement.

Conclusion

This chapter has argued that by its very nature defence is a highly politicised area of government policy and it is inevitably affected by the political context in which it is located. It cannot be divorced from either its international or domestic environments and sits somewhat precariously between the two. Any analysis of defence policy needs to take this into account as well as the moral sensitivities that defence frequently brings to the political debate.

Defence continues to have an impact far beyond mere electioneering. It became one of the central battlegrounds during the 1980s. However, there were attendant costs. The Conservative's success in making defence a litmus test by which the various parties were judged by the public had an adverse effect upon the armed forces themselves as the Conservatives sought to avoid making defence decisions which might have been construed as weakening Britain's conventional forces. Moreover, in the post-Cold War period this legacy prevented the Conservatives undertaking an adequate reconsideration of Britain's defence policy. Periods of defence consensus, therefore, cannot be considered indefinite because the issues that surround defence are too politically sensitive for cross-bench support to last. Moreover, where they have occurred, such as in the early 1990s, they tend to lead to a stagnation in policy development.

This chapter has also emphasised that defence is not just a political issue between the parties but also within the main parties. Within the Conservative Party defence became a key battleground for the two wings of the party. As a result of this, during the 1980s, far more emphasis was given by the various factions of the Conservative Party to the management of defence and the procurement decisions within the MoD and far less to a consideration of matching threat assessment with procurement decisions, military doctrine and force deployments. Moreover, the defence post has become useful as a means of sidelining the most vociferous opponents of the Prime Minister within the Cabinet and preventing them organising opposition within the party.

Within Labour also, defence has posed problems and proved to be a major factor keeping them out of office throughout the 1980s. It is also clear that successive Labour governments have been far freer to undertake defence reviews than their Conservative counterparts. Defence has not been viewed as a poison chalice for individual ministers. Nevertheless, defence has been one of the principal battlegrounds within the Labour Party and there has always been a unilateralist element within the party, which has sought to achieve a far more radical shift in defence policy.

What is also clear from this chapter is the degree of choice available to individual governments, whether this be about issues of procurement or the amount of money devoted to defence. This conclusion is at odds with the declinist view of defence policy and suggests that even if decline is inevitable its conduct and pace can be altered. Moreover, the politics of defence is not solely about managing decline. Individual ministers have the opportunity to make significant procurement decisions, based on the political agenda of the day, which will, in turn, impact upon Britain's industrial base and regional policy.

Notes

1. Sir E. Broadbent, *The Military and Government: from Macmillan to Heseltine*, Basingstoke: Macmillan for RUSI, 1988, pp. 59–60.
2. P. Calvocoressi, 'Deterrence, the Costs, the Issues, the Choices', *The Sunday Times*, 6 April 1980.
3. N. Lawson, *The View From No. 11: Memoirs of a Tory Radical*, London: Bantam Press, 1992, p. 32.
4. B. Castle, *The Castle Diaries, 1964–70*, London: Weidenfeld & Nicolson, 1984, p. 5.
5. See, for example, George Robertson, Speech to the Labour Party Conference, 1997.
6. S. P. Huntington, *The Common Defence: Strategic Programs in National Politics*, Colombia: Columbia University Press, 1961, pp. 1–7.
7. S. L. v. Gorka, 'NATO After Enlargement: Is the Alliance Better Off?', *NATO Review*, 47 (3) Autumn 1999, p. 33.
8. H. Wynn, *RAF Nuclear Deterrent Forces*, London: HMSO, 1994, pp. 398–9.
9. *Statement on the Defence Estimates, 1978*, Cmnd. 7,099, London: HMSO, 1978, p. 13.
10. L. Freedman, *The Politics of British Defence, 1979–98*, Basingstoke: Macmillan, 1999, p. 6.
11. House of Commons Defence Committee, *Fourth Report: United Kingdom Peace-keeping and Intervention Forces: Report together with the Proceedings of the Committee relating to the report, minutes of evidence and memoranda*, House of Commons Papers No. 188, session 1992–93, London: HMSO, 1993, p. xxvi.
12. *The Strategic Defence Review*, Cmnd. 3,999, London, The Stationery Office, 1998, p. 4; see also article by the Prime Minister in *Newsweek International*, 19 April 1999, available at www.fco.gov.uk
13. P. M. Jones, 'British Defence Policy: the Breakdown of the Inter-Party Consensus', *Review of International Studies*, 13 (2) April 1987, pp. 111–31.
14. D. Keohane, *Labour Party Defence Policy since 1945*, Leicester: Leicester University Press, 1993, p. 22.
15. Lord Carrington, *Reflect on Things Past: The Memoirs of Lord Carrington*, Glasgow: William Collins, 1988, p. 218.
16. P. M. Jones, op. cit., p. 113.
17. Michael Clarke, 'A British View', in R. Davy (ed.), *European Détente: A Reappraisal*, London: Sage Publications for the RIIA, 1992, p. 101. It was notable that one of Thatcher's early advisers on foreign affairs was the historian Robert Conquest, a fellow member of the New Right. Margaret Thatcher, *The Downing Street Years*, London: HarperCollins, 1993, p. 351. For Conquest's point of view see R. Conquest, *Present Danger: Towards a Foreign Policy*, Oxford: Basil Blackwell, 1979. For a background of the evolution of the New Right within the Conservative Party see N. Ridley, *My Style of Government: the Thatcher Years*, London: Fontana, 1992, pp. 1–22.
18. D. Keohane, op. cit., p. 22.
19. A. Benn, *The End of an Era: Diaries 1980–90*, London: Random House, 1992, pp. 46, 154.

20. For details of the SDP's initial success see J. Cole, *As It Seemed to Me: Political Memoirs*, London: Weidenfeld & Nicolson, 1995, pp. 230–45.

21. See F. Noguera and Peter Willets, 'Public Attitudes and the Future of the Islands', in A. Danchev (ed.), *International Perspectives on the Falklands Conflict*, Basingstoke: Macmillan, 1992, particularly pp. 241–2.

22. Jones, op. cit., p. 111.

23. B. George and C. Pawlisch, 'Defence and 1983 Election', *ADIU Report*, 5 (4) July/August 1983, p. 2.

24. Idem.

25. Tom King, *House of Commons Parliamentary Debates*, Vol. 177, sixth series, session 1989–90, 23 July–19 October 1990, Statement to the House, 25 July 1990, cols. 468–86.

26. C. McInnes, 'Labour's Strategic Defence Review', *International Affairs*, 74 (4) October 1998, pp. 823–45, at p. 828.

27. Ibid., p. 845.

28. *Defence Outline of Future Policy, 1957*, Cmnd. 124, London: HMSO, 1957.

29. *The United Kingdom Defence Programme: The Way Forward*, Cmnd. 8,288, London: HMSO, 1981.

30. D. Healey, *The Time of My Life*, London: W. W. Norton, 1989, p. 270.

31. R. Mason, *House of Commons Parliamentary Debates*, vol. 883, fifth series, 9–20 December 1974, Statement to the House, 16 December 1974, col. 1,148.

32. Quoted by A. Raphael, 'Nott fights reargard action in Whitehall whispering war', *The Observer*, 20 June 1982.

33. Italics in original. A. G. Jordan and J. J. Richardson, *British Politics and the Policy Process: an Arena Approach*, London: Allen and Unwin, 1987, pp. 105–6.

34. Sir E. Broadbent, *The Military and Government: from Macmillan to Heseltine*, Basingstoke: Macmillan for RUSI, 1988, pp. 59–60.

35. C. Parkinson, *Right at the Centre*, London, Weidenfeld & Nicolson, 1992, p. 149.

36. W. Wallace, 'Britain's search for a new role in the world,' *The Observer*, 15 August 1993, p. 16.

37. W. van Eekelen, 'WEU on the way back to Brussels', Speech at Chatham House on 22 September 1992, p. 3, reprinted in *WEU Press Review*, No. 161, 24 September 1992.

38. P. Madgwick, *British Government: The Central Executive Territory*, London: Philip Allan, 1991, p. 15.

39. R. Jenkins, *A Life at the Centre*, London: Macmillan, 1991, p. 219.

40. Healey, op. cit., p. 401.

41. Stuart Croft and Phil Williams, 'The United Kingdom' in R. C. Karp (ed.), *Security with Nuclear Weapons? Different Perspectives on National Security*, Oxford: Oxford University Press for SIPRI, 1991, p. 147.

42. See Robin Cook, 'British Foreign Policy', Speech made at the launch of the FCO Mission Statement, London: FCO, 12 May 1997.

43. The incoming Labour government indicated its commitment in this area by strengthening the Department for International Development (formerly the Overseas Development Administration) and substantially increasing its budget.

44. In 1979 only 2 per cent of the electorate thought defence was a major issue in the election. By 1983 this had risen to 38 per cent. Michael Heseltine, 'The United Kingdom's Strategic Interests and Priorities', *The RUSI Journal*, 128 (4), p. 3.
45. J. Simpson, *The Independent Nuclear State: Britain, the United States and the Military Atom*, Basingstoke: Macmillan, second edition 1986, pp. 41–2.
46. Only a select few in Wilson's and Callaghan's Cabinets knew of the ongoing Chevaline programme or Callaghan's decision to initiate studies into a replacement for Polaris. D. Owen, *Time to Declare*, London: Michael Joseph, 1991, pp. 380–1.
47. *Defence – Outline of Future Policy*, Cmnd. 124, London: HMSO, 1957, para. 7.
48. F. Pym, *House of Commons Parliamentary Debates*, vol. 988, fifth series, session 1979–80, 7–18 July 1980, written answer 14 July 1980, cols. 420-1w.
49. Private discussion.
50. K. Speed, *Sea Change: The Battle for the Falklands and the Future of Britain's Navy*, Bath: Ashgrove Press, 1982, p. 79.
51. The UK Mobile Force consisted of an air-portable brigade of four infantry battalions, an armoured reconnaissance regiment, an armoured squadron, one-plus SAM battery and a logistical support group. IISS, *The Military Balance, 1987–88*, London: IISS, 1987, p. 79.
52. H. Barnes and D. Buchan, 'Danes Worried by UK Review of Defence Force's Role', *The Financial Times*, 22 January 1987.

Chapter 7

Defence Procurement and Industrial Policies

Matthew Uttley

Introduction

Defence procurement and industrial policies have been central themes in debates about Britain's relative postwar economic decline. This has reflected the national economic significance of post-1945 military–industrial activity: the UK armed services have been British industry's single largest customer[1] and defence has consumed a sizeable proportion of national scientific and technical resources.[2] The focus of the 'declinist debate' has traditionally been on whether Britain's relatively high levels of military equipment expenditure have 'crowded out' civil investment and undermined overall national economic performance.[3] This chapter addresses a separate but equally important aspect of the relationship between defence procurement and British 'decline'. Rather than investigating the impact of military equipment expenditure on the UK economy, this chapter analyses decline in terms of the postwar procurement policy shifts Britain has undertaken in its adjustment from 'great power' to 'medium power' status.

In 1945, only Britain, the United States and the Soviet Union emerged from hostilities with a comprehensive defence industrial capacity. Subsequently, Britain has undergone the transition from a 'first' division weapon producer to being a 'leader of the second division, though following an order of magnitude behind the superpowers'.[4] This relative decline has reflected postwar trends in military equipment costs and defence budgetary constraints. Since 1945, the unit production cost of major weapons systems has increased rapidly in real terms:[5] the real costs of tactical combat aircraft have been growing at 10 per cent per annum, with similar rates of growth for submarines, frigates, attack helicopters and self-propelled artillery.[6] A significant variable accounting for these cost trends has been the military imperative for major equipment performance enhancements when the armed services have acquired successive generations of weapon systems. Though British defence budgets have grown at the same time as equipment costs have been rising, budgetary increases have been smaller than, and 'only partially compensated for the concurrent escalation in the unit cost of defence equipment'.[7]

Given these trends, postwar British defence decision-makers have been confronted with objective constraints. However, rather than merely acknowledging these constraints, this chapter surveys the various assumptions, choices and trade-offs that policy-makers have made in Britain's adjustment from 'first' division weapon producer status.

The 'broad front' approach and national self-sufficiency, 1945–60

In 1945, Britain inherited 'a fully operating arms industry, a level of advanced military technology not too distant in many areas from the United States, and access to nuclear technology'.[8] Between 1945 and 1960, defence procurement policies rested on two dominant assumptions. The first was that Britain could and should sustain a 'broad front approach' to weapon procurement, or 'large-scale and extensive [government] sponsorship of nearly all the sciences and engineering fields considered to be important militarily'[9] in industry and government research establishments. The second assumption was that Britain should seek to retain an independent national research and development (R&D) and production capability across the spectrum of defence-related technologies.

The 'broad front' philosophy had two main elements. The first was the 'multiplicity of companies'[10] concept, or the maintenance of numerous design teams and production lines for each class of weapon.[11] In the aircraft sector, for example, government contracting sustained 22 major aircraft design groups with associated manufacturing facilities, and nine major aero-engine development groups between 1945 and 1959.[12] Underpinning this approach was the view that sustaining a range of firms in each weapon sector ensured surge production capability in the event of general war[13] and technical competition between the various design teams.[14]

The second element was 'parallel development', or government sponsorship of two or three designs of equipment in each class in order to safeguard against the failure of any one type. In the aircraft sector, for example, parallel development was manifest in four distinct strategies.[15] Government sponsored parallel 'competition aircraft', or aircraft whose development was financed along with one or more other similar types, all competing to fulfil the same operational requirement. 'Reinsurance' policies were adopted whereby multiple projects were funded by government as insurance against potential development problems on more advanced types. Government also provided extensive funding for parallel 'research' programmes in industry, each of which invariably involved the building of flying prototypes or models. Finally, multiple experimental projects were sponsored at the government's own research establishments, including the Royal Aircraft Establishment and the Royal Radar Establishment.[16] 'Parallel development' reflected a consensus among policy-makers that investment on multiple R&D lines offered a hedge against unforeseen technical difficulties on individual programmes and ensured the emergence of suitable weapon systems to meet foreseeable military requirements.[17]

Implicit in the 'broad front' approach was the imperative that Britain should retain a comprehensive and self-sufficient domestic military R&D and production capability. At the most general level, self-sufficiency was equated with 'strategic autarky', or national self-determination in defence and foreign policy that complete control over weapons and their replacement parts could provide.[18] National autonomy in weapons development was also viewed as a source of national independence, a means of achieving security of equipment supply and a way of tailoring equipment requirements to the precise needs of the British armed services. Finally, self-sufficiency was equated with national economic benefits in the form of domestic employment, support for balance of payments and tax revenues,[19] as well as a source of technological 'spin-offs' that civilian industry could exploit.[20]

Between 1945 and the late 1950s, Britain sustained these tenets of defence procurement policy for two reasons. First, the relatively low cost and simplicity of contemporary military equipment meant that government could afford to sponsor multiple projects and design teams with available budgetary resources.[21] Moreover, Britain's decision to undertake substantial rearmament during the Korean War, coupled with funding provided by the US for British military equipment programmes, expanded the finances available for development and production. Second, though the UK imported some American equipment under the Mutual Defence Assistance Programme and manufactured American aircraft designs under license, there was 'sufficient across-the-board competence [in domestic industry] and special military requirements for Britain to attempt to develop and produce new weapons alone'.[22] Consequently, governments viewed the equipment imported or produced under license during this period as a 'stop-gap' until alternative British designs emerged.

By the late 1950s, however, major strains were showing in Britain's ability to maintain a 'broad front' approach, and in 1960 the 'multiplicity of companies' and 'parallel development' philosophies were largely abandoned. At one level, this policy shift reflected official concerns about the limited number of postwar projects that had finally entered production:[23] a trend attributed to government sponsorship of 'too many' firms and projects, and procurement policies which had spread 'the country's industrial and design effort too thinly'.[24] More fundamentally, government realised that Britain no longer had the financial and technical resources to sustain an extensive array of competing design teams and projects. During 1954 a total of 155 combat aircraft represented a value of approximately £6.2 million, whereas by 1958, the production of 178 combat aircraft was valued at £29 million.[25] As these cost increases were entirely attributable to increased technological complexity, decision-makers recognised that government contracting should be used to reduce the number of firms and design teams, and that scarce resources should be targeted on fewer projects for which production was likely.[26]

By the early 1960s, government aspirations of comprehensive national self-sufficiency in weapon development and manufacture were also reassessed. In the face of rapidly accelerating R&D and production costs, policy-makers realised that Britain had insufficient technical resources to remain at the technological frontier across the spectrum of defence-related development.[27] This realisation was reflected in the Plowden Committee of Inquiry into the British aircraft industry which advocated, *inter alia*, that Britain should form international partnerships for future aerospace development and production.[28]

'National champions' and international equipment partnerships, 1960–79

By the late 1950s, defence decision-makers had accepted that budgetary constraints and spiralling equipment costs necessitated a policy re-evaluation. This reappraisal ushered in a second discrete phase in postwar procurement and defence-industrial policy which endured between 1960 and 1979. The revised approach had three central tenets. The first was recognition and acceptance that government contracting should encourage the formation of larger industrial groupings in the aerospace, shipbuilding and jet engine sectors. This reflected the view that industrial mergers would ameliorate the growing cost and technological sophistication of weapons development as larger design teams would focus R&D expenditure and technical manpower on fewer but better resourced projects, and generate economies of scale in manufacture.[29] The assumptions here were that large firms with consolidated equipment orders could achieve 'learning effects', or the fall in unit costs per unit of output as workers became more accustomed to particular operations, and exploit scale economies as the fixed costs of weapons development were spread over longer production runs.[30]

By 1960, government had played a central role in reshaping the aerospace sector in the hope that it would be 'more able to survive in an age of high R&D costs and advanced technology'.[31] During 1959, the government engineered the merger of the UK's engine firms into Rolls-Royce and Bristol Siddeley and the airframe companies into the Hawker Siddeley Group and British Aircraft Corporation.[32] A further step towards market concentration occurred in 1966 when Rolls-Royce took over Bristol Siddeley. To preserve an indigenous engine development and production capability, the government nationalised Rolls-Royce in 1971 when the firm went into liquidation.[33] Similar trends occurred in the airframe and shipbuilding sectors: during 1977, British Aerospace and British Shipbuilders were formed by mergers and nationalisation in the Aircraft & Shipbuilding Industries Act. Government intervention and takeovers meant that GEC emerged as a 'national champion' electronics company. Finally, by the late 1970s production of land armaments had become concentrated in the government-owned Royal Ordnance Factories.

The second policy tenet was overt government protection of key domestic suppliers in public and private ownership from the commercial risks of weapon development. During the 1940s and 1950s, relatively low equipment development costs meant that defence firms could initiate new projects on a speculative basis employing their own capital. By the early 1960s, however, the increases in equipment costs and sophistication led to government recognition of the need for public funding to shoulder the financial risks of development and production in industry. One manifestation of this was the growth in 'cost-plus' contracting, whereby government reimbursed defence firms with their actual development and production outlays on a weapon project regardless of their levels, plus a fixed-fee or government-determined percentage profit.[34] Another was government protection of major domestic suppliers through the use of 'preferred supplier' lists which distributed defence contracts across industry to ensure the long-term viability of firms in each weapon sector. Finally, given the growing complexity of weapon designs, the MoD intervened directly on large weapon programmes, directing and managing design and development work undertaken in industry.

The third tenet was government policies to foster international defence procurement partnerships and other forms of non-national equipment sourcing. The realisation in the early 1960s that Britain lacked the resources to sustain a 'broad front approach' raised two interrelated policy issues: the choices between alternative acquisition strategies and types of partnerships in weapon sectors where national self-sufficiency was deemed too costly.

After the early 1960s, Britain employed three discrete weapon acquisition strategies where independent development ceased to be viable. For some acquisitions it avoided domestic R&D and manufacture altogether by importing foreign weapon systems off-the-shelf. In other cases, licensed production and co-production strategies enabled Britain to bypass the costly R&D stages of weapon acquisition and focus instead on domestic manufacture of non-national designs. Finally, Britain participated in a series of international collaborative ventures involving joint R&D and production of defence items with at least one partner state.

After the early 1960s, the mix of off-the-shelf, licensed/co-production and international collaboration in British defence procurement reflected pragmatic responses to equipment requirements on a case-by-case basis. The UK imported major weapon platforms from the United States, notably Polaris and Trident missile technology.[35] The scale of British off-the-shelf purchases, however, was limited by wider economic, industrial and political concerns. Balance of payments considerations, government anxieties about UK job losses, and fears that domestic technological and manufacturing capabilities would be eroded if major contracts were placed overseas, all militated against large-scale importation of major weapon platforms. As a consequence, off-the-shelf procurement was largely restricted to purchases where US industry had a clear technological edge over other procurement alternatives.

For some requirements, governments perceived that co-production and licensed production provided economic and industrial benefits over both national sourcing and off-the-shelf acquisition. Unlike independent national development, co-production and licensed production offered a mechanism to circumvent the costly and lengthy R&D stages of weapons development and the opportunity for industry to focus instead on the manufacture of proven equipment. Correspondingly, unlike direct imports, licensed production also offered the prospect of technology transfer and a role for British industry, albeit at the manufacturing stage. After 1960, licensed production was relied on extensively in the helicopter sector where successive generations of British production technology were of US design origin.[36]

However, from the early 1960s, governments viewed international collaboration as the 'least-worst' procurement alternative where independent development ceased to be viable.[37] In part, this reflected government assessments of the potential benefits of collaboration over comparable national projects. In economic terms, collaboration enabled fixed R&D costs to be shared with partner states and offered the potential for economies of scale through combined production orders. In operational terms, Britain, and its NATO partners, saw collaborative projects as a route to increased equipment rationalisation, standardisation and interoperability (RSI) within the alliance as member states developed and operated common items of equipment.[38] Unlike direct imports and licensed/co-production, an attraction of collaborative ventures was the inclusion of British industry in the R&D and production phases of weapon development. In this regard, international collaboration was equated with preserving an indigenous design and production capability in weapon sectors where national self-sufficiency was no longer affordable. The significance of UK participation in major defence-related collaborative ventures is illustrated by the range of programmes undertaken between 1960 and 1990 (Table 7.1).

Table 7.1 British participation in major military-related collaborative projects, 1960–90

	Project start	Nations/companies involved	Details
Aircraft			
Jaguar	05/65	France, UK	Strike/trainer
Gazelle	02/67	France, UK	Light utility helicopter
Lynx	02/67	France, UK	Multipurpose helicopter
Tornado	07/67	UK, FRG, Italy	Strike/fighter
EH101	06/80	UK, Italy	Military helicopter
Harrier II	08/81	USA, UK	V/STOL strike
EFA	12/83	FRG, Italy, Spain, UK	Combat aircraft
Engines			
RB 153	1960	Rolls-Royce, MTU	For supersonic VTOL
M 45	1964	Rolls-Royce, SNECMA	Military version for AFVG
TF 41	1965	Rolls-Royce, Allison	For Vought A-7 Corsair
T 112	1965	Rolls-Royce, KHD	Auxiliary power for V/STOL
RB 193	1965	Rolls-Royce, MTU	For VAK 191B V/STOL
Adour	1966	Rolls-Royce, Turbomeca	For Jaguar
RB 199	1969	Rolls-Royce, MTU, Fiat	For Tornado
RTM 322/321	1978	Rolls-Royce, Turbomeca	For military/civil helicopters
V 2500	1983	Rolls-Royce, Pratt & Whitney, Japanese Aero-Engines, MTU, Fiat	Advanced technology turbofan
EJ 2000	1985	Fiat, MTU, Rolls-Royce, Sener	For EFA
MTR 390	1986	MTU, Turbomeca, Rolls-Royce	For Eurocopter
Missile projects			
Marcal	1964	France, UK	Air-surface missile
ASRAAM	1982	FRG, UK, Norway	
TRIGAT	1987	France, FRG, UK	
NAAWS	1988	Canada, France, FRG, Italy, Netherlands, Spain, UK, USA	Shipborne missile

After 1960, British policy-makers also had to confront difficult choices about the balance between defence–industrial cooperation with European NATO partners and the US. This issue stemmed from wider NATO concerns during the 1970s over transatlantic weapon trade imbalances, highlighted by the fact that the European alliance members were purchasing approximately $8 billion worth of US defence equipment, while the US spent just $700 million on European equipment.[39] In response to political tensions over this imbalance, America and its European partners investigated policy options to encourage a more equitable 'two-way street' in transatlantic weapons trade. Both the 1976 Culver-Nunn legislation in the US and the 1978 Klepsch Report identified closer intra-European procurement cooperation as the mechanism to rationalise European defence–industrial activity and balance transatlantic arms flows.[40]

For Britain and its European partners, the basic dilemma was one of balancing the benefits and costs of transatlantic and intra-European procurement cooperation. Britain recognised that transatlantic partnerships offered two sets of benefits when compared with European collaborative arrangements. After 1945, American defence industries had enjoyed greater economies of scale in production than their European counterparts because they catered for the much larger unit requirements of the US armed services.[41] As a consequence, US industry could develop and manufacture lower cost equipment than European single national or collaborative ventures. Moreover, the scale of US investment in a range of equipment sectors provided American firms with a clear technological lead over their European counterparts measured in equipment delivery times and performance. Consequently, access to US technology through transatlantic equipment partnerships offered a means to exploit American investment and acquire state-of-the-art equipment. Correspondingly, for the European NATO states, close transatlantic procurement cooperation had the potential cost that reliance on US-designed weapon systems could lead to the erosion of European defence R&D and production capabilities. From the 1960s, this concern led to concerted policies in the UK and elsewhere designed to foster intra-European procurement cooperation as a way to offset the scale of US weapon investment.[42]

After the late 1960s, Britain reconciled these dilemmas by adopting a twin-track approach. On the one hand, it pragmatically purchased major American weapon platforms and collaborated with US firms on a case-by-case basis, notably the Harrier aircraft programme. On the other hand, this was balanced with Britain's growing involvement in intra-European collaborative ventures, primarily in the aerospace sector (Table 7.1).

Between 1960 and the late 1970s, the legacies of British procurement policies were twofold. As Gummett points out, the combination of policies and initiatives meant that Britain did retain 'the capacity for the autonomous development of a wide range of weapon systems, including nuclear weapons and all the major weapon platforms except long range ballistic missiles, heavy bombers and large aircraft carriers'.[43] However, by the late 1970s anxieties began to emerge about poor equipment reliability, major cost overruns and delivery slippages on major domestic programmes,[44] and the future direction that Britain should take in international weapon partnerships. In addressing these concerns, the Conservative government elected in 1979 ushered in the third major postwar shift in British procurement and defence–industrial policies.

Competitive procurement policies, 1979–98

Despite domestic defence–industrial consolidation and participation in international collaborative ventures, British policy-makers throughout the 1960s and 1970s witnessed major unit cost increases in major weapon platforms. After 1979, the Conservative government's aim was 'to flatten or even reverse the established curve which shows the trend towards increasing equipment costs'.[45] The key driver for the new administration's reappraisal of defence procurement was financial: by the early 1980s, and despite the short-term savings measures outlined in the Nott Review, the perception in Whitehall was of a 'funding gap' between resources assigned to defence and Britain's stated military commitments. The government could have addressed the 'funding gap' by increasing the defence budget, reducing service personnel and salaries, or abandoning a major defence role. However, each of these options was deemed politically unacceptable.[46] Instead, the preferred solution was to bring procurement costs under stringent control.

The Conservative reforms intended to reduce procurement costs were to have important effects on government relations with major domestic equipment suppliers, the focus of international weapon partnerships and UK arms exports policy.

After 1979, the government's analysis was that by privatising defence contractors under public ownership, introducing greater competition for defence contracts and making 'value for money' the guiding principle in the procurement process, then military goals could still be achieved but within a tighter defence budget.[47] Set against the 'value for money' imperative, the procurement arrangements the Conservatives inherited appeared to offer considerable scope for economies: major defence contractors under public ownership, extensive use of 'cost-plus' contracts with little risk to industry, and overt protectionism in the form of 'buy-British' policies were all equated with financial waste and poor 'value for money'.[48] Instead, the Conservative analysis was that privatisation, the introduction of market forces and a shift in the risk of weapon development away from government to industry would generate major economies from the procurement budget.[49]

Reinforced by the government's 'overall faith in private enterprise',[50] state-owned enterprises including British Aerospace, the Royal Dockyards, the naval shipyards of British Shipbuilders, the Royal Ordnance Factories and Rolls-Royce were privatised on the assumption that this would bring more efficient management.[51] By the mid-1980s Defence Secretary Michael Heseltine sought to introduce a systematic competition policy which was developed by the Chief of Defence Procurement, Sir Peter Levene.[52] Under the so-called 'Levene Reforms' it became axiomatic that a greater proportion of MoD contracts would be awarded competitively. Measures were introduced to generate rivalry between UK suppliers and encourage overseas bids for MoD contracts. Competitive bidding was also extended to all stages of major projects from concept, feasibility and project definition to full development. Finally, increased pressure was exerted on major suppliers to demonstrate the use of competition in their dealings with subcontractors.

Other elements of the Levene Reforms included measures to transfer the risk of project failure from the MoD to its suppliers and in return, reward efficiency in industry through higher profits. Measures here included a shift away from cost-plus forms of contracting towards the use of firm or fixed price contracts and the adoption of the 'prime contractor' approach, whereby a single firm acted as a prime contractor with responsibility for managing an entire project and organising its subcontractors. Finally, the MoD was required to adopt 'Cardinal Points Specifications', whereby equipment requirements were expressed in terms of key performance criteria and industry was left to decide how best to meet them. Taken collectively, the ethos of the 'Levene Reforms' was that 'defence procurement was to become more like other kinds of purchasing of goods and services'.[53]

In parallel with domestic procurement reform, Conservative administrations reviewed the form and nature of Britain's international procurement partnerships. Between 1979 and 1989, *de facto* policy was to continue the 'twin-track' strategy of balancing procurement cooperation with the US and the European NATO states. Important tensions did emerge, however, over the extent to which Britain should pursue an overtly European focus in defence–industrial matters. This issue came to a head in the 'Westland affair' of 1985.[54] In question was the future of Westland, Britain's sole helicopter manufacturer which was encountering financial difficulties. In essence, debates over

Westland's future reflected a basic policy choice. Government could have intervened to encourage Westland's absorption by a consortium of European helicopter manufacturers, thereby encouraging the build-up of a European industrial pillar in the helicopter sector. In the event, and in line with its broader hands-off approach to defence–industrial restructuring, the government avoided direct intervention and allowed Westland to be taken-over by UTC, a major American manufacturer. The Westland affair highlighted a more general reluctance among British policy-makers to foster an overtly European defence–industrial focus, and a preference instead for pragmatic transatlantic and intra-European partnerships on a case-by-case basis.[55]

After the Cold War, pressures for Britain and its western European partners to rationalise and integrate procurement policies became more acute. On the demand side, changing threat perceptions were reflected in reduced procurement budgets at a time when equipment unit costs were rising in real terms at approximately 10 per cent per annum. On the supply side, reduced equipment orders became instrumental in west European defence–industrial restructuring, reflected in a gradual breakdown of national ownership patterns and an increase in intra-European transnational consortia.[56] After 1989, these trends, coupled with the domestic consolidation of American defence firms, created pressures for Britain to pursue closer European integration in defence–industrial and procurement policies.

At the same time, there were post-Cold War incentives for Britain to enhance its transatlantic defence–industrial linkages. These stemmed from the so-called 'Revolution in Military Affairs' (RMA), or the marriage of systems that collect, process and communicate information with those that apply military force. As Freedman points out, the extent to which the RMA was underway after the Cold War was 'rather particular. Only the United States ha[d] the economic resources and the military infrastructure to begin to follow this path.'[57] In terms of the enabling technologies of the RMA – precision guided munitions, stealth weapons, sensors and defence suppression techniques – US defence industries were acquiring a clear development and manufacturing edge over their counterparts in western Europe. In the face of US technological leadership in key weapon sectors, incentives were created, and remain, for Britain to access this know-how through technology transfers from America.

Confronted with these trends, British procurement policy under the Conservative administrations of the 1990s was characterised by a remarkable degree of continuity. Britain worked with its partners to foster the gradual process of European defence industrial restructuring.[58] In parallel, governments continued to develop collaborative links with the US to meet equipment requirements that were either too costly or beyond the technological capability of European industries. In the case of direct equipment purchases from the US, the trend has been for Britain to seek 'offsets', or domestic industrial compensation and benefits. For example, the UK government contract for $1,150 million placed with Boeing for the AWACS system was accompanied with an agreement by the American supplier to invest similar funds in British industry to offset the industrial impact of the overseas purchase.[59]

A final strand of post-1979 procurement policy related to UK arms exports. Underpinning the Levene Reforms was the expectation that efficiency improvements in domestic industry would translate into a growth in British arms sales. Throughout the Cold War, the UK had been the world's fourth-ranking exporter (by sales value), behind the US, USSR and France.[60] Until the mid-1970s, Britain was the third-ranking supplier to the Third World behind the US and USSR, a position overtaken subsequently by France and briefly by Italy in the mid-1980s. However, after the late-1980s, the combination of major arms transfer agreements with Middle Eastern countries and aggressive government-led export strategies enabled the UK market share in developing states to increase steadily. As a consequence, the UK emerged as the third-ranking exporter of major conventional weapons after the Cold War.[61]

The aggressive arms export policies pursued during the Conservative administrations had two main drivers.[62] First, in economic terms, governments saw exports as a way of offsetting inflationary trends in domestic R&D and production. The assumption was that because exports increased domestic manufacturing runs beyond what they otherwise would have been, then UK procurement costs would reduce as the fixed R&D costs of weapons development were spread over a larger production output. In addition, longer domestic production runs to meet export orders were seen as a source of economies of scale and 'learning economies'. A further expectation was that defence exports could 'help to smooth production rates, keep production lines open and companies in business in times of low domestic demand'.[63] Finally, exports were expected to help ensure the economic viability of UK contractors which, in turn, would preserve domestic competition and maintain the scope of the defence industrial base.

Second, in politico-military terms, decision-makers assumed that arms transfers could enhance Britain's influence and leverage over the domestic and foreign policies of importing states.[64] For example, major arms sales were viewed as mechanisms to promote democracy in recipient countries, as an indirect means to deter aggression against UK allies and a means to enhance regional stability. In essence, therefore, weapons exports were equated with maintaining linkages with strategically important allies as well as promoting wider British interests.

The 1980s and 1990s witnessed a series of government-led export promotion strategies. The Defence Export Services Organisation (DESO), originally established in 1966, was tasked to provide extensive support to industry in the marketing of defence products. Governments also subsidised arms transfers in the form of 'export credits' which were designed to shift the financial risk from exporting companies to the British government through the extension of credit lines to overseas customers. Finally, government fostered the offset of export sales against trade commitments backed or undertaken by national governments. Saudi Arabia, for example, a country with very little manufacturing capability, was awarded UK offsets to abate the sales price of major weapons imports by some 35 per cent.[65]

Taken collectively, procurement policies under the Conservative administrations of the 1980s and 1990s were intended to ameliorate budgetary pressures and inflationary trends in major weapon platforms. However, the practical implications of Conservative policies remain controversial. A major area of contention is the impact of the Levene Reforms. Official reports have presented competition policy as 'a very effective way of improving value for money'.[66] In 1988, for example, the MoD informed the House of Commons Defence Committee that six equipment projects valued at £2,000 million that were exposed to competition policy yielded savings of £250 million.[67] Subsequent reports claimed the reforms had reduced the overall costs of defence procurement by over £1 billion per annum throughout the early 1990s.[68] Moreover, scrutinies maintained that competition had increased the efficiency of UK defence contractors which had, in turn, enhanced industry's export competitiveness. Illustrative is former Minister of State for Defence Procurement Jonathan Aitken's assertion that UK defence firms 'themselves would admit that their competitiveness in . . . international markets owe[d] a great deal to the competitive procurement policies . . . [adopted during] the mid-1980s'.[69]

Conversely, the Levene Reforms have been criticised in a number of respects. First, commentators have argued that the purported cost savings reflected MoD tactics of reducing equipment unit orders, delays in ordering, or stretching programmes in the face of declining post-Cold War procurement budgets.[70] Second, evidence suggests that MoD changes to equipment requirements and specifications undermined the discipline of competition and fixed price contracting on various programmes.[71] Third, concerns have been raised about the high costs of competition for industry, and whether contractors shifted these costs to the MoD in the form of overheads.[72] Fourth, some analysts have called into question the Conservative administrations' commitment to international competition for major UK defence contracts. Schofield, for example, claims that 'in some areas there [was] an unstated policy of preferred suppliers':[73] where national monopolies existed, some MoD contracts were let without reference to non-national suppliers, and where international tendering was adopted British firms maintained an unblemished record of winning major orders. Finally, critics point out that the reforms had only a marginal impact on rates of inflation on major defence projects. Kirkpatrick, for example, argues that the savings from Conservative procurement reform were limited and 'offset only a small fraction of the observed unit-cost growth between successive defence equipment'.[74] This observation is reinforced by the 1997 National Audit Office report on major defence programmes which found evidence of cost overruns on 24 of the top 25 projects (by value), and delays in 20 of the 25 projects.[75]

A second area of controversy has been UK arms exports policy. Despite government expectations of economic and political benefits, critics have challenged the efficacy of British arms exports on a number of levels. Concern has emerged about the financial implications of UK arms transfers. Some critics have argued that British government export subsidies including, *inter alia*, export promotion policies and offsets, have outweighed sales revenues.[76] Others claim that reliance on arms exports to offset the costs of domestic procurement has been costly and inefficient when compared with other procurement alternatives. In terms of the purported politico-military benefits of weapon sales, critics have argued that arms transfers to regions of tension have increased, rather than decreased, political instability[77] and point out that some major importers have become Britain's adversaries. For example, the UK government supplied arms to the Shah of Iran, only for the Ayatollah to turn against the West after the Iranian Revolution. Similarly, as the Scott Report highlighted, after UK companies aided the development of Iraq's military capabilities British forces faced domestically-produced equipment during Operation Desert Storm.[78] Rather than supporting the emergence of democratic regimes, Britain has also been accused of exporting military equipment to states with questionable human rights records.[79] Finally, the claim that arms exports have increased British influence and leverage has been challenged on the grounds that importers have been 'able to choose from a number of arms suppliers, freeing them away from dependence on a single arms supplier'.[80]

The Conservative administrations after 1979 adopted policies designed to balance equipment budgets and military requirements. Evidence suggests that these policies enhanced the efficiency and competitiveness of UK defence firms, achieved a desirable balance in international equipment cooperation and exploited the potential of arms exports. However, the critiques of Conservative policies that emerged during the mid-1990s set a new agenda for procurement reform under the Blair administration.

The post-Strategic Defence Review era

In response to perceived limitations in the Levene Reforms the Blair government undertook a major review of procurement policy in 1998. The 'Smart Procurement' initiative that emerged stemmed in part from a perception that Conservative competition policies failed to achieve the savings they promised, but also a desire to build on the fact that 'during the last years of Conservative rule, [government had recognised] the value of moving to a closer relationship with industry in general and defence industry in particular'.[81] A central tenet of 'Smart Procurement' is a rejection of the confrontational approach in relations between government and industry, reflected in recent moves towards long-term cooperative relationships and overt acceptance that domestic defence contractors are legitimate 'stakeholders' in the acquisition process. Through partnering and other initiatives subsumed under the banner of procurement reform, the 1998 Strategic Defence Review assumed £2 billion savings from the UK equipment programme over the subsequent ten-year period.

The detailed impact of 'Smart Procurement' on defence acquisition costs is unlikely to emerge for some time. As Codner points out, 'the Defence Programme in the past has usually erred on the side of optimism. Indeed, it is the cost aspect of the [Strategic Defence] Review that has been the only real source of criticism by analysts and commentators.'[82] For the analysts of contemporary procurement policy, the question remains whether 'Smart Procurement' provides the management tools to achieve these economies.

The Blair government has also signalled Britain's continued commitment to the 'twin-track' approach of procurement cooperation with Europe and the US. The government has stated that collaborative procurement will account for approximately 40 per cent of future UK equipment expenditure.[83] To foster European defence–industrial rationalisation, Britain has become a member of the Organisme Conjointe de Co-operation en matière d'Armament (OCCAR) – a quadrilateral armaments structure with France, Germany and Italy – which intends to 'improve collaborative practices' and deliver European defence systems 'able to compete effectively in world markets'.[84] At the same time, the Blair government has pursued closer transatlantic procurement links, illustrated by preliminary cooperation on an Anglo-US replacement for the Harrier aircraft in the form of the Joint Strike Fighter project.[85]

Since the 1960s, the UK's 'twin-track' approach to international procurement cooperation has been pragmatic. However, future governments will continue to face difficult policy choices as the unit costs of sophisticated defence platforms keep rising. Pressures are likely to continue for UK policy-makers to decide explicitly between systematic European defence industrial integration on the one hand, and forms of transatlantic equipment cooperation on the other. For procurement analysts, these scenarios raise important research issues. There is the need to address the potential economic and political benefits and costs of different models of European defence integration.[86] Correspondingly, in the context of RMA debates, there are major questions about the extent to which US administrations will allow genuine technology transfer to Britain and other NATO states.[87]

In addition, the Blair government is attempting to balance the economic imperative to export arms with measures to control the dangers of conventional weapon proliferation as part of its ethical dimension to foreign policy. On the one hand, declining defence procurement budgets and the growing costs of domestic R&D and production continue to provide an imperative for aggressive arms export policies. On the other hand, government has recognised the need for national restraint in arms transfers, prompted in part by Britain's military operations against states deploying weapons originally exported by the UK. Notable British initiatives to encourage multilateral arms transfer restraints include proposals forming the basis for the 1998 European Union Code of Conduct on Arms Exports, which outlined broad moral and political considerations to which national arms licensing authorities should have regard.

For analysts of arms transfer policy, Britain's attempt to reconcile the drivers for arms exports with an ethical foreign policy dimension raises ongoing issues. First, there is scope for a comprehensive assessment of the real contribution of arms exports to the domestic defence manufacturing sector and the UK economy as a whole. Second, there are questions about the approach that Britain should adopt in future conventional arms control negotiations, and the implications of such negotiations for UK industry. Finally, important questions remain about what an 'ethical dimension' to foreign policy will really mean in practical terms. At issue here will be the efficacy of government policy in reconciling the economic imperative to export arms with a stated desire to control the flow of defence technology, *inter alia*, to undemocratic regimes.

Conclusion

Since 1945, British governments have faced an ongoing structural constraint: defence equipment budgets have failed to keep pace with the dramatic increase in the unit costs of major defence platforms. The net effect of this constraint has been a relative decline in the scale and scope of defence–industrial activity as Britain has adjusted from 'first' division weapons producer status to a 'leader of the second division'. However, this adjustment has not simply been a mechanistic response to structural pressures. Instead, successive administrations have attempted to 'manage' Britain's relative decline by striving to reconcile a range of difficult choices. The way in which policy-makers have attempted to reconcile these choices represents, in shorthand, the 'British way' in postwar defence procurement policy.

This chapter shows that the 'British way' has comprised a number of discrete themes. One theme concerns the degree of consensus and controversy in debates over the content and direction of defence procurement and industrial policies. Confronted with the structural constraint of rising equipment costs, a postwar consensus emerged on three issues: the premise that British governments should intervene to maintain a broad domestic defence–industrial capability; acceptance that Britain should offset the costs and risk of domestic weapon development through international equipment partnerships; and broad agreement among policy-makers on the economic and political desirability of UK arms exports. Where controversy has emerged it has been over how best to meet these goals. At issue here has been the optimum size and scope of the UK defence industrial base, the appropriate balance between national and non-national sourcing, the form that international procurement partnerships should take, and the precise criteria for arms exports policy.

A second theme in the 'British way' has been the adoption by governments of grand procurement reforms which they perceived would 'solve' the structural problem of equipment affordability. The policy reappraisal in the early 1960s, which led to the emergence of big firms and the growth in international collaborative ventures, was viewed as an overarching solution to offset trends in equipment costs. Again, during the 1970s and 1980s, the Conservative procurement reforms were presented as a panacea for spiralling equipment costs. In many respects, the economies envisaged by the Blair government from the 'Smart Procurement' initiative mark the latest in a series of panaceas to ameliorate the affordability problem.

A third theme has been the gradual blurring of the dichotomy between the 'domestic' and the 'international' as it relates to defence–industrial activity. During the 1940s and 1950s, policies of national 'self-sufficiency' were contrasted sharply with reliance on non-national defence technology. Since the 1960s, however, distinctions between domestic and international have become less clear as Britain has become an active participant in international equipment ventures and defence industries have rationalised on a pan-European basis. The consequence of this trend has been an iterative redefinition by governments of what constitutes an essential minimum 'national' defence–industrial capability and a gradual acceptance of the economic necessity for 'internationalised' solutions to meet the UK's defence needs.

History suggests that defence equipment costs will continue to increase at a higher rate than procurement budgets. Given this structural constraint, the central challenge for future British governments is likely to reflect those of their postwar predecessors: how to manage defence procurement and industrial policies in the face of relative national decline. A central issue for policy analysts will be to identify areas of continuity and change as governments address this complex and perennial issue.

Notes

1. K. Hartley, *The Economics of Defence Policy*, London: Brassey's, 1991, p. 75.
2. See, for example, J. P. Dunne and R. P. Smith, 'The Economic Consequences of Reduced UK Military Expenditure', *Cambridge Journal of Economics*, 8 (3) 1984, pp. 297–310; Council for Science and Society, *UK Military R&D*, Oxford: Oxford University Press, 1986; and, P. Gummett, 'Britain's Military Research and Development', *Defense Analysis*, 2 (2) 1986, pp. 158–9.
3. See, for example, M. Chalmers, *Paying for Defence*, London: Pluto Press, 1985; and, R. P. Smith, 'Military Expenditure and Investment in OECD Countries, 1954–1973', *Journal of Comparative Economics*, 4 (1) 1980, pp. 19–32.
4. P. Gummett, 'Problems for UK Military R&D', in I. Bellany and T. Huxley (eds), *New Conventional Weapons and Western Defence*, London: Frank Cass, 1987, p. 49.

5. See, for example, D. L. I. Kirkpatrick and P. G. Pugh, *Towards Starship Enterprise – are Current Trends in Defence Unit Costs Inexorable?*, London: Aerospace, 1983.

6. D. Kirkpatrick, 'Rising Costs, Falling Budgets and their Implications for Defence Policy', *Economic Affairs*, 17 (4) 1997, p. 11.

7. Ibid., p. 10.

8. M. Edmonds, 'International Military Equipment Procurement Partnerships: The Basic Issues', in M. Edmonds (ed.), *International Arms Procurement: New Directions*, Oxford: Pergamon, 1981, p. 5.

9. R. Head, 'The Weapons Acquisition Process: Alternative National Strategies', in F. B. Horton, A. C. Rogerson and E. L. Warner (eds), *Comparative Defense Policy*, London: Johns Hopkins University Press, 1974, p. 414.

10. See J. Lovering, 'Restructuring the British Defence Industrial Base after the Cold War: Institutional and Geographical Perspectives', *Defence Economics*, 4 (2) 1993, pp. 123–39.

11. See D. Wood, *Project Cancelled: The Disaster of Britain's Abandoned Aircraft Projects*, London: Tri-Service Press, 1990, p. 16.

12. For more details, see E. Devons, 'The Aircraft Industry', in D. Burns (ed.), *The Structure of British Industry*, Volume II, Cambridge: Cambridge University Press, 1964, pp. 45–92.

13. See T. Geiger, '"The Next War is Bound to Come": Defence Production Policy, Supply Departments and Defence Contractors in Britain, 1945–57', in H. Mercer, N. Rollings and J. D. Tomlinson (eds), *The Labour Governments and Private Industry: The Experience of 1945 to 1951*, Edinburgh: Edinburgh University Press, 1992, pp. 95–118.

14. P. Gummett, 'Civil and Military Aircraft in the UK', in J. Krige (ed.), *Choosing Big Technologies*, Reading: Harwood, 1993, p. 206.

15. Second Report from the Select Committee on Estimates, *The Supply of Military Aircraft*, HCP 34, Session 1956–57, London: HMSO, 1956, p. ix.

16. See, for example, M. J. Lighthill, 'The Royal Aircraft Establishment', in J. Cockcroft (ed.), *The Organisation of Research Establishments*, Cambridge: Cambridge University Press, 1965, pp. 28–54.

17. For a detailed discussion on the assumptions underpinning 'parallel development', see R. R. Nelson, *The Economics of Parallel R&D Efforts: A Sequential-Decision Analysis*, Santa Monica: RAND, 1959; and C. J. Hitch and R. N. McKean, *The Economics of Defence in the Nuclear Age*, Cambridge, MA: Harvard University Press, 1960, pp. 249–50.

18. Head, op. cit., p. 413.

19. For an extended discussion, see T. Sandler and K. Hartley, *The Economics of Defense*, Cambridge: Cambridge University Press, 1995, pp. 185–7.

20. For an extended discussion, see J. Molas-Gallart, *Military Production and Innovation in Spain*, Reading: Harwood, 1992, pp. 7–40.

21. F. Gregory and J. Simpson, 'The Acquisition of Military Aircraft in Great Britain and West Germany', in F. B. Horton, A. C. Rogerson and E. L. Warner (eds), *Comparative Defense Policy*, London: Johns Hopkins University Press, 1974, p. 459.

22. Edmonds, op. cit., p. 6.

23. These concerns reflected the findings of the Second Report from the Select Committee on Estimates, *The Supply of Military Aircraft*, HCP 34, Session 1956–57, London: HMSO, 1956. The trend is documented statistically by Worcester. Between 1945 and 1965 some 196 manned aircraft projects were undertaken in the UK, of which ten types were ultimately produced in quantities of 500 or more. See R. Worcester, *The Roots of British Air Policy*, London: Hodder & Stoughton, 1966, p. 9.

24. Second Report from the Select Committee on Estimates, *The Supply of Military Aircraft*, HCP 34, Session 1956–57, London: HMSO, p. xvi.

25. K. Hartley, 'The Mergers of the UK Aircraft Industry, 1957–60', *Journal of the Royal Aeronautical Society*, December 1965, p. 864.

26. *Defence – Outline of Future Policy*, Cmnd. 124, London: HMSO, 1957.

27. For a general discussion of the problems the UK confronted, see A. J. Alexander and J. R. Nelson, *Measuring Technological Change: Aircraft Turbine Engines*, Santa Monica: RAND Corporation, 1972.

28. *Report of the Committee of Inquiry into the Aircraft Industry*, Cmnd. 2853, London: HMSO, 1965.

29. See K. Hartley, 'The Learning Curve and its Application to the Aircraft Industry', *Journal of Industrial Economics*, 13 (2) March 1965, pp. 122–8.

30. For a wider discussion of these assumptions, see G. C. Allen, *British Industries and their Organisation*, London: Longman, 1970, p. 186.

31. T. Taylor and K. Hayward, *The Defence Industrial Base: Development and Future Policy Options*, London: Brassey's, 1989, p. 100.

32. See D. Egerton, *England and the Aeroplane: An Essay on a Militant and Technological Nation*, London: Macmillan, 1991, pp. 95–100.

33. See A. Reed, *Britain's Aircraft Industry: What Went Right? What Went Wrong?*, London: J.M. Dent, 1973.

34. For a general discussion of this contracting mechanism, see C. C. Turpin, *Government Procurement and Contracting*, Harmondsworth: Penguin, 1972.

35. For a general discussion, see G. M. Dillon, *Dependence and Deterrence: Success and Civility in the Anglo-American Special Nuclear Relationship, 1962–82*, Aldershot: Gower, 1983.

36. For a discussion of UK postwar licensed production in the helicopter sector, see M. R. H. Uttley, 'British Helicopter Developments, 1945–1960: A Case Study of Technology Transfer and Market Dominance', *Science and Public Policy*, 18 (4) August 1991, pp. 235–43.

37. For a wider discussion of the UK's assumptions in entering collaborative procurement, see A. G. Draper, *European Defence Equipment Collaboration: Britain's Involvement, 1957–87*, London: RUSI, 1990; and, R. Matthews, *European Armaments Collaboration: Policy, Problems and Prospects*, Reading: Harwood, 1992.

38. Matthews, op. cit.

39. Cited in C. Cannizzo, 'Procurement Via the Two-Way Street: Can it Achieve its Objectives?', in M. Edmonds (ed.), *International Arms Procurement: New Directions*, Oxford: Pergamon, 1981, p. 59.

40. See, for example, S. Shaffer, 'Linking Arms: Weapons Cooperation in NATO', in M. Edmonds (ed.), *International Arms Procurement: New Directions*, Oxford: Pergamon, 1981, pp. 24–52.

41. See, for example, K. Hartley, 'Development Time Scales for British and American Military Aircraft', *Scottish Journal of Political Economy*, 19 (2) June 1972, pp. 115–34.

42. See K. Hartley, *NATO Arms Co-operation: A Study in Economics and Politics*, London: Allen & Unwin, 1983.

43. P. Gummett, 'Problems for UK Military R&D', op. cit., p. 49.

44. See: House of Commons Defence Committee, *The Procurement of Major Defence Equipment 5th Report*, Session 1987–88, HCP 431, London: HMSO, 1988; and the collection of articles in T. Francis (ed.), *Managing the Costs of Defence: Proceedings of a Foundation Seminar*, London: Public Finance Foundation, 1986.

45. Taylor and Hayward, op. cit., p. 73.

46. Ibid.

47. W. Walker and P. Gummett, 'Britain and the European Armaments Market', in *International Affairs*, 65 (3), 1989, p. 421.

48. J. Bourn, *Securing Value for Money in Defence Procurement*, Whitehall Paper No. 25, London: RUSI, 1994.

49. For a general discussion of these assumptions, see Taylor and Hayward, op. cit., pp. 70–89.

50. Ibid., p. 74.

51. See: M. J. Rawlinson, 'Government Defence Factories and Dockyards: the Defence Implications of Privatization', *Defence Force*, January/February 1989, pp. 27–35; and, House of Commons Defence Committee, First Report from the Defence Committee Session 1985–1986, *Further Observations on the Future of the Royal Dockyards*, HMSO: London, 1985.

52. See P. Levene, 'Competition and Collaboration: UK Defence Procurement Policy', *RUSI Journal*, 132 (2) 1987, pp. 3–6.

53. Gummett, 'Civil and Military Aircraft in the UK', op. cit., p. 214.

54. For a more detailed discussion, see L. Freedman, 'The Case of Westland and the Bias to Europe', *International Affairs*, 63 (1), pp. 1–19; and, Stuart Croft, 'The Westland Helicopter Crisis: Implications for the British Defence Industry', *Defense Analysis*, 3 (4) 1987, pp. 291–303.

55. See P. Levene, 'Maintaining the Two Way Street: UK/US Defence Procurement', *NATO's Sixteen Nations*, October 1989, pp. 77–80.

56. See, for example, W. Walker and S. Willett, 'Restructuring the European Defence Industrial Base', *Defence Economics*, 4 (1) 1993, pp. 141–60.

57. L. Freedman, 'The Revolution in Strategic Affairs', *Adelphi Paper 318*, Oxford: Oxford University Press, 1998, p. 56.

58. See M. R. H. Uttley, 'The Integration of West European Defence Procurement: Issues and Prospects', *Defense Analysis*, 11 (3) 1995, pp. 279–91; P. De Vestel, 'Defence Markets and Industries in Europe: Time for Political Decisions', *Chaillot Paper 21*, Paris: WEU, 1995; and, RUSI Working Group, '1992: Protectionism or Collaboration in Defence Procurement', *Whitehall Paper No. 6*, London: RUSI, 1990.

59. For a detailed discussion of UK offsets policy, see S. Martin and K. Hartley, 'The UK Experience with Offsets', in S. Martin (ed.), *The Economics of Offsets: Defence Procurement and Countertrade*, Reading: Harwood, 1996, pp. 337–55.

60. See C. Catrina, *Arms Transfers and Dependence*, London: Taylor & Francis, 1988, p. 48.

61. Stockholm International Peace Research Institute, *SIPRI Yearbook 1998*, Oxford: Oxford University Press, 1998, p. 294.

62. For an extended discussion and a summary of the literature, see Catrina, op. cit., pp. 70–3.

63. Ibid., p. 71.

64. See House of Commons Committee of Public Accounts, *Support for Defence Exports: Minutes of Evidence*, Wednesday 26 April 1989, London: HMSO, 1989.

65. See A. M. Al-Ghrair and N. Hooper, 'Saudi Arabia and Offsets', in S. Martin (ed.), *The Economics of Offsets: Defence Procurement and Countertrade*, Reading: Harwood, 1996, pp. 219–44.

66. Bourn, op. cit., p. 22.

67. House of Commons Defence Committee, *The Procurement of Major Defence Equipment, 5th Report*, Session 1987–88, HCP 431, London: HMSO, 1988.

68. National Audit Office, *Ministry of Defence: Defence Procurement in the 1990s*, HCP 390, London: HMSO, 1994.

69. J. Aitken, 'Defence Procurement: Past, Present and Future', *RUSI Journal*, 139 (1) 1994, p. 41.

70. S. Schofield, 'The Levene Reforms: An Evaluation', *Defense Analysis*, 11 (2) 1995, p. 163.

71. For a discussion, see K. Hartley, 'Defence Procurement in the UK', *Defence and Peace Economics*, 9 (1–2), 1998, pp. 54–5.

72. Ibid., p. 51.

73. Schofield, op. cit., p. 160.

74. Kirkpatrick, op. cit., p. 11.

75. Ministry of Defence *Major Projects Report 1996*, Report by the Comptroller and Auditor General, London: HMSO, HC 238, 15 August 1997, pp. 2–4.

76. See S. Martin, 'The Subsidy Savings from Reducing UK Arms Exports', *Journal of Economic Studies*, 26 (1), 1999, pp. 15–37.

77. See, for example, P. Eavis and O. Sprague, 'Does Britain Need to Sell Weapons?', in J. Gittings and I. Davis (eds), *Britain in the 21st Century: Re-Thinking Defence and Foreign Policy*, Nottingham: Spokesman, 1996, p. 128.

78. See: D. Miller, 'The Scott Report and the Future of British Defense Sales', *Defense Analysis*, 12 (3) 1996, pp. 359–69; and, D. Miller, *Export or Die: Britain's Defence Trade with Iraq*, London: Cassell, 1996.

79. Eavis and Sprague, op. cit.

80. Ibid., p. 129.

81. T. Taylor, 'Smart Procurement and Partnership with Industry', *RUSI Journal*, 143 (2) 1998, p. 41.

82. M. Codner, 'Policy topped but Treasury tailed? The Strategic Defence Review', *The Officer*, July/August 1998, p. 33.

83. Taylor, op. cit., p. 45.

84. *Strategic Defence Review*, p. 10-9.

85. See J. Elliott, 'JSF for Everybody? The JSF Programme and its International Implications', *Military Technology*, 22 (3) 1988, pp. 20–9.
86. See Uttley, 1995, op. cit.
87. See M. R. H. Uttley, 'Licensed Production and the RMA: The Scope and Limitations for the United Kingdom', in R. Matthews (ed.), *Managing the RMA*, Reading: Harwood, 2001 (forthcoming).

Conclusion

Stuart Croft and Wyn Rees

One of the purposes of this volume has been not only to illustrate the broad and broadening nature of British defence policy and policy-making over more than a fifty-year period, but also to focus on its ideational element. British defence policy over the latter half of the twentieth century is traditionally portrayed as a dependent variable; that is, it has been fundamentally conditioned by the material reality of a declining economic base. This declinist argument is not being refuted here. The authors are not trying to suggest that economic decline did not take place nor that decline did not play a fundamental part in the British defence condition. However, we are arguing that traditional declinism, with all of its positivist elements as just set out, is insufficient to understand the nature of British defence policy. A deeper understanding demands an appreciation that defence policy has been the product as much of ideas as it has of material decline. To do otherwise would be to accept a deterministic explanation. It would deny the influence that a strategic community within the UK has been able to impress on the conduct of policy-making. This community has comprised governments of various political hues, influential ministers of defence – such as Duncan Sandys and Denis Healey – civil servants, academics, journalists and senior representatives of the three armed services.

The Introduction to this book set out five elements that would shape the volume. It was suggested that the role of epistemology was crucial, and that the book would focus upon change. These two elements are of course interrelated. The view that British defence policy, as with all other areas of public policy, has been about managing decline in circumstances of objective reduction in the material base is too simplistic. We have not sought to argue that by the sheer force of political will it would have been possible for the decline in the material base to be reversed. Even the Thatcher administration was forced to make choices in its military priorities, despite its avowed commitment to a strong defence. The problem of defence resources has been a real one as costs have escalated and as relatively modest economic growth rates have struggled to keep pace with the rising price of military equipment.

Instead, it is important to provide a more balanced perspective to that of the narrow declinist thesis. This requires an acknowledgement of the interrelationship between material circumstance and the way it is interpreted. Successive postwar governments were aware of the pressure on resources and the need to balance commitments and capabilities. Yet changes in policy occurred at specific moments because of the impact of changing ideas and because orthodoxies did not remain constant. The decision to withdraw from East of Suez, for example, could have been justified on financial grounds many years earlier but the political climate in which such a decision could be taken was insufficiently mature until the end of the 1960s.

Material decline after all, has been relative rather than absolute. By any measurement, the United Kingdom and its population is much richer in 2000 than it was in 1945 when wartime rationing was still in operation. And in narrowly military terms, although Britain's armed forces may be much smaller in scale in 2000 compared with 1945 – indeed, in 2000 it may have fewer people under arms than in 1780 – nevertheless the potency of the contemporary force outweighs its predecessors by incalculable degrees.[1] The range, speed and lethality of British weapon systems are now many times that of their predecessors. One only needs to look at weapons platforms such as the Trident submarine, the Type 23 frigate, the Challenger II tank or the Tornado multi-role combat aircraft to appreciate this.

The themes of declining resources versus the power of ideas have run throughout the chapters of this book. When examining crises, it was argued that Britain's defence reviews was as much about apportioning resources within government budgets as it was about objective notions of decline. For example, the 1957 Sandys Review believed that technological advances would enable Britain to fulfil the same commitments but through different means. The 1981 Nott Review was concerned with reordering spending priorities yet preserved the same defence roles. In the chapter on Britain's global role, it was suggested that the UK's sense of its unique contribution to international order was a key element in its policies, irrespective of resource constraints. Although the broad outlines of policy were accepted by Labour and Conservative governments, there were differences over how interests were interpreted. While in opposition both parties decried the policies of the incumbent administration, but modified them only slightly when they were returned to office.

Britain's commitment to European security has similarly been explicable as a combination of notions of objective threat (above all, a military threat during the Cold War), and the means with which these threats have been interpreted and reinterpreted. For example, Serb action in Bosnia was not seen to be the same threat to Europe as Serb military activity in Kosovo. Europe grew over the years into the foremost military commitment of the UK and, since the end of the Cold War, it has remained the preoccupation of those responsible for the state's security. In the nuclear sphere, again the impact of ideas regarding the role, nature and usability of the British deterrent are central to understanding the impact of the military hardware. Here there was an influential alternative school of thought that challenged the orthodoxy of the strategic elite. The chapter examining the organisation of British defence stressed the diversity of approaches in the quest for management solutions to Britain's defence needs, and that this has been central to the way in which the conduct of defence must be understood.

The third theme in the Introduction was that notions of structure and agency had to be reassessed if the view of an objective decline in Britain's defence policy was refuted. This is not to say that structural pressures were unimportant in framing British defence decisions; nor that Britain had free reign in determining policy. The key here is that structure and agency have been mutually constituted and, as such, cannot be separated. Cold War structures may have been in part external to the UK, but they framed the nature of defence thinking for decades. Conversely, the way in which the British government perceived its obligations was vital in the way it constructed its policies. For instance, military commitments were retained to many former colonies after independence was formally granted, even in cases where the material resources to carry them out were lacking. This was because the UK believed it had a special obligation to uphold international order. These same attitudes account for the unilateral actions of the UK in intervening in crises such as Kuwait, and with Indonesia in the 1960s, in an effort to resist territorial aggression by regional powers.

A fourth theme in the Introduction was that the traditional dichotomy between the international and the domestic spheres, in relation to explaining defence policy, was simply inadequate. As the chapters on the politics of defence and the organisation of defence indicated, external and internal factors have been closely intertwined. In procurement policy, governments have been influenced on the one hand by external demands; such as the desire to sell arms to valued allies and the choice between cooperation on developmental and manufacturing projects with either the United States or Europe. On the other hand, domestic considerations have also been integral to defence decision-making; such as employment pressures within the UK, the need to support the defence–industrial base and the potential to influence voting behaviour in marginal constituencies. In regards to the orientation of national defence policy, Britain has found itself influenced by the process of decolonisation in its former dependent territories and by progress in European economic and political integration which encouraged a reassessment of priorities.

Lastly, the Introduction suggested that there had been a change in the meaning of the term 'defence policy' over the course of the latter half of the twentieth century. Defence policy used to be made not by the Ministry of Defence, a relatively new name, but by the Ministry of War. The linguistic shift from 'war' to 'defence' was important. It implied that whereas there used to be benefits to offensive military operations (notably in acquiring the Empire, if that could be termed 'beneficial') those days were over as the Cold War implications of nuclear weaponry began to be integrated into thinking. But by the end of the Cold War, defence itself began to be seen to have been practised in too limited a fashion. Whereas military forces were once involved in conquering territory and unwilling peoples, and then had become to be seen as some sort of shield against malevolent violence, military force began to be seen to have a role in protecting 'other' people.

The experience of the 1990s has shown that contemporary 'security' is a broad and multifaceted concept. It is now recognised that British forces must be ready to engage in operational tasks of greater diversity, ranging from the rescue of citizens from a civil conflict, such as Sierre Leone, through to peacemaking and high intensity military operations. The inclusion of defence diplomacy as an operational task and the recent focus on issues of human rights has helped to underpin this expanding agenda. The 1999 White Paper reflected these evolving attitudes within the Blair government and acknowledged that the purposes for which military forces were deployed was changing. It noted that the 1998 Strategic Defence Review had 'focused attention on the consequences of the break-up of states, and on ethnic and religious conflict, population and environmental pressures, competition for scarce resources, on the effects of illegal drugs, terrorism and crime. Nothing in the past two years has changed that assessment.'[2]

But of course, there are continuities in British defence policy across the period from 1945 to 2000. There is still concern that Britain cannot meet its defence obligations, that British forces are over-stretched and that the government is too eager to involve this country in the latest diplomatic crisis around the world. Defence expenditure in the UK by 2000 had fallen to 2.6 per cent of GDP per head and many argue that this level is inadequate to fund the demands of the future.[3] There remains the perennial concern of balancing Britain's commitment to Europe as well as to the United States. In opening the way for a defence capacity with the EU there is the attendant fear that the UK will be contributing towards the alienation of the US. With 20 per cent of Britain's civil servants in the Ministry of Defence's area by 2000, concerns over the appropriate management of defence remain. And Britain is still unsure of to what extent it should be pursuing autarky in defence procurement as compared with collaborative structures with either its transatlantic or European partners. Such issues as these appear to remain the constants of the British defence debate. They are addressed by an approach that is pragmatic and problem-solving in nature. The predisposition of British defence officials to seek panaceas to age-old problems, that preserve options and try to avoid making hard choices, seems to be alive and well.

In retrospect, does all of this add up to a characteristically British 'way of defence'? Probably yes, but only because of the historical circumstances in which Britain found itself. All decision-making units are the products of time and circumstance, and so produce their own 'way'. But that does not translate into 'unique'; nor necessarily into any form of model. That there is a British way perhaps tells us little more than that there is a unit labelled 'British defence' that is worthy of study.

Notes

1. G. Wheatcroft, 'Arms and the money', *The Guardian*, 19 May 2000.
2. Internet, http://www.mod.uk/policy/wp99/ch1.htm
3. D. Walker and R. Norton-Taylor, 'Missions: impossible', *The Guardian*, 16 May 2000.

Bibliography

Books/Journal Articles

Adler, E. (1997), 'Seizing the Middle Ground', *European Journal of International Relations*, 3 (3), pp. 319–63.

Airey, S. E. (1995), 'Does Russian Seapower Have a Future?', *RUSI Journal*, 140 (6), pp. 15–22.

Aitken, J. (1994), 'Defence Procurement: Past, Present and Future', *RUSI Journal*, 139 (1), pp. 39–42.

Alexander, A. J. and J. R. Nelson (1972), *Measuring Technological Change: Aircraft Turbine Engines*, Santa Monica: RAND Corporation.

Al-Ghrair, A. M. and N. Hooper (1996), 'Saudi Arabia and Offsets', in S. Martin (ed.), *The Economics of Offsets: Defence Procurement and Countertrade*, Reading: Harwood, pp. 219–44.

Allen, G. C. (1970), *British Industries and their Organisation*, London: Longman.

Ascher, K. (1987), *The Politics of Privatisation: Contracting Out Public Services*, London: Macmillan.

Bagehot (2000), 'Who Hoon Is. And Why He Matters', *The Economist*, 11 March, p. 45.

Banks, M. (1985), 'The Inter-Paradigm Debate', in M. Light and A. J. R. Groom (eds), *International Relations: A Handbook of Current Theory*, London: Pinter, pp. 7–26.

Barker, E. (1983), *The British Between the Superpowers, 1945–50*, London: Macmillan.

Barnes, H. and D. Buchan (1987), 'Danes Worried by UK Review of Defence Force's Role', *The Financial Times*, 22 January.

Barry, C. (1996), 'NATO's Combined Joint Task Forces in Theory and Practice', *Survival*, 38 (1), pp. 81–97.

Bartlett, C. J. (1972), *The Long Retreat: A Short History of British Defence Policy, 1945–70*, London: Macmillan.

Bartlett, C. J. (1977), *A History of Post-war Britain, 1945–74*, London: Longman.

Baylis, J. (1989), *British Defence Policy: Striking the Right Balance*, Basingstoke: Macmillan.

Baylis, J. (1995), *Ambiguity and Deterrence: British Nuclear Strategy, 1945–1964*, Oxford: Clarendon Press.

Baylis, J. and A. Macmillan (1993), 'The British Global Strategy Paper of 1952', *Journal of Strategic Studies*, 16 (2), pp. 200–26.

Bellany, I. (1994), *Reviewing Britain's Defence*, Aldershot: Dartmouth.

Benn, A. (1992), *The End of an Era: Diaries 1980–90*, London: Random House.

Blackett, P. M. S. (1948), *Fear, War and the Bomb: Military and Political Consequences of Atomic Energy*, London: Turnstile Press.

Blackett, P. M. S. (1956), *Atomic Weapons and East–West Relations*, Cambridge: Cambridge University Press.

Blackett, P. M. S. (1962), *Studies of War, Nuclear and Conventional*, Edinburgh: Oliver & Boyd.

Blackett, P. M. S. (1962), 'Steps Towards Disarmament', *Scientific American*, 206 (4), pp. 45–53.

Booth, K. (1983), 'Unilateralism: A Clausewitzian Reform?', in N. Blake and K. Pole (eds), *Dangers of Deterrence: Philosophers on Nuclear Strategy*, London: Routledge and Kegan Paul, pp. 41–83.

Booth, K. (1989), 'Part One: Alternative Defence', in K. Booth and J. Baylis, *Britain, NATO and Nuclear Weapons: Alternative Defence Versus Alliance Reform*, London: Macmillan, pp. 1–232.

Booth, K. (1991), *New Thinking About Strategy and International Security*, London: HarperCollins 1991.

Booth, K. (1992), '"Loose Nukes" and the Nuclear Mirror', *Arms Control: Contemporary Security Policy*, 13 (1), pp. 140–50.

Bourn, J. (1994), *Securing Value for Money in Defence Procurement*, Whitehall Paper No. 25, London: RUSI.

Brenner, M. (1998), 'Terms of Engagement: The United States and the European Security Identity', *The Washington Papers*, CSIS.

Broadbent, Sir E. (1988), *The Military and Government: from Macmillan to Heseltine*, Basingstoke: Macmillan for RUSI.

Bullock, A. (1983), *The Life and Times of Ernest Bevin. Volume III. Foreign Secretary, 1945–51*, London: Heinemann.

Bullock, A. (1985), *Ernest Bevin Foreign Secretary*, Oxford: Oxford University Press.

Cahen, A. (1989), 'The Western European Union and NATO: Building a European Defence Identity Within the Context of Atlantic Solidarity', in *Brassey's Atlantic Commentaries*, No. 2, London: Brassey's.

Calvocoressi, P. (1980), 'Deterrence, the Costs, the Issues, the Choices', *The Sunday Times*, 6 April.

Campbell, D. (1986), *The Unsinkable Aircraft Carrier*, London: Paladin.

Cannizzo, C. (1981), 'Procurement Via the Two-Way Street: Can it Achieve its Objectives?', in M. Edmonds (ed.), *International Arms Procurement: New Directions*, Oxford: Pergamon, pp. 53–70.

Carrington, Lord, P. (1989), *Reflect on Things Past: The Memoirs of Lord Carrington*, London: Fontana.

Carver, M. (1989), *Out of Step: The Memoirs of Field Marshal Lord Carver*, London: Century Hutchinson.

Carver, M. (1992), *Tightrope Walking: British Defence Policy since 1945*, London: Hutchinson, 1992.

Castle, B. (1984), *The Castle Diaries, 1964–70*, London: Weidenfeld & Nicolson.

Catrina, C. (1988), *Arms Transfers and Dependence*, London: Taylor & Francis.

Chalmers, M. (1985), *Paying for Defence*, London: Pluto Press.

Chalmers, M. (1992), *Biting the Bullet, European Defence Option for Britain*, London: Institute for Public Policy Research.

Chalmers, M. (1995), 'Military Spending and the British Economy', reprinted in D. Coates and J. Hillard (eds), *UK Economic Decline*, London: Harvester Wheatsheaf, pp. 287–91.

Clarke, M. (1985), 'The Alternative Defence Debate: Non-Nuclear Defence Policies for Europe', *ADIU Occasional Paper*, Number 3, Science Policy Research Unit, University of Sussex.

Clarke, M. (1992), 'A British View', in Richard Davy (ed.), *European Détente: A Reappraisal*, London: Sage for the RIIA.

Clarke, M. (1997), 'Britain', in M. Brenner (ed.), *NATO and Collective Security*, Basingstoke: Macmillan, pp. 6–38.

Codner, M. (1998), 'Policy topped but Treasury tailed? The Strategic Defence Review', *The Officer*, July/August, pp. 30–3.

Coker, C. (1986), *A Nation in Retreat?*, London: Brassey's.

Cole, J. (1995), *As It Seemed to Me: Political Memoirs*, London: Weidenfeld & Nicolson.

Collins, B. (1987), 'The Rayner Scrutinies', J. Gretton and A. Harrison (eds), *Reshaping Central Government*, Oxford: Policy Journals, pp. 11–22.

Conquest, R. (1979), *Present Danger: Towards a Foreign Policy*, Oxford: Basil Blackwell.

Cooper, F. (1987), 'Ministry of Defence', in J. Gretton and A. Harrison (eds), *Reshaping Central Government*, Oxford: Policy Journals, pp. 107–30.

Cornish, P. (1996), *British Military Planning for the Defence of Germany 1945–50*, Basingstoke: Macmillan in association with King's College London.

Council for Science and Society (1986), *UK Military R&D*, Oxford: Oxford University Press.

Croft, S. (1987), 'The Westland Helicopter Crisis: Implications for the British Defence Industry', *Defense Analysis*, 3 (4), pp. 291–303.

Croft, S. (1994), 'Continuity and Change in British Thinking About Nuclear Weapons', *Political Studies*, 42 (2), pp. 228–42.

Croft, S. (1994), *The End of a Superpower*, Aldershot: Dartmouth.

Croft, S. and D. H. Dunn (1994), 'Anglo-German Disagreement over CFE', in S. Croft (ed.), *The Conventional Armed Forces in Europe Treaty: The Cold War Endgame*, Aldershot: Dartmouth, pp. 106–35.

Croft, S. and P. Williams (1991), 'The United Kingdom', in R. C. Karp (ed.), *Security with Nuclear Weapons? Different Perspectives on National Security*, Oxford: Oxford University Press for SIPRI, pp. 145–61.

Croft, S., J. Redmond, W. Rees and M. Webber (1999), *The Enlargement of Europe*, Manchester: Manchester University Press.

Danchev, A. (1986), *Very Special Relationship: Field Marshal Sir John Dill and the Anglo-American Alliance 1941–44*, London: Brassey's.

Dando, M. and P. Rogers (1984), *The Death of Deterrence*, London: CND Publications.

Darby, P. (1973), *British Defence Policy East of Suez, 1947–68*, Oxford: Oxford University Press.

Davis, B. (1990), *Qaddafi, Terrorism and the Origins of the US Attack on Libya*, New York: Praeger.

Dawson, R. and R. Rosencrance (1966), 'Theory and Reality in the Anglo-American Alliance', *World Politics*, 19 (1), pp. 21–51.

Deighton, A. (1990), *The Impossible Peace*, Oxford: Clarendon.

Devereux, D. (1990), *The Formulation of British Policy Towards the Middle East, 1948–56*, Basingstoke: Macmillan.

Devons, E. (1964), 'The Aircraft Industry', in D. Burns (ed.), *The Structure of British Industry*, Volume II, Cambridge: Cambridge University Press, pp. 45–92.

Dillon, G. M. (1983), *Dependence and Deterrence: Success and Civility in the Anglo-American Special Nuclear Relationship, 1962–82*, Aldershot: Gower.

Dillon, M. (1977), 'Recurring Dilemmas and Decision-Making for Defence', in J. Baylis (ed.), *British Defence Policy in a Changing World*, London: Croom Helm, pp. 208–28.

Dodd, T. and M. Oakes (1998), *The Strategic Defence Review White Paper*, Research Paper 98/91, House of Commons Library, London: The Stationery Office.

Dorman, A., M. Smith and M. R. H. Uttley (1998) 'Jointery and Combined Operations in an Expeditionary Era: Defining the Issues', *Defense Analysis*, 14 (1), pp. 1–8.

Dowding, K. (1995), *The Civil Service*, London: Routledge.

Draper, A. G. (1990), *European Defence Equipment Collaboration: Britain's Involvement, 1957–87*, London: RUSI.

Driver, C. (1964), *The Disarmers*, London: Hodder & Stoughton.

Dunne, J. P. and R. P. Smith (1984), 'The Economic Consequences of Reduced UK Military Expenditure', *Cambridge Journal of Economics*, 8 (3), pp. 297–310.

Eavis, P. and O. Sprague (1996), 'Does Britain Need to Sell Weapons?', in J. Gittings and I. Davis (eds), *Britain in the 21st Century: Re-Thinking Defence and Foreign Policy*, Nottingham: Spokesman, p. 128.

Economist, The (1980), 17 May, p. 49.

Eden, A. (1960), *Full Circle*, London: Cassell.

Editorial (1990), 'Options for Change Review', in *The Independent*, 26 July.

Edmonds, M. (1981), 'International Military Equipment Procurement Partnerships: The Basic Issues', in M. Edmonds (ed.), *International Arms Procurement: New Directions*, Oxford: Pergamon, pp. 1–23.

Edmonds, M. (1985), 'Central Organizations of Defence in Great Britain', in M. Edmonds (ed.), *Central Organizations of Defence*, London: Frances Pinter, pp. 85–107.

Edmonds, M. (1986), 'The Higher Organisation of Defence in Britain, 1945–85: the Federal–Unification Debate', in M. Edmonds (ed.), *The Defence Equation*, London: Brassey's, pp. 57–78.

Edmonds, M. (1998), 'Defense Management and the Impact of Jointery', *Defense Analysis*, 14 (1), pp. 9–28.

Eekelen, W. van (1992), 'WEU on the way back to Brussels', Speech at Chatham House on 22 September 1992, reprinted in *WEU Press Review*, No. 161, 24 September.

Egerton, D. (1991), *England and the Aeroplane: An Essay on a Militant and Technological Nation*, London: Macmillan.

Elliott, J. (1988), 'JSF for Everybody? The JSF Programme and its International Implications', *Military Technology*, 22 (3), pp. 20–9.

Fairhall, D. (1981), 'The Battle of the Cuts', *The Guardian*, 7 January.

Francis, T. (ed.) (1986), *Managing the Costs of Defence: Proceedings of a Foundation Seminar*, London: Public Finance Foundation.

Freedman, L. (1980), *Britain and Nuclear Weapons*, London: Macmillan for the Royal Institute of International Affairs.

Freedman, L. (1981), *The Evolution of Nuclear Strategy*, London: Macmillan.

Freedman, L. (1986), 'The Case of Westland and the Bias to Europe', *International Affairs*, 63 (1), pp. 1–19.

Freedman, L. (1995), 'Bosnia: Does Peace Support Make any Sense?', *NATO Review*, 43 (6), pp. 19–23.

Freedman, L. (1998), 'The Revolution in Strategic Affairs', *Adelphi Paper 318*, Oxford: Oxford University Press.

Freedman, L. (1999), *The Politics of British Defence, 1979–98*, Basingstoke: Macmillan.

Fursdon, E. (1980), *The European Defence Community: A History*, London: Macmillan.

Geiger, T. (1992), ' "The Next War is Bound to Come": Defence Production Policy, Supply Departments and Defence Contractors in Britain, 1945–57', in H. Mercer, N. Rollings and J. D. Tomlinson (eds), *The Labour Governments and Private Industry: The Experience of 1945 to 1951*, Edinburgh: Edinburgh University Press, pp. 95–118.

George, B. and C. Pawlisch (1993), 'Defence and 1983 Election', *ADIU Report*, 5 (4) July/August.

Gilbert, M. (1991), *Churchill: A Life*, London: Heinemann.

Gorka, S. L. v. (1999), 'NATO After Enlargement: Is the Alliance Better Off?', in *NATO Review*, 47 (3), p. 33.

Gowing, M. (1964), *Britain and Atomic Energy 1939–45*, London: Macmillan.

Gowing, M. (1974), *Independence and Deterrence*, London: Macmillan.

Gray, V. (1996), 'Beyond Bosnia: Ethno-National Diasporas and Security in Europe', *Contemporary Security Policy*, 17 (1) , pp. 146–73.

Greenwood, D. (1991), 'Expenditure and Management', in P. Byrd (ed.), *British Defence Policy: Thatcher and Beyond*, London: Philip Allan, pp. 36–66.

Greenwood, J. and D. Wilson (1989), *Public Administration Today*, London: Unwin Hyman.

Gregory, F. and J. Simpson (1974), 'The Acquisition of Military Aircraft in Great Britain and West Germany', in F. B. Horton, A. C. Rogerson and E. L. Warner (eds), *Comparative Defence Policy*, London: Johns Hopkins University Press, pp. 453–64.

Groom, A. J. R. (1974), *British Thinking About Nuclear Weapons*, London: Pinter.

Grove, E. (1987), *Vanguard to Trident*, London: Bodley Head.

Gummett, P. (1986), 'Britain's Military Research and Development', *Defense Analysis*, 2 (2), pp. 158–9.

Gummett, P. (1987), 'Problems for UK Military R&D', in I. Bellany and T. Huxley (eds), *New Conventional Weapons and Western Defence*, London: Frank Cass, pp. 49–68.

Gummett, P. (1993), 'Civil and Military Aircraft in the UK', in J. Krige (ed.), *Choosing Big Technologies*, Reading: Harwood. Also published in *History and Technology*, 9 (1–4), pp. 203–24.

Hall, S. (1958), *Breakthrough*, London: Combined Universities CND.

Halliday, F. (1982), 'The Sources of the New Cold War', in E. Thompson, M. David, R. Williams, R. Bahro, L. Magri, E. Balibar, R. and Z. Medvedev, J. Cox, S. Kugai, M. Raskin, N. Chomsky, A. Wolfe, M. Kaldor and F. Halliday, *Exterminism and the Cold War*, London: Verso for the New Left Review, pp. 289–328.

Halliday, F. (1983), *The Making of the Second Cold War*, London: Verso.

Hartley, K. (1965), 'The Mergers of the UK Aircraft Industry, 1957–60', *Journal of the Royal Aeronautical Society*, December, pp. 846–53.

Hartley, K. (1965), 'The Learning Curve and its Application to the Aircraft Industry', in *Journal of Industrial Economics*, 13 (2), pp. 122–8.

Hartley, K. (1972), 'Development Time Scales for British and American Military Aircraft', *Scottish Journal of Political Economy*, 19 (2), pp. 115–34.

Hartley, K. (1983), *NATO Arms Co-operation: A Study in Economics and Politics*, London: Allen & Unwin.

Hartley, K. (1991), *The Economics of Defence Policy*, London: Brassey's.

Hartley, K. (1992), 'Defence', in A. Harrison (ed.), *From Hierarchy to Contract*, London: Policy Journals, p. 60.

Hartley, K. (1998) 'Jointery – Just Another Panacea? An Economist's Perspective', *Defense Analysis*, 14 (1), pp. 79–86.

Hartley, K. (1998) 'Defence Procurement in the UK', *Defence and Peace Economics*, 9 (1–2), pp. 39–61.

Head, R. (1974), 'The Weapons Acquisition Process: Alternative National Strategies', in F. B. Horton, A. C. Rogerson and E. L. Warner (eds), *Comparative Defense Policy*, London: Johns Hopkins University Press, pp. 412–25.

Healey, D. (1989), *The Time of My Life*, London: Penguin.

Heseltine, M. (1983), 'The United Kingdom's Strategic Interests and Priorities', *The RUSI Journal*, 128 (4), pp. 3–5.

Hitch, C. J. and R. N. McKean (1960), *The Economics of Defence in the Nuclear Age*, Cambridge, MA: Harvard University Press.

Hobkirk, M. D. (1984), *The Politics of Defence Budgeting: A Study of Resource Allocation in the United Kingdom and the United States*, London: Macmillan.

Holden Reid, B. (1984), 'Civil War Between Services', in *Military History*, January, pp. 1–7.

Howard, M. (1970), *The Central Organisation for Defence*, London: RUSI.

Howard, M. (1991), 'P. M. S. Blackett', in J. Baylis and J. Garnett (eds), *The Makers of Nuclear Strategy*, London: Pinter Publishers.

Howe, G. (1994), *Conflict of Loyalty*, London: Pan.

Huntington, S. P. (1961), *The Common Defense: Strategic Programs in National Politics*, Colombia: Columbia University Press.

Jackson, W. (1990), *Britain's Defence Dilemma: An Inside View*, London: B. T. Batsford.

Jenkins, D. (1993), 'Simplicity of Death, Complexities of Life', in David Martin and Peter Mullen (eds), *Unholy Warfare: The Church and the Bomb*, Oxford: Basil Blackwell, pp. 81–97.

Jenkins, R. (1991), *A Life at the Centre*, London: Macmillan.

Johnson, P. (1985), *Neutrality: A Policy for Britain*, London: Temple Smith.

Jones, P. M. (1987), 'British Defence Policy: the Breakdown of the Inter-Party Consensus', *Review of International Studies*, 13 (2), pp. 111–31.

Jordan, A. G. and J. J. Richardson (1987), *British Politics and the Policy Process: an Arena Approach*, London: Allen and Unwin.

Kaldor, M. (1982), 'Warfare and Capitalism', in E. Thompson, M. David, R. Williams, R. Bahro, L. Magri, E. Balibar, R. and Z. Medvedev, J. Cox, S. Kugai, M. Raskin, N. Chomsky, A. Wolfe, M. Kaldor and F. Halliday, *Exterminism and the Cold War*, London: Verso for the New Left Review, pp. 261–87.

Kaldor, M. (1982), 'Is there a Soviet Military Threat?', in M. Clarke and M. Mowlam (eds), *Debate on Disarmament*, London: Routledge and Kegan Paul, pp. 29–44.

Kelly, S. and A. Gorst (1999), 'Whitehall and the Suez Crisis', Special edition of *Contemporary British History*, 13 (2), pp. 1–11.

Kemp, P. (1990), 'Can the Civil Service Adapt to Managing by Contract?', *Public Money & Management*, 10 (3), pp. 25–32.

Kent, J. and J. Young (1992), 'British Overseas Policy: The "Third Force" and the Origins of NATO – in Search of a New Perspective', in B. Heuser and R. O'Neill (eds), *Securing Peace in Europe 1945–62: Thoughts for the Post-Cold War Era*, Basingstoke: Macmillan, pp. 41–64.

Keohane, D. (1993), *Labour Party Defence Policy since 1945*, Leicester: Leicester University Press.

King, D. (1987), *The New Right*, London: Macmillan.

King-Hall, S. (1958), *Defence in the Nuclear Age*, London: Gollancz.

Kirkpatrick, D. (1987), 'Rising Costs, Falling Budgets and their Implications for Defence Policy', *Economic Affairs*, 17 (4), pp. 10–14.

Kirkpatrick, D. L. I. and P. G. Pugh (1983), *Towards Starship Enterprise – are Current Trends in Defence Unit Costs Inexorable?*, London: Aerospace.

Kissinger, H. (1984), *The Times*, 23 March.

Kitson, F. (1971), *Low Intensity Operations*, London: Faber and Faber.

Lawson, N. (1992), *The View From No.11: Memoirs of a Tory Radical*, London: Bantam Press.

Leurdijk, D. (1994), *The United Nations and NATO in Former Yugoslavia: Partners in International Cooperation*, The Hague: Netherlands Atlantic Commission and the Netherlands Institute of International Relations.

Levene, P. (1987), 'Competition and Collaboration: UK Defence Procurement Policy', *RUSI Journal*, 132 (2), pp. 3–6.

Levene, P. (1989), 'Maintaining the Two Way Street: UK/US Defence Procurement', *NATO's Sixteen Nations*, October, pp. 77–80.

Lighthill, M. J. (1965), 'The Royal Aircraft Establishment', in J. Cockcroft (ed.), *The Organisation of Research Establishments*, Cambridge: Cambridge University Press, pp. 28–54.

Louis, W. R. and H. Bull, (1986), *The Special Relationship: Anglo-American Relations Since 1945*, Oxford: Clarendon.

Louis, W. R. and R. Owen (eds) (1998), *The Suez Crisis and its Consequences*, Oxford: Clarendon Press.

Lovering, J. (1993), 'Restructuring the British Defence Industrial Base after the Cold War: Institutional and Geographical Perspectives', *Defence Economics*, 4 (2), pp. 123–39.

McGwire, M., K. Booth and J. Connell (eds) (1975), *Soviet Naval Policy: Objectives and Constraints*, New York: Praeger.

McInnes, C. (1988), 'BAOR in the 1980s: Changes in Doctrine and Organisation', *Defense Analysis*, 4 (4), pp. 377–94.

McInnes, C. (1998), 'Labour's Strategic Defence Reivew,' *International Affairs*, 74 (4),
  pp. 823–45.
McIntosh, M. (1990), *Managing Britain's Defence*, London: Macmillan.
Macmahan, J. (1981), *British Nuclear Weapons For and Against*, London: Junction Books.
Macmillan, H. (1972), *Pointing the Way, 1959–61*, London: Macmillan.
Madgwick, P. (1991), *British Government: The Central Executive Territory*, London: Philip
  Allan.
Malone, P. (1984), *The British Nuclear Deterrent*, London and New York: Croom Helm and
  St Martins Press.
Martin, S. (1999), 'The Subsidy Savings from Reducing UK Arms Exports', *Journal of Economic
  Studies*, 26 (1), pp. 15–37.
Martin, S. and K. Hartley (1996), 'The UK Experience with Offsets', in S. Martin (ed.), *The
  Economics of Offsets: Defence Procurement and Countertrade*, Reading: Harwood, pp. 337–55.
Mathews, K. (1993), *The Gulf Conflict and International Relations*, London: Routledge.
Matthews, R. (1992), *European Armaments Collaboration: Policy, Problems and Prospects*, Reading:
  Harwood.
Mellon, E. (1993), 'Executive Agencies: Leading Change from the Outside-in', *Public Money
  and Management*, 13 (2), pp. 5–11.
Metcalfe, L. and S. Richards (1990), *Improving Public Management*, London: Sage.
Miller, D. (1990), 'Planning Programme Budgeting Systems and the Case of Rational Decision-
  Making in Britain's Ministry of Defence', in *Defense Analysis*, pp. 131–45.
Miller, D. (1996), *Export or Die: Britain's Defence Trade with Iraq*, London: Cassell.
Miller, D. (1996), 'The Scott Report and the Future of British Defense Sales', *Defense Analysis*,
  12 (3), pp. 359–69.
Molas-Gallart, J. (1992), *Military Production and Innovation in Spain*, Reading: Harwood.
Mountbatten, Earl (1980), 'The Final Abyss?', in *Apocalypse Now?*, Nottingham: Spokesman for
  the Atlantic Peace Foundation in Support of the World Disarmament Campaign.
Nailor, P. (1978), 'British Defence Policy in the 1960s', in F. Gregory, M. Imber and
  J. Simpson (eds), *Perspectives upon British Defence Policy*, Southampton: Southampton
  University Press, pp. 62–7.
Nelson, R. R. (1959), *The Economics of Parallel R&D Efforts: A Sequential-Decision Analysis*,
  Santa Monica: RAND.
Newhouse, J. (1989), *The Nuclear Age: From Hiroshima to Star Wars*, London: Michael Joseph.
Noel-Baker, P. (1960), *The Arms Race*, London: Calder.
Noguera, F. and P. Willets (1992), 'Public Attitudes and the Future of the Islands', in
  A. Danchev (ed.), *International Perspectives on the Falklands Conflict*, Basingstoke: Macmillan.
Nuttall, S. (1992), *European Political Cooperation*, Oxford: Clarendon Press.
Ovendale, R. (1994), *British Defence Policy since 1945*, Manchester: Manchester University
  Press.
Owen, D. (1991), *Time to Declare*, London: Michael Joseph.
Owen, D. (1995), *Balkan Odyssey*, London: Indigo.
Palin, R. (1988), 'A Military Perspective', in P. Sabin (ed.), *The Future of UK Air Power*,
  London: Brassey's, pp. 139–42.
Parkinson, C. (1992), *Right at the Centre*, London: Weidenfeld & Nicolson.
Pickering, J. (1989), *Britain's Withdrawal from East of Suez: The Politics of Retrenchment*,
  Basingstoke: Macmillan in association with the Institute of Contemporary British History.
Pierre, A. (1972), *Nuclear Politics*, London: Oxford University Press.
Pirie, M. (1988), *Micropolitics*, London: Wildwood House.
Ponting, C. (1989), *Breach of Promise: Labour in Power 1964–70*, London: Hamish Hamilton.

Porter, T. (1994), 'Postmodern Political Realism and International Relations Theory's Third Debate', in C. T. Sjolander and W. S. Cox (eds), *Beyond Positivism: Critical Reflections on International Relations*, Boulder, CO: Lynne Rienner, pp. 105–28.

Raphael, A. (1982), 'Nott fights rearguard action in Whitehall whispering war', *The Observer*, 20 June.

Rawlinson, M. J. (1989), 'Government Defence Factories and Dockyards: the Defence Implications of Privatization', *Defence Force*, January/February, pp. 27–35.

Reed, A. (1973), *Britain's Aircraft Industry: What Went Right? What Went Wrong?*, London: J.M. Dent.

Reed, B. and G. Williams (1971), *Denis Healey and the Politics of Power*, London: Sidgwick and Jackson.

Rees, W. (1989) 'The 1957 Sandys White Paper: New Priorities in British Defence Policy', *Journal of Strategic Studies*, 12 (2), pp. 215–29.

Rees, W. (1998), *The Western European Union at the Crossroads: Between Trans-Atlantic Solidarity and European Integration*, Boulder, CO: Westview Press.

Ridley, N. (1992), *My Style of Government: The Thatcher Years*, London: Fontana.

Rogers, P. (1997), 'Reviewing Britain's Security', *International Affairs*, 73 (4), pp. 655–69.

Rogers, P. and M. Dando (1992), *A Violent Peace: Global Security after the Cold War*, London: Brassey's.

Rogers, P., M. Dando and P. van der Dungen (1981), *As Lambs to the Slaughter*, London: Arrow Books.

Rose, C. (1986), *Campaigns Against Western Defence*, London: Macmillan for the RUSI.

Russell, B. (1959), *Common Sense and Nuclear Warfare*, London: George Allen & Unwin.

Sander, D. (1990), *Losing an Empire, Finding a Role: British Foreign Policy since 1945*, Basingstoke: Macmillan.

Sandler, T. and K. Hartley (1995), *The Economics of Defense*, Cambridge: Cambridge University Press.

Scholte, J. A. (1993), *International Relations of Social Change*, Buckingham: Open University Press.

Schofield, S. (1995), 'The Levene Reforms: An Evaluation', *Defense Analysis*, 11 (2), pp. 147–74.

Shaffer, S. (1981), 'Linking Arms: Weapons Cooperation in NATO', in M. Edmonds (ed.), *International Arms Procurement: New Directions*, Oxford: Pergamon, pp. 24–52.

Shultz, G. (1993), *Turmoil and Triumph. My Years as Secretary of State*, New York: Macmillan.

Simpson, J. (1986), *The Independent Nuclear State: Britain, the United States and the Military Atom*, London: Macmillan.

Slater, J. (1993), 'A Fleet for the 90s', *RUSI Journal*, 138 (1), pp. 8–10.

Slessor, J. (1957), 'British Defence Policy', *Foreign Affairs*, 35 (4), pp. 551–63.

Smith, D. (1982), 'Non-Nuclear Military Options for Britain', *Peace Studies Papers*, Number 6, Bradford University School of Peace Studies: Housemans.

Smith, M. J. (1998), 'Reconceptualizing the British State: Theoretical and Empirical Challenges to Central Government', *Public Administration*, 76 (1), pp. 45–72.

Smith, R. and J. Zametica (1985), 'The Cold Warrior: Clement Attlee Reconsidered, 1945–7', *International Affairs*, 61 (2), pp. 237–52.

Smith, R. P. (1980), 'Military Expenditure and Investment in OECD Countries, 1954–1973', *Journal of Comparative Economics*, 4 (1), pp. 19–32.

Snyder, W. P. (1964), *The Politics of British Defense Policy, 1945–1962*, Ohio: Ohio University Press.

Sokolsky, J. J. (1991), *Seapower in the Nuclear Age: The United States Navy and NATO, 1949–80*, London: Routledge.

Speed, K. (1982), *Sea Change: The Battle for the Falklands and the Future of Britain's Navy*, Bath: Ashgrove Press.

Stewart, M. (1993), 'Future Resource Management in Defence', *RUSI Journal*, 138 (2), pp. 73–76.

Stocker, J. R. (1996), 'Canadian Joint Operations', *RUSI Journal*, 141 (3), pp. 36–8.

Straw, S. and J. Young (1997), 'The Wilson Government and the Demise of TSR-2, October 1964–April 1965', *Journal of Strategic Studies*, 20 (4), December, pp. 18–44.

Stromseth, J. E. (1988), *The Origins of Flexible Response: NATO's Debate over Strategy in the 1960s*, Basingstoke: Macmillan.

Taylor, T. (1998), 'Smart Procurement and Partnership with Industry', *RUSI Journal*, 143 (2), pp. 41–6.

Taylor, T. and K. Hayward (1989), *The Defence Industrial Base: Development and Future Policy Options*, London: Brassey's.

Thatcher, M. (1993) *The Downing Street Years*, London: HarperCollins.

Thomas, H. (1967), *The Suez Affair*, London: Weidenfeld & Nicolson.

Thompson, E. (1982), 'Notes on Exterminism: the Last Stage of Civilisation', in E. Thompson, M. David, R. Williams, R. Bahro, L. Magri, E. Balibar, R. and Z. Medvedev, J. Cox, S. Kugai, M. Raskin, N. Chomsky, A. Wolfe, M. Kaldor and F. Halliday, *Exterminism and the Cold War*, London: Verso for New Left Review.

Thompson, E. P. (1980), *Protest and Survive*, London: Penguin Books.

Thompson, E. P. (1982), 'A Mid-Atlantic Moderate', in M. Clarke and M. Mowlam (eds), *Debate on Disarmament*, London: Routledge and Kegan Paul.

Thompson, E. P. (1982), *Zero Option*, London: The Merlin Press 1982.

Thursfield, H. G. (ed.) (1951), *Brassey's Annual: The Armed Forces Yearbook, 1951*, London: William Clowes.

Tonge, R. (1993), 'Financial Management', in D. Farnham and S. Horton (eds), *Managing the New Public Services*, London: Macmillan, pp. 78–98.

Turpin, C. C. (1972), *Government Procurement and Contracting*, Harmondsworth: Penguin.

Uttley, M. R. H. (1991), 'British Helicopter Developments, 1945–1960: A Case Study of Technology Transfer and Market Dominance', *Science and Public Policy*, 18 (4), pp. 235–43.

Uttley, M. R. H. (1993), 'Competition in the Provision of Defense Support Services: The UK Experience', *Defense Analysis*, 9 (3), pp. 271–88.

Uttley, M. R. H. (1995), 'The Integration of West European Defence Procurement: Issues and Prospects', *Defense Analysis*, 11 (3), pp. 279–91.

Uttley, M. R. H. (2001), 'Licensed Production and the RMA: The Scope and Limitations for the United Kingdom', in R. Matthews (ed.), *Managing the RMA*, Reading: Harwood, (forthcoming).

Vestel, P. De (1995), 'Defence Markets and Industries in Europe: Time for Political Decisions', *Chaillot Paper 21*, Paris: WEU.

Vincent, J. (1962), *Christ in a Nuclear World*, Manchester: Crux Press.

Walker, D. and R. Norton-Taylor (2000), 'Missions: impossible', *The Guardian*, 16 May.

Walker, W. and P. Gummett (1989), 'Britain and the European Armaments Market', in *International Affairs*, 65 (3), pp. 419–42.

Walker W. and S. Willett (1993), 'Restructuring the European Defence Industrial Base', *Defence Economics*, 4, pp. 141–60.

Wallace, W. (1993), 'Britain's search for a new role in the world,' *The Observer*, 15 August, p. 16.

Weinberger, C. (1990), *Fighting for Peace: Seven Critical Years at the Pentagon*, London: Michael Joseph.

Wendt, A. (1987), 'The Agent–Structure Problem in International Relations Theory', *International Organisation*, 41 (3), pp. 335–70.

Wendt, A. (1992), 'Anarchy is What States Make of It: The Social Construction of Power Politics', *International Organisation*, 46 (2), pp. 391–425.

Wendt, A. (1995), 'Constructing International Politics', *International Security*, 20 (1), pp. 71–81.

Wendt, A. (1999), *Social Theory of International Politics*, Cambridge: Cambridge University Press.

Wettern, D. (1982), *The Decline of British Seapower*, London: Jane's.

Wheatcroft, G. (2000), 'Arms and the money', *The Guardian*, 19 May.

Winand, P. (1993), *Eisenhower, Kennedy and the United States of Europe*, New York: St Martin's Press.

Wood, D. (1990), *Project Cancelled: The Disaster of Britain's Abandoned Aircraft Projects*, London: Tri-Service Press.

Worcester, R. (1966), *The Roots of British Air Policy*, London: Hodder & Stoughton.

Wynn, H. (1994), *RAF Nuclear Deterrent Forces*, London: HMSO.

Yost, D. (1998), *NATO Transformed: The Alliance's New Roles in International Security*, Washington: United States Institute of Peace.

Young, H. (1998), *This Blessed Plot: Britain and Europe from Churchill to Blair*, London: Macmillan.

Ziegler, P. (1985), *Mountbatten: the Official Biography*, London: William Collins.

Ziegler, P. (1993), *Wilson: The Authorised Life*, London: Weidenfeld & Nicolson.

Zuckerman, S. (1980), 'Defence is Indivisible', in *Apocalypse Now?*, Nottingham: Spokesman for the Atlantic Peace Foundation in Support of the World Disarmament Campaign.

Documents

Public Record Office Documents

Public Record Office, Reference FO 371/66546.

Public Record Office, Reference FO 800/517.

Public Record Office, 'Report by the Chiefs of Staff on Defence Policy and Global Strategy', D.O. (50) 45, CAB 131/9, 7 June 1950.

Public Record Office, DG 1/11/56 MD (50) 12 'Western Union Defence Organisation', 5/7/1950.

Public Record Office, 'Report by the Chiefs of Staff on Defence Policy and Global Strategy,' PREM 11/49, COS (52) 362. fos 85, 80, 15 July 1952.

Public Record Office, DEFE 4/87 JP (56) 7, Discussed in COS (56) 55th Meeting, UK Requirements in the Middle East, 31/5/1956.

Public Record Office, CAB 129/84 CP (56) 269, 'UK Forces in Germany', 28/11/1956.

Public Record Office, RO, DEFE 5/72 COS (56) 428, 'Relations Between ANZAM and SEATO', 4/12/1956.

Public Record Office, DEFE 4/94, Annex to JP (57) 8 (Final) 'Long Term Defence Policy', 24/1/1957.

Public Record Office, DEFE 4/96 Annex to JP (57) 28 (Final) CPX 7, 22/3/1957.

Public Record Office, DEFE 5/80 COS (57) 280 Appendix, 'Minimum Essential Force Requirements for the Period up to 1963', 19/12/1957.

Public Record Office, DEFE 5/84 COS (58) 155, Definition of Terms, 13/6/1958.

Public Record Office, DEFE 6/51 COS (58) 110 (Final) Baghdad Pact: Review of Existing Plans and Studies, 22/8/1958.

Public Record Office, RO, DEFE 5/88 COS (59) 17 Brief for the 6th Meeting of the Military Committee of the Baghdad Pact, 22/1/1959.

Public Record Office, RO, DEFE 4/117 COS (59) 18th Meeting of the Baghdad Pact, 12/3/1959.

Public Record Office, DEFE 4/129 COS (60) 55th Meeting, 'NATO Strategy', 13/9/1960.
Public Record Office, CAB 139/1929, FP (60) 1, 'Future Policy Study', 24/2/1960.
Public Record Office, CAB 148/40, OPD (0) (64) 'Defence Policy', 30/10/1964.
Public Record Office, CAB 130/213, Misc 17/1st, 'Defence Review 1964–5', 21/11/64.
Public Record Office, CAB 148/18, OPD (65) 29th Meeting, 16/6/1965.
Public Record Office, CAB 130/213 'Miscellaneous 17/5', 13 June 1965.
Public Record Office, PREM 13/214 'Record of a conversation between the Prime Minister and Dean Rusk', May 1965.
Public Record Office, CAB 128/41, CC 38 (66) 'Germany', 20/7/1966.
Public Record Office, RO, CAB 148/30, OPD (67) 17th Meeting, Defence and Overseas Policy Committee, 21/4/1967.

Select Committee Reports

Second Report from the Select Committee on Estimates, *The Supply of Military Aircraft*, HCP 34, Session 1956–57, London: HMSO, 1956.
Report of The Management Committee on the Management and Control of Research and Development, London: HMSO, 1961.
Report of the Committee of Inquiry into the Aircraft Industry, Cmnd. 2853, London: HMSO, 1965.
House of Commons Defence Committee, First Report from the Defence Committee Session 1985–1986, *Further Observations on the Future of the Royal Dockyards*, HMSO: London, 1985.
House of Commons Defence Committee, *The Procurement of Major Defence Equipment*, 5th Report, Session 1987–88, HCP 431, London: HMSO, 1988.
House of Commons Defence Committee, *Seventh Report, Statement on the Defence Estimates 1988*, HCP 495, London: HMSO, 1988.
House of Commons Committee of Public Accounts, *Forty-First Report, Ministry of Defence: Control and Use of Manpower*, Session 1988–89, HCP 397, London: HMSO.
House of Commons Committee of Public Accounts, *Support for Defence Exports: Minutes of Evidence*, Wednesday 26 April 1989, London: HMSO, 1989.
House of Commons Defence Committee, *Fourth Report: United Kingdom Peacekeeping and Intervention Forces: Report together with the Proceedings of the Committee relating to the report, minutes of evidence and memoranda*, House of Commons Papers No. 188, Session 1992–93, London: HMSO, 1993.
Treasury and Civil Service Committee, *Private Finance for Public Projects*, Session 1992–93, London: HMSO, 1993.

Statement on the Defence Estimates

Statement Relating to Defence 1948, Cmnd. 7,327, London: HMSO.
Statement on Defence 1956, Cmnd. 9,691, London: HMSO.
Defence Outline of Future Policy 1957, Cmnd. 124, London: HMSO.
Statement on the Defence Estimates 1965, Cmnd. 2,592, London: HMSO.
Statement on the Defence Estimates 1966, Part I: The Defence Review, Cmnd. 2,901, London, HMSO.
Supplementary Statement on Defence Policy 1967, Cmnd. 3,357, London: HMSO.
Statement on the Defence Estimates 1968, Cmnd. 3,540, London: HMSO.
Supplementary Statement on Defence Policy 1968, Cmnd. 3,701, London: HMSO.
Statement on the Defence Estimates, Cmnd. 3,390, London: HMSO.
Supplementary Statement on Defence Policy 1970, Cmnd. 4,521, London: HMSO.

Statement Relating to the Defence Estimates 1973, Cmnd. 5,231, London: HMSO.
Statement on the Defence Estimates 1975, Cmnd. 5,976, London: HMSO.
Statement on the Defence Estimates 1978, Cmnd. 7,099, London: HMSO.
Statement on the Defence Estimates 1981, Cmnd. 8212-I, London: HMSO.
Statement on the Defence Estimates 1984, Cmnd. 9227-I, London: HMSO.
Statement on the Defence Estimates 1987, London: HMSO.
Statement on the Defence Estimates 1989, Cmnd. 675-I, London: HMSO.
Statement on the Defence Estimates 1991, Britain's Defence for the 1990s, Cmnd. 1,559, London: HMSO.
Statement on the Defence Estimates 1992, Cmnd. 1,981, London: HMSO.
Statement on the Defence Estimates 1996, Cmnd. 3,223, London: The Stationery Office.

Government Reports

Central Organisation for Defence, Cmnd. 6923, London: HMSO, 1946.
Defence – Outline of Future Policy, Cmnd. 124, London: HMSO, 1957.
Central Organisation for Defence, Cmnd. 476, London: HMSO, 1958.
Central Organisation for Defence, Cmnd. 2097, London: HMSO, 1963.
Reorganisation of the Army Reserves, Cmnd. 2,855, London: HMSO, 1965.
Ministry of Technology, *Report of the Steering Group on Development Cost Estimating*, London: HMSO, 1969.
The United Kingdom Defence Programme: The Way Forward, Cmnd. 8,288, London: HMSO, 1981.
Central Organisation for Defence, Cmnd. 9315, London: HMSO, 1984.
HM Treasury, *Using Private Enterprise in Government*, London: HMSO, 1986.
Audit Commission, *Competitiveness and Contracting Out of Local Authorities' Services*, Occasional Paper No. 3, London: HMSO, 1987.
Efficiency Unit, *Improving Management in Government: The Next Steps*, London: HMSO, 1988.
National Audit Office, *Ministry of Defence: Control and Use of Manpower*, London: HMSO, 27 April 1989.
HM Treasury, *Competing for Quality: Buying Better Public Services*, Cmnd. 1730, London: HMSO, 1991.
Centre for Public Services, *Monitoring Public Services*, Sheffield: CPS, 1991.
Defending Our Future, Cmnd. 2,270, London: HMSO, 1993
Front Line First: The Defence Costs Study, London: HMSO, 1994.
National Audit Office Report by the Comptroller and Auditor General, *The New Management Strategy in the Ministry of Defence*, London: HMSO, 1994.
National Audit Office, *Ministry of Defence: Defence Procurement in the 1990s*, HCP 390, London: HMSO, 1994.
Ministry of Defence, *United Kingdom Doctrine for Joint and Combined Operations*, Joint Warfare Publication 0-10, 3rd Study Draft, 1997.
Ministry of Defence *Major Projects Report 1996*, Report by the Comptroller and Auditor General, London: HMSO, HC 238, 15 August 1997.
Strategic Defence Review, Cmnd. 3,999, London: The Stationery Office, 1998.

Hansards/House of Commons Debates

Roy Mason, *House of Commons Parliamentary Debates*, vol. 882, fifth series, session 1974–75, 25 November–6 December 1974, Statement to the House, 3 December 1974, col. 1,352.

Roy Mason, *House of Commons Parliamentary Debates*, vol. 883, fifth series, session 1974–75, 9–20 December 1974, Statement to the House, 12 December 1974, col. 1,148.

Roy Mason, *House of Commons Parliamentary Debates*, vol. 883, fifth series, 9–20 December 1974, Statement to the House, 16 December 1974, col. 1,148.

Hansard, 13 May 1980, p. 1050.

Hansard, Vol. 977, Col. 679, 24 January 1980.

Francis Pym, *House of Commons Parliamentary Debates*, vol. 988, fifth series, session 1979–80, 7–18 July 1980, written answer 14 July 1980, cols. 420-1w.

Hansard, Vol. 128, Col. 1,294, 4 March 1988.

Tom King, *House of Commons Parliamentary Debates*, vol. 177, sixth series, session 1989–90, 23 July–19 October 1990, Statement to the House, 25 July 1990, cols. 468–86.

Speeches/Statements

NATO Press Communiqué S-1 (91) 85, 7 November 1991.

George Robertson, Speech to the Labour Party Conference, 1997.

Robin Cook, 'British Foreign Policy', Speech made at the launch of the FCO Mission Statement, London: FCO, 12 May 1997.

Ministry of Defence Press Release, No. 213/98, 12 August 1998.

Declaration on European Defense', St Malo, 3–4 December 1998, www.fco.gov.uk.

Speech of Prime Minister Tony Blair, www. fco.gov.uk, March 1999.

Presidency Conclusions, Helsinki European Council, 10–11 December 1999.

A. Vershbow, Speech at Wilton Park, England, 26 January 2000.

Labour Party Publications

Modern Britain in a Modern World, London: The Labour Party, 1987.

Opportunity Britain, London: The Labour Party, 1991.

Miscellaneous

The Alternative Defence Commission, First report, *Defence Without the Bomb*, London: Taylor & Francis, 1983.

Diminishing the Nuclear Threat, London: British Atlantic Committee Report, 1984.

IISS, *The Military Balance, 1987–88*, London: IISS, 1987, p. 79.

The Alternative Defence Commission, *The Politics of Alternative Defence*, London: Paladin 1987.

RUSI Working Group, '1992: Protectionism or Collaboration in Defence Procurement', *Whitehall Paper No. 6*, London: RUSI, 1990.

Stockholm International Peace Research Institute, *SIPRI Yearbook 1998*, Oxford: Oxford University Press, 1998.

Centre for Defence Studies, *The Strategic Defence Review: How Strategic? How Much of a Review?*, London: Brassey's, July 1998.

'Britain Survey: A Power in the World', *The Economist*, 6 November 1999.

Index